THE

IRISH RACE

IN

AMERICA

THE
IRISH RACE
IN
AMERICA

Edward O'Meagher Condon

Bicentennial Edition

Foreword by

Hon. PAUL O'DWYER

President, City Council of New York

 OGHAM HOUSE
NEW YORK

Copyright © 1976, Ogham House, Inc.

Printed in the United States of America

OGHAM HOUSE, INC.
6 Sherri Lane
Spring Valley, N.Y. 10977

Library of Congress catalogue card number: 75-35480
ISBN 0-916590-01-1

To

BRIGID BOOKLE LEE

FOREWORD

Our nation was founded two hundred years ago by people of many different races and cultures whose desire for freedom was their common bond. Out of this mixture came the strength of purpose which led to the success of the American Revolution and which has sustained our country ever since. Of all the groups, not the least were the immigrants from Ireland. They had known the yoke of centuries of English oppression and, although unable to attain freedom in their native land, they were determined to live free in their new home.

Colonists of other racial strains had also been exposed to the arrogance of the Stamp Act and similar laws aimed at exploiting our earliest settlers. Failure to give heed to these grievances was sufficient to spark revolt against distant masters. The Irish not only had these reasons to spur them on, but memories of savage wrongdoing in the homeland provided the added impetus which drove them into Washington's army in numbers and proportions far exceeding those of their fellow Americans. Some came to the military with skills which qualified them for high ranks; however, for the most part they could be found among the non-commissioned class.

People of Irish extraction, in their devotion to the new nation, continued to support it in 1812 when the fledgling Republic was again in danger of capture and in 1861 when the call to arms was heard in far off Dublin City.

Between the wars, men of brawn and women of industry

made their way up through the obstacle course which lay in the path of the newcomer. Theirs is no romantic story of the energetic stranger and his ultimate triumph. At times it is a sad tale of inhumanity and at other times, a love story.

It is all there in Captain Edward O'Meagher Condon's *The Irish Race in America,* written when some of the events were almost contemporary history. In simple style, he tells the story of the foundation of our nation's traditions and the odyssey of the Children of Ir in their flight from cruelty as they sought entrance through the Golden Door.

As we celebrate our Bicentennial, this book has special significance to all Americans. Irish Americans will be grateful to Gerry Lee for his discovery of this long forgotten account of the Irish experience in their Promised Land.

HON. PAUL O'DWYER
President of the Council,
The City of New York

November, 1975

INTRODUCTION

The Irish Race in America first appeared in 1887 as part of a series of works on Irish topics issued under the imprint of Ford's National Library. The publishers were A.E. and R.E. Ford, whose brother Patrick founded the *Irish World,* a New York based newspaper still in publication. Edward O'Meagher Condon was on the staff of this paper when he wrote the book, which he dedicated to Patrick Ford.

The book apparently received wide circulation at the time, although it has not been possible to ascertain the number or size of the printings. In keeping with the policy of the publishers to produce "The Cheapest Books in America", the paperbound version sold for twenty-five cents and the clothbound for one dollar. Economy was achieved through the use of low-quality paper so only a few copies of the original remain, such as that in the rare book section of the New York Public Library. The particular copy used for this reprint was discovered, brown and brittle to the touch, about three years ago among the collection of the now defunct Catholic Lending Library, which was operated for many years by Father Bertrand L. Conway, C.S.P. at St. Paul the Apostle Church in Manhattan.

This bicentennial edition includes the original text in its entirety; in addition, it contains a name-index and some biographical material about the author. Condon was a patriot of both the United States and Ireland: for one, he fought and was wounded; for the other, he fought and was imprisoned. He served as a Captain in the famous Irish Brigade of the Union Army during the Civil War and, shortly thereafter, played a leading role in the abortive Fenian Rising of the Irish against English rule. Sentenced to be hung for his part in the Manchester Martyr affair during this insurrection, his defiant statement from the dock, "God Save Ireland", so aroused public opinion, particularly in the United States, that he was spared the fate of his companions, Allen, Larkin and O'Brien. Instead, his sentence was commuted to life imprisonment. He spent eleven years at hard labor before being freed in 1878 through the intervention of President Hayes who acted on an unanimous resolution of Congress decrying the harsh treatment of Condon. Upon his release, The New York Times carried a front-page report detailing London newspaper editorial comments inveighing against such blatant interference on behalf of a common criminal.

In 1909, by special permission of Winston Churchill, then Home Secretary, Captain Condon was allowed to visit Ireland and England from which he had been permanently banished. He was welcomed with open arms in Manchester, and in Dublin he was made an honorary freeman of the city; the proclamation to this effect is presently displayed in the Fifth Avenue mansion which houses the headquarters and library of the American Irish Historical Society. This society was founded in 1897 "to make better known the Irish chapter in American history" and Condon joined it one year later. He was an architect by profession and an historian by avocation. He remained active in Irish American affairs until his death in 1915 and was survived by his wife and one daughter who now share his grave in a remote corner of Calvary Cemetery in New York; there were no grandchildren.

The Irish Race in America by Edward O'Meagher Condon was a pioneering effort to bring to public attention the significance and extent of the Irish involvement in the birth and development of the United States. Certainly, he undertook an herculean task. Even in his day, it was generally assumed that the Irish impact was minimal until the Great Famine brought hordes of emigrants to these shores.

The book opens in the sixth century, a time when Irish sailor saints roamed the seas, with the story of St. Brendan the Navigator's seven year voyage to the Land of Promise. It is a tale which has lain for centuries in that limbo between fact and fiction, withstanding translations in many languages including Latin, English, French and Flemish. Columbus is understood to have visited Ireland seeking details of Brendan's voyage and twelfth century Norse writings describe expeditions to Great Ireland or Vinland (now known to be North America). A recent archeological find of a boulder in Newfoundland may finally prove the Irish claim to the discovery of America. The stone is inscribed in Ogham, the alphabet of the Druids of ancient Ireland, which remained in use two centuries after the conversion of Ireland to Christianity in the fifth century.

The purported travels of St. Brendan are followed in O'Meagher Condon's book by equally controversial material about the Anglo-Saxon. To the author, the assumption of superiority over the Irish by the ruling class in England was incongruous in light of the origins of the people inhabiting that country and he correctly noted that the Celtic presence was greatly underestimated and ignored. From there, he proceeded to examine the effects of Irish migration on the history of the United States.

His book will probably be an eye-opener for those unfamiliar with Irish influence on the early affairs of this nation. This bicentennial edition is not offered as the definitive work on the subject, but as a starting point on the road to knowledge.

GERALD F. LEE
Ogham House

CONTENTS.

THE IRISH RACE IN AMERICA.

CHAPTER I.

AMERICA DISCOVERED BY IRISHMEN.—COLUMBUS AND HIS FOL-
LOWERS.

THE history of the Irish race in America is one which
those in whose veins its blood runs may read with pride and
pleasure.   It is, in the main, a record of privations endured
with manly fortitude, of difficulties overcome by invincible
determination, of unselfish patriotism often displayed under
the most unfavorable circumstances, of unremitting industry, too seldom successful in obtaining its just rewards, and
of unswerving fidelity and devotion to the cause of freedom
and persistent attachment to the principles to whose successful assertion and maintenance this Republic owes, not
only its origin but its glory, progress and prosperity.   The
desire on the part of Irish Americans to preserve the memory of the share taken by men of their blood, in establishing
and building up this nation, is not an unworthy, but rather
a laudable and patriotic one, and in order to gratify it to
some extent, the following brief outline of the principal
facts of American history, in which they may feel special
interest, has been prepared.

From the earliest ages, the Irish have been remarkable for
their love of adventure and travel.   Their Phœnician progenitors swept westward in their galleys, along the Mediterranean to Spain, and past the pillars of Hercules, and like

them, disdaining the slow mode of progress by land, the children of Milesius ere long sailed across the sea, to seek the Isle of·Destiny, the western limit of the Old World, and the nearest land to this great, but then unknown, continent, whereon in God's good time was to be established the mightiest Republic upon earth, and where millions of their race were to find a home and freedom. For many centuries after the settlement of the Gaelic tribes in Ireland, the spirit of enterprise of the people found vent in commercial intercourse with the ports of southern Europe and the Mediterranean. At a later period, they became indignant at the near approach of the Roman eagles to their shores, and often their fleets swept down on the coasts of Britain and Gaul, in defiance of those who claimed to be masters of the world. But when St. Patrick had declared to them the divine truths of the Christian faith, and they had embraced it with a fervor and a fidelity never to be chilled or shaken, their thoughts took a new direction. They devoted themselves to the duties of religion and the advancement of learning, with quenchless zeal and tireless industry. Not satisfied with welcoming to their monasteries and schools countless strangers from every land—who received gratuitously, not only education, but shelter, food and clothing—large numbers of Irish monks went abroad, through France, Germany, Switzerland and Italy, as well as Britain, and throughout the whole extent of Europe their voices were heard proclaiming the dread mystery of man's Redemption, bringing the erring to penance, enlightening the ignorant, and building churches and monasteries for the glory and service of God, and schools for the diffusion of knowledge. With them it was declared "the habit of travelling had become a second nature." * "What shall I say of Ireland,"

---

* Walafrid Strabo, Vita S. Galli.

asks a writer of the period, " which, despising the dangers of the ocean, emigrates entirely with her troops of philosophers and descends on our shores "? *

But the Irish missionaries did not confine their attention entirely to Britain and the Continent. They founded colonies and planted the Christian faith in Iceland and, before all others, crossed the Atlantic and trod the shores of America. Records still in existence show that when the Northmen landed in Iceland in the ninth century, they found already there settlements of Irish Christians. The latter, however, some time after withdrew from that island, leaving behind them books in their own language, bells and croziers, distinct indications of their origin and their faith, as well as of the presence among them of bishops and priests.

Owing to the wanton destruction of large numbers of ancient Irish archives by the English, our knowledge of the first discovery of America is not as exact as could be desired, but quite enough is known to justify us in claiming the honor of that achievement for St. Brendan, bishop of Clonfert, who flourished in the sixth century. According to the Irish annals this prelate, after investigating the traditions which even in his time were prevalent in Ireland respecting the existence of a great continent to the West, resolved to seek it out, and convert its people to the faith of Christ. Having made all necessary preparations, he set sail with some faithful companions, in 545, from the bay on the coast of Kerry which still bears his name, and after a difficult voyage landed, as is generally believed, upon the shores of Virginia. He then penetrated inland until he came to a large river flowing from east to west, supposed to be the Ohio. After having preached the Gospel for seven years, in various parts of the country, he returned to Ireland, and

---

* Heiric, Pref. Vitæ S. Germani.

according to some authorities, remained there and founded
several monasteries, but others assert that having obtained
a reinforcement for his missionary company, he again set
sail for the West, and was never heard of more.   The latter
statement appears the more probable, from the fact that we
find no mention of a bishop filling the see of Ardfert, over
which he presided at the time of his departure, until the
middle of the eleventh century.

The story of St. Brendan's voyage and discoveries was
soon made known in every part of Europe.   There are still
to be found in the libraries of Paris, several manuscripts containing accounts of it in Latin, and throughout France in
various places, are preserved similar narrations in the Romance and old French dialects, while versions in Irish,
German, Spanish, Portuguese and Italian are scattered in
all parts of the continent.   Wynkyn de Worde, the first English printer, published nine years before Columbus sailed
from Palos, a relation of the Irish saint's voyage * and adventures, but owing to the want of accurate information,
his story was embellished with numerous imaginary incidents.   In the *Nova Legenda* written by Capgrave, or as
some believe by John of Tynemouth, and published in 1516,
another sketch of St. Brendan's discoveries is given.   Vora-
ginius, Provincial of the Dominicans, and bishop of Genoa, in
the latter part of the thirteenth century, speaks particularly
of "St. Brandan's Land" in his *Golden Legend,* and Paulo
Toscannelli the Florentine, who prepared for Columbus the
charts used on his first voyage, gave this name to the territory which, in accordance with the custom of the Italian
geographers of that period, he marked down as being opposite to "Europe and Africa from the south of Ireland to the
end of Guinea."   Otway, in a work published in Dublin, in

---

* "Lyfe of Saynt Brandan," in the Golden Legend. Published by
Wynkyn de Worde, 1483.   Fol. 357.

1845, gives an interesting account of the traditions preserved among the people of the west of Ireland respecting St. Brendan's voyage.*

---

* In a note to "Otway's sketches in Erris and Tyrawley," the following appears : " We are informed that Brendan, hearing of the previous voyage of his cousin, Barinthus, in the western ocean, and obtaining an account from him of the happy isles he had landed on in the far west, determined, under the strong desire of winning heathen souls to Christ, to undertake a voyage of discovery himself. And aware that, all along the western coast of Ireland, there were many traditions respecting the existence of a western land, he proceeded to the islands of Arran, and there remained for some time, holding communication with venerable St. Enda, and obtaining from him much information on what his mind was bent. There can be little doubt that he proceeded northward along the coast of Mayo, and made inquiry, among its bays and islands, of the remnants of the Tuatha Danaan people, that once were so expert in naval affairs, and who acquired from the Milesians, or Scots, that overcame them, the character of being magicians, for their superior knowledge. At Inniskea, then, and Innisgloria, Brendan set up his cross; and, in after times, in his honor were erected those curious remains that still exist. Having prosecuted his inquiries with all diligence, Brendan returned to his native Kerry ; and from a bay sheltered by the lofty mountain that is now known by his name, he set sail for the Atlantic land; and, directing his course towards the southwest, in order to meet the summer solstice, or what we would call the tropic, after a long and rough voyage, his little bark being well provisioned, he came to summer seas, where he was carried along, without the aid of sail or oar, for many a long day. This, it is to be presumed, was the great gulf-stream, and which brought his vessel to shore somewhere about the Virginian capes, or where the American coast tends eastward, and forms the New England States. Here landing, he and his companions marched steadily into the interior for fifteen days, and then came to a large river, flowing from east to west ; this, evidently, was the river Ohio. And this the holy adventurer was about to cross, when he was accosted by a person of noble presence,—but whether a real or visionary man does not appear,—who told him that he had gone far enough ; that further discoveries were reserved for other men, who would, in due time, come and Christianize all that pleasant land. The above, when tested

America was known to the Scandinavians as *Irland it Mikla,* or "Great Ireland." Their records contain accounts of three voyages made thither, after the time of St. Brendan, and before the advent of Columbus. The *Landnamabock,* compiled in the thirteenth century, tells us that in 983 Ari Marson, a kinsman of Eric the Red,"was driven by a tempest to *Huitramannaland* or 'White Man's Land,' which some call *Irland it Mikla,* and which lies in the western ocean near to Vinland the Good, west from Ireland." Ari, it is said, on the authority of Thorfinn, Jarl of the Orkneys, was not permitted to return home, but was still held in great honor, by those who insisted on his remaining among them, and received the sacrament of baptism while living there, from which last fact we may perceive, that the seed sown by St. Brendan, had, up to that time at least, borne fruit. Another adventurer, Biorn, crossed the Atlantic, some time after Ari Marson's voyage, and, toward the middle of the eleventh century; he was followed by Gudlief, son of Gudlang, according to the statements found in the book above mentioned, which were based on the testimony of Rafn, a merchant of Limerick.

In the Scandinavian Sagas, "Great Ireland" is described in the following manner. "To the south of habitable Greenland there are uninhabited and wild tracts and enormous icebergs. The country of the Skrælings lies beyond these; Markland beyond this, and Vinland the Good beyond the last. Next to this and something beyond it lies Albania,

---

by common sense, clearly shows that Brendan landed on a continent, and went a good way into the interior, met a great river running in a different direction from those he heretofore crossed ; and here, from the difficulty of transit, or want of provisions, or deterred by increasing difficulties, he turned back ; and, no doubt, in a dream, he saw some such vision which embodied his own previous thought and satisfied him that it was expedient for him to return home."

that is Huitramannaland, whither formerly vessels came
from Ireland. There, several Irishmen and Icelanders saw
and recognized Ari (Marson), concerning whom nothing
had been heard for a long time and who had been made
their chief by the inhabitants of the land.''

Eminent writers believe that '' the country of the Skræl-
ings '' here referred to, was the Esquimaux coast, that
'' Markland '' was what is known to us as Labrador, that
'' Vinland '' included what is now New England, and that
'' Huitramannaland '', or as it was usually called, '' Great
Ireland '' extended from the last named territory to Florida.

The Irish would doubtless have turned the discoveries of
St. Brendan to good account, and established, and kept up
communication with America, were it not that their attention
was drawn in another direction by the savage contest carried
on between the Britons and their treacherous Saxon ''allies,'' who sought to become masters of their country, and
who, it seemed not improbable, after their expected triumph,
might endeavor to obtain a footing in Ireland. At a later
period the long continued incursions of the Danes, and the
confusion and excitement which they caused, brought about
a condition of affairs extremely unfavorable for the carrying
out of peaceful enterprises. From the final overthrow of
the northern marauders at Clontarf, to the landing of the
Normans, internal disputes similar to those which in that age
disturbed the peace of almost all other countries, kept the
minds of the Irish princes and people fixed upon incidents
occurring on their own soil, and the consequences which
followed the last named event were of such a character, as
to compel thenceforth their almost exclusive and uninter-
rupted attention to be given to domestic affairs. So it was
left for other nations to colonize permanently the '' Great
Ireland '' across the Atlantic, though that was nevertheless

destined to become in time, the chosen home and country of the great majority of the Irish race.

Nearly nine hundred and fifty years after St. Brandan's voyage, Columbus sailed from Palos on his mission of discovery. The constant intercourse maintained between Ireland and Spain from the earliest ages, gives good ground for believing the statements made, with respect to the presence of Irishmen amongst his crews. An old Italian writer asserts, that one of these was the first to plant his foot upon the soil of St. Salvador, having presumed to leap ashore, even before the illustrious Admiral himself. However this may be, it is certain that among the forty men left by Columbus to guard the fort which he built on the island of St. Domingo, previous to his return to Spain from his first transAtlantic voyage, there was a native of Galway named William Eyres. The latter, of course shared the fate of his companions, who were all slain and the fort destroyed by the Indians, soon after the Admiral's departure. The list containing the names of the fated garrison was found by Navarrette * among the archives of Seville, early in the present century, while searching for materials for his great history of Spanish maritime discovery.

---

* " *Coleccion de los viajes y descubrimientos que hicieron por mar los Españoles desdes fines del siglo XV,*" written by Martino Fernandez Navarrette ; vols. 1 and 2 published in 1825.

CHAPTER II.

BEFORE proceeding to glance at the part, which men of Irish blood have taken in the affairs of this continent, it may be well to call attention to the absurd use of the term "Anglo-Saxon" by British and pro-British writers, and speakers, especially those among them, who are accustomed to contrast the alleged virtues of the people to whom the designation is applied, with the assumed faults and defects of the Celt or Gael. The persons referred to, assume that the "Angles" were, like the Saxons, a Germanic tribe, and that both overran nearly the whole of Britain, almost extirpating the native Celts, except a few who were driven into the mountains of Wales and Scotland; that in fact the original inhabitants were dealt with as Cromwell a thousand years later, endeavored to deal with the Irish, when he ordered the people of three provinces to cross the Shannon, and not to return under pain of death.

Those assumptions are now beginning to be recognized by the best informed students of history, as groundless. No Teutonic tribe was ever known by the name of "Angles." In the language of a distinguished writer * who recently dis-

---

* Charles Mackay, L.L.D., of London, who in a very interesting article, which appeared in the New York *Independent* of August 13, 1885, said on this subject:

" A very large proportion of the British people are accustomed to boast of their ' Anglo-Saxon ' descent, without acknowledging or even suspecting that their ancestry is to a much larger extent British than Teutonic, and that they are the descendants, more or less mixed, with

cussed the question, "the German 'Angles' were an imaginary people who never existed." The much misused and misunderstood word is in fact a corruption of *An-Gael* which signifies "the Celt." Recent investigations have shown that the Celtic Britons formed a considerable portion of the

---

other races of the Celtic inhabitants who possessed the whole country before the Roman, German, Danish and Norman invaders set foot on the soil or usurped the Government. In all this they show their ignorance of the meaning of the words 'British,' 'English' and 'Anglo-Saxon.' The error is of old growth and originated in the pretentious half-knowledge of the early writers, who compiled their traditional, and for the most part untrustworthy histories, in the later languages. Latin was at that time the only medium of the little literature which existed. None of the Celtic languages was reduced to writing except by the Druidical priests, who kept their learning to themselves, and only communicated orally with the people. And German and its off-shoot, the early English, was in its infancy and almost wholly inchoate and unformed."

"The error with which I am at present more particularly concerned is of more than a thousand years' standing, and derives the name of the Southern frontier of Great Britain from a supposed German tribe, who with the Jutes and Saxons, invaded the island after the departure of the Romans. It happens, however, that the name of "Angles" was never borne by, or known to any German tribes. The invaders of the East coast of Britain came from the opposite coast of the continent, principally from Denmark, Holland and Belgium, and brought their barbarous laws, and rude language along with them. The true origin of the word 'Angles' is the Celtic or Gaelic '*an*,' the definite article, and '*gaidheil*', (in which the consonants *dh* are not pronounced), which signifies the 'gael' or the '*Celts;*' whence *An-gael*, and not Angles."

"The epithet 'Anglo-Saxon,' now so frequently applied to South Britain, is of much more recent origin, and was not known in the golden age of English literature, when Shakespeare and Spencer flourished, nor until the second half of the eighteenth century. Britain was known to the Romans as Anglia, centuries before the Saxons or that section of them erroneously supposed to have been called Angles, established themselves in any part of the country. It was not until the Hanoverian (a Saxon) family of the Georges had given three sovereigns to the country, that courtly writers began to talk of the 'Anglo-Saxon' origin of the

population of England, even after the Saxons became its masters through treachery; that when the Danes had, in their turn subjugated the latter, they brought over large colonies of their own people, whose descendants still predominate in northeastern England, and that finally the Norman Con-

---

people, and that the epithet finally became synonymous with 'English.' It is true that in the time of the Romans, a small portion of the eastern coast of Anglia, immediately opposite Belgium and Holland, was called ' the Saxon shore.' The name was given to it from the fact that successive swarms of Dutch and Danish pirates had succeeded in forming such settlements on the littoral, though they had never been able to penetrate into the interior of the country. The Gael, or Celts, called these pirates *Sassenach*, as the Southern English are called to this day by the Gaelic and Celtic speaking people of Wales, Ireland and Scotland. The word did not originally signify a German or native of Saxony, but a robber and an assassin, in which sense it still obtains currency among such of the Irish people as retain a hereditary hatred of British rule."

Referring to the influence which " popular usage " in England has produced on the minds of the Scotch, in regard to this question Dr. Mackay continues:

" It cannot be affirmed that the objection taken by the northern nation to the southern usurpation of the epithet English, is in any way unreasonable, founded as it is upon the commonly received if not universal opinion, that the English receive their name from the German 'Angles,' an imaginary people who never existed. The Southern English believed this fable, and not aware of the fact that they are not half so much German as they think themselves, made light of the Scottish objection, and called it sentimental, and unworthy of practical consideration. But if Angles are in reality " Angael " or the Gael, the Scottish and Northern Britain people are quite as much Angael or English as those of the south, and the English Government is rightfully the designation of government of the whole kingdom. This fact should remove the natural jealousy of the Scotch, and cut away from the conceit of the South British the very slender and rotten foundation on which it is based. But until the Southern English admit the fact that a colony of Germans did not give name to England, but that the whole country of Britain, otherwise Anglia, as the Romans called it, derives its name from the Celtic *Angael*, the North British are quite right in objecting to being called English."

quest was followed by an immense immigration, of the kindred of those who swept away forever Saxon supremacy and power at Hastings. Of the four principal elements, Celtic, Saxon, Danish and Norman-French, which compose the mass of the population of Britain, the first named is certainly strongest in point of numbers, but it is questionable whether the second be entitled to the next place in that respect. The descendants of the tribes who accompanied and followed, in the wake of Hengist and Horsa, form but a comparatively small minority of the British people. The application to them of the epithet " Anglo-Saxon," is absurd and misleading, as is the assumption, that they form the bulk of the nation, and the extravagant conceit, that they compose the great mass of the citizens of this republic.* A little consideration given to this question, would lead to the removal of erroneous impressions still existing in many quarters with respect to it, and prevent in future the mischievous effects, which they have too often caused.

---

* In this connection the remark made by Brodhead in his " *History of the State of New York* " may be quoted. " Much," he says, " of what has been written of American history, has been written by those who, from habit or prejudice, have been inclined to magnify the influence and extol the merit of the Anglo-Saxon race at the expense of every other element which has assisted to form the national greatness."

The following from the *American Medical Monthly*, Dec., 1855, may be added here:

" The history of emigration, and the peculiarity of our language, so different from the Saxon dialects of east and north England, prove that our ancestors came from the Celtic south and west of England, and the other persecuted Celtic parts of the three kingdoms,—not to mention Celtic Spain, Celtic France and Celtic Belgium. The Celto-Germans, from the borders of the Rhine, probably outnumbered the Gothic immigrants from North Europe, whose type has been submerged in the general Celtic tide. The true American type is therefore not a hybrid Anglo-Saxon, but a pure-bred Celtic race, as their language, their history, their physique, and impulsive versatile genius testify."

It may be further said that the number of emigrants of all elements, from England to this country previous to the Revolution, did not greatly exceed that of those who came here from Ireland, though the contrary opinion has long been prevalent. It is not difficult to account for the erroneous views entertained until recently on this subject. Through the rigid enforcement of the infamous penal "laws," the British government sought to deprive the great mass of the Irish people, of the blessings of religion and the benefits of education. Its efforts to obliterate the ancient faith from the soil of Ireland were unsuccessful, but, it to a great extent, accomplished its other object. The descendants of those who in past days had diffused knowledge throughout Britain and Europe, were deprived of the right to educate themselves, because of their fidelity to their religious convictions. The inevitable result followed. Ignorance overspread the land, except where hunted priests might find time, amid the dangers to which they were exposed, to instruct their people, or daring devotees of the forbidden art of teaching, might, at the risk of imprisonment and death, endeavor in the shade of a hedge, or under the shelter of a ruined hut, to communicate the rudiments of knowledge to those who aspired after the prohibited luxury.

The early Irish immigrants found the British penal "laws" in force here. The great scarcity of priests rendered the practice of the duties of their religion almost impossible, and its profession deprived them in almost every quarter, of the right to share in the privileges enjoyed by others. Their immediate descendants might cherish traditions of their origin and belief, but these under the circumstances by which they were surrounded, naturally grew fainter in course of time, and within a few generations, became necessarily vague, even if they were not entirely effaced. Americans of Irish and Catholic ancestry, without the means of practising or preserving a correct knowledge of their father's faith, were gradually drawn into the ranks of the various sects, with whose members they grew up and mingled. Moreover in the books of instruction which they studied at school, and the works on history and other subjects which they read, they found England extolled above all other nations, while the Irish were represented as rude, insubordinate and ignorant. With no opportunity afforded them of obtaining truthful information on these subjects, they became to some extent impressed with a belief in the correctness of the misleading statements and views so persistently promulgated; lost pride in preserving the memory of their origin, and at length yielded a tacit assent to the assumptions of British writers; that the descendants of the countrymen of the latter, formed the great mass of the people of this continent. But it is by no means too late to correct this error, or to remove the mischievous effects to which it has led.

With regard to Irish immigrants of the various Protestant denominations who sought a home on this soil before the Revolution, it is to be remembered that they were subjected to few restrictions or disqualifications. Free from the embarrassments under which their Catholic countrymen who came here labored, they could avow more boldly their nationality, and manifest more freely and fearlessly their pride in it. As, moreover, from the circumstances alluded to, they occupied a more prominent position and took a more active part in public affairs, than their Catholic kindred here, the proportion between their numbers and those of the latter, seems much greater than that which obtained in Ireland at that time, though in reality, there was but little difference. These facts should not be lost sight of by those who wish to form a correct estimate of the strength of the Irish race in America.

CHAPTER III.

The Irish in Maryland.

The first considerable emigration from Ireland to America took place in 1629, when a colony of Irish and English effected a permanent settlement in Guiana.* George Calvert, first Lord Baltimore, had endeavored to establish a colony of a similar character on the peninsula of Avalon, in Newfoundland, three years earlier, but owing to the rigor of the climate, he after spending over $100,000, and passing two winters in the place, reluctantly abandoned his project and returned home.

This distinguished man was born in 1580, and at an early age obtained a position at Court, through the influence of Sir Robert Cecil, the "artful" Minister whom James I., continued in the position he had held under Elizabeth. In 1620 Calvert was made Secretary of State, and he afterwards entered the English Parliament as member, first for Yorkshire, his native county, and later for the University of Oxford. In 1624 he became a Catholic, and at once resigned his position as Secretary, saying to James, " I must now be wanting to my trust or violate my conscience in the discharge of this office." The King was "so moved by Calvert's honest avowal, that while he accepted his resignation, he continued him as a member of the Privy Council for life, and soon after created him Lord Baltimore," † his

---

* Marmion's " History of the Maritime Ports of Ireland."
† McSherry, " History of Maryland."

title being taken from the town of that name in southwestern Cork, anciently known as a sanctuary of the Druids.

Soon after his return from Newfoundland, Lord Baltimore went to Virginia with the intention of establishing himself there, but unfortunately, religious bigotry was at that period too strong in the province to allow him to carry out his purpose. He was urged to take the oath of supremacy, which was considered equivalent to a renunciation of his faith, and upon his refusal to comply, was compelled to go away. He then ascended the Chesapeake, and surveyed a portion of the present State of Maryland, after which he returned to England, and in a short time made application to Charles II., for a grant of that territory. Henrietta Maria, the Catholic wife of the ill-starred sovereign, supported the request, which was acceded to, but before the charter had received the royal signature, Calvert died, "leaving a name against which the breath of calumny has hardly dared whisper a reproach." * His eldest son, Cecil, who inherited his title and privileges, obtained however the grant intended for his father and undertook to carry out his purpose. Leonard Calvert, brother of the proprietary, was placed in charge of the undertaking, and he with about two hundred Irish and English emigrants "nearly all of whom were Catholics and gentlemen of fortune and respectability, who desired to fly from the spirit of intolerance which pervaded England, and to rear up their altars in freedom in the wilderness," † set sail from the Isle of Wight in November 1633, having "first placed their ships under the protection of God, imploring the intercession of the Blessed Virgin and of St. Ignatius and all the guardian angels of Maryland." ‡ The expedition was accompanied by Fathers

---

* Bancroft.   † McSherry.
‡ Father White, " *Relatio itineris in Marylandiam.*"

White and John Altham of the Society of Jesus, and was supplied by the generosity of Calvert with stores of provisions, clothing, agricultural implements, and whatever else was deemed necessary for the comfort of the intending settlers. After a weary voyage of four months, the emigrants landed on the island of St. Clements, and as became them, first sought the blessing of God upon their enterprise. "On the day of the Annunciation of the Holy Virgin Mary," says Father White, "the twenty-fifth of March, in the year 1634, we offered in this island for the first time the Sacrifice of the Mass; in this region of the world it had never been celebrated before. The sacrifice being ended, having taken upon our shoulders the great cross, which we had hewn from a tree, and going in procession to the place that had been designated, the governor, commissioners and other Catholics participating in the ceremony, we erected it as a trophy to Christ the Saviour, while the Litany of the Cross was chanted humbly, on our bended knees with great emotion of soul." * The Governor at once bought from the Indians a tract of territory on the mainland, about thirty miles in length, which is now included in St. Mary's county, and on March 27, the city of St. Mary was founded. Speaking of this event Bancroft says that on the day mentioned, "the Catholics took quiet possession of the little place and religious liberty obtained a home, its only home in the wide world, at the humble village which bore the name of St. Mary's." †

The new colony made rapid progress. During the first two or three years after its settlement, the proprietary expended upon its improvement more than $200,000. All who believed in Christ were cordially welcomed there, and Puritans banished from Virginia and Quakers driven out of

---

* Relatio.   † Bancroft.

New England, found a refuge and freedom upon a soil un-
stained by the blood of its original possessors, and among a
people free from the fell spirit of religious bitterness, which
then ruled supreme in the other colonies, subject to England.
Nor were the Indians neglected, or looked upon, as in Massachusetts and elsewhere as "the devil's own children and
agents, whom the saints were in duty bound to exterminate
and send back to the powers of darkness whence they
came." *   The devoted and zealous Jesuit Fathers divided
their time between them and the settlers.   Native tribes and
communities were converted, and the " Our Father" and the
"Hail Mary" were heard in the wigwam of the savage, as well
as in the home of the pale-face.   Hymns in honor of the
Crucified, and of the Sinless Mother, who stood beneath
His cross on Calvary, echoed alike through the paths of
the forest and in the streets of the little town, and peace
and harmony reigned, between the children of the soil and
those who sought to found upon it, a refuge for the oppressed
and persecuted of every clime and creed.   The Jesuits applied themselves with their characteristic ardor, to the study
of the Indian language and its many dialects, and soon
became able to instruct the native neophytes in their own
tongue.   The success of the Fathers in their "spiritual
plantations " was rapid and remarkable.   Within five years
from the time of their first landing they had baptized Chilo-
macon, King of the Piscataways, who dwelt near where
to-day stands the Capital of the Republic, with his family
and a considerable number of his tribe.   This example was
followed by the young Queen of the Potopacos, with the
wife and children of another chief, and nearly all their followers.   The spirit which animated the missionaries will
be understood from the words of one of their number,

---

* Upham's " Salem Witchcraft, etc."

Father Block, uttered in 1641, a short time before his death. " For my part," he wrote, " I would rather, laboring in the conversion of these Indians, expire on the bare ground deprived of all human succor and perishing with hunger, than once think of abandoning this holy work of God from fear of want." The good Fathers were so devoted to their sacred duties, that they declined to take any part in purely secular affairs. Though summoned to sit in the first Legislature of the colony, convened in 1635, they " desired to be excused from giving voice in this Assembly " * and though their names were retained on the list of members, they took no part in the deliberations of that body.

But ere long troubles arose which owed their formidable character, to the intolerance of those who had sought and found in Maryland, a refuge from persecution. A trader named Clayborne, who had received a royal license to traffic with the Indians in 1631, and had established himself in Kent Island, refused to acknowledge the authority of Lord Baltimore, and endeavored to arouse the hostility of the Indians against the new settlers. His efforts in this direction proved abortive, but in 1645 he was enabled by the aid of the Protestant refugees from other colonies, to raise a rebellion and drive Leonard Calvert, the Governor, to take shelter in Virginia. The insurgents remained masters of the situation for nearly a year and a half, but at length Calvert returned with a body of troops and succeeded in re-establishing his authority. In 1649 the General Assembly was again convened. It was composed of eleven Catholics and three Protestants † and by it was passed the Toleration Act, a convincing and memorable proof of the truly Christian and patriotic spirit of its authors. It ran as follows:

---

* Bozman.   † Davis's " Day Star of American Freedom."

" Whereas the enforcing of conscience in matters of religion hath frequently fallen out to be of dangerous consequence in those commonwealths where it has been practised, and for the more quiet and peaceable government of this province, and the better to preserve mutual love and unity among the inhabitants; therefore be it enacted, that no person or persons whatsoever within this province or the islands, ports, harbors, creeks or havens thereunto belonging, professing to believe in Jesus Christ, shall from henceforth be anyways troubled, or molested, or discountenanced for, or in respect of his or her religion, nor in the free exercise thereof, within this province or the islands thereunto belonging, nor anyway compelled to the belief or exercise of any other religion, against his or her consent." *

But this admirable law was not long permitted to remain in force, by those who, while loudly clamoring for religious liberty for themselves, shamefully denied it to those who differed from them in belief. Cromwell, supported by a Parliament which had decreed in 1644 that " no quarter should be given to any Irishman," who resisted its usurped authority over his country,† had become supreme in Britain and Ireland, and his adherents in the colony sought to obtain control of its government. They were successful. The Long Parliament in 1651 appointed commissioners, one of whom was Clayborne, to assume the government of Maryland. The natural result followed. An Assembly, from which Catholics were totally excluded, was called in 1654, which revoked the Toleration Act, and declared that those who professed the Faith of Columbus and Calvert were not entitled to the protection of the law. Referring to these outrageous proceedings Bancroft says ‡ " The Puritans had neither the gratitude to respect the rights of

---

* Bacon's laws.   † Rushworth.
‡ Bancroft, i., 261.

the government by which they had been received and fostered, nor magnanimity to continue the toleration, to which alone they were indebted for their residence in the colony." Stone, Lord Baltimore's representative, made an effort in the following year to assert his authority, but he was unsuccessful, and fell with his followers into the hands of his enemies, who put four of his party to death. In 1660, however, on the restoration of Charles II., the proprietary was restored to his rights, and by his direction Philip Calvert was appointed governor.

Matters went on quietly enough until the English changed masters in 1689, when the spirit of intolerance again displayed itself. A notorious atheist named Coode formed an "Association in arms for the defence of the Protestant religion etc.," and this body called a convention, which made various frivolous or false charges against Lord Baltimore, to William of Orange, and demanded that the government of the colony should be taken by the latter, into his own hands. Although the Protestants of Kent county sent a petition to the King, declaring that there was no ground for the accusation of Coode and his associates, and denouncing his falsehood and unfaithfulness, the request of the malcontents was complied with, and Sir Lionel Copley was sent over as royal governor. He convened a General Assembly in 1692, which established the Anglican church as the religion of the state and imposed a tax upon Catholics and members of other denominations for the support of the dominant sect. In 1704 new laws were passed "to prevent the further growth of Popery," of which, the following were some of the provisions:

"Catholic bishops and priests were forbidden to say Mass, or in any way exercise their ministry. Catholics were deprived of the right of elective franchise, unless they renounced their faith. They were forbidden to teach, were obliged to support the established (Anglican) Church, and were forced to pay a double tax. It was strongly recommended that "children were to be taken from the pernicious influence of Popish parents." And it was decreed that a Catholic child, by becoming a Protestant, could exact his share of property from his parents, 'as though they were dead.' Catholic emigrants were moreover forbidden to enter Maryland."*

In 1706 the Quakers were allowed to hold meetings by the Assembly, though that "privilege" was denied to those who professed the faith of the founders of the colony. In the same year it was decreed that "Papists" should pay double the tax required from Protestants, and later those of the proscribed religion were "forbidden to appear in certain parts of the towns." The oppression and indignities to which the Catholics were subjected, at length drove them to think of obtaining deliverance from it by expatriation. In 1752 Daniel Carroll, father of Archbishop Carroll, went to France to endeavor to make arrangements for the removal of himself and his co-religionists to Louisiana, but although he had several interviews on the subject with the ministers of Louis XV., his mission led to no definite results. So matters remained until the period of the Revolution, when the Convention held at Annapolis, December 8, 1774, passed unanimously a resolution in which it was said, "As our opposition to the settled plan of the British administration to enslave America, will be strengthened by an union of all ranks of men in this province, we do most earnestly recommend, that all former differences about religion or politics * * * from henceforth cease and be buried forever in oblivion, and we entreat, we conjure every man by his duty to God, his country and his posterity, cordially

---

* O'Kane Murray, "History of the Catholic Church in the United States."

to unite in defence of our common rights and liberties."
In 1775 Charles Carroll of Carrollton was chosen a member
of the Maryland "Committee to prepare a Declaration of
rights and a form of government for this State," and the
result of his labors was, that Catholics were again admitted,
to the enjoyment of all rights and privileges granted to their
fellow-citizens, in the following year.

Notwithstanding all the disabilities, under which those inhabitants of Maryland who professed the faith of the great
majority of the Irish people labored, the latter continued at
intervals, in considerable numbers to seek a home there.
According to Bozman the issue of the Irish Confederate
war, 1641-52, "affected the population of the province," as
indeed it also affected the other colonies, through the transportation thither of vast numbers of the Irish people by
the Cromwellians. The violation of the Treaty of Limerick
by William of Orange, drove many of those who had supported James II., but had remained in Ireland trusting to
"British faith" to seek a new home beyond the Atlantic.
Among the immigrants into Maryland somewhat later was
the father of Archbishop Carroll. Of the vast numbers of
Irish, the great majority of whom were members of the
ancient faith, who were compelled by landlord enactions
and "laws" against liberty of conscience as well as against
national industries, to emigrate during the eighteenth century, prior to the Revolution, a very large proportion preferred to settle in Pennsylvania, owing to the comparative
toleration accorded there to Catholics. It is to be observed,
however, that considerable numbers of these, located near
the borders of Maryland, a circumstance which seems to
show, that while they did not wish to subject themselves to
the disabilities imposed on those of their religion, in the
province founded by Calvert, they at the same time were
anxious to settle in the vicinity, of the large settlements of

their countrymen and kindred, who had at an early period made their home there.

Irish immigrants driven from their native land by land-lord enactments and the coercive measures of the British government, poured in extraordinary numbers into Mary-land, as indeed they did into all the other colonies, during the five or six years just preceding the Revolution. In a Baltimore paper of August 20, 1773, the following item is found, " Within this fortnight three thousand five hundred emigrants have arrived from Ireland.* They brought with them bitter memories, which inspired them to become the most active and uncompromising enemies of British rule.† It is not assumed that immigration on this scale was kept up through the year, nor would it be correct to suppose that considerable numbers of Irish immigrants did not arrive in the " Land of the Sanctuary " during all the years above mentioned, because no accurate information on the subject has been handed down to us. The events then occurring in Ireland, and the enormous emigration to America to which they led, which will be alluded to later, justify the belief that the increase of Maryland's population from 85,000 in 1749 to 174,000 in 1775,‡ an increase of nearly ninety thousand in twenty-six years, was in great part owing to the rapid influx of Irish immigrants.

Before closing this chapter, attention may be called to the absurd view entertained by Englishmen of a certain class, with regard to the pride which Marylanders feel, in

---

* *Maryland Journal and Baltimore Advertiser.*

† Lossing says, vol. 2, p, 193, referring to the events of 1776: " A large number of Presbyterians from the north of Ireland had settled in the province, and the principles of their ecclesiastical polity being favor-able to Republicanism they exerted a powerful influence in casting off the royal yoke."

‡ Compendium of the seventh census, De Bow, Washington, 1854.

dwelling on the memory of the founder of their State. One of these wiseacres declared recently that "the good people of Baltimore pique themselves on being planted by a lord, while the neighboring States were planted by commoners." To lower their conceit he tells them that Lord Baltimore's title was derived from a mere honorary Irish barony, which gave him no place in the British House of Lords.* His disclosure evidently failed to produce the appalling effect intended, for an eminent jurist of the Monumental City commenting on it, said, "Whether Calvert was lord or commoner, or commoner made lord, is to us a matter of profound indifference. * * * We are proud of his great charter as one of the noblest works that human hands have ever reared, the most glorious proclamation ever made of the liberty of thought and worship. Had he been an Irish peasant instead of an Irish baron we should reverence him perhaps the more, and certainly feel none the less the honor of descending from the good brave men who made the precepts he bequeathed them, a practical and living truth." †

---

* London *Athenæum.*

† S. T. Wallis—quoted in McSherry's Essay on the Early History of Maryland.

CHAPTER IV.

THE IRISH IN PENNSYLVANIA.

WILLIAM PENN, while a student at Oxford in 1660, became favorably impressed by the religious opinions professed by the members of the Society of Friends. A few years later, while living at Cork, he joined the Quakers of that city and thenceforth became an ardent advocate of their doctrines. On his return to England, the persecution to which he and his brethren were subjected made him desirous of securing for the latter a home in the New World, where they could enjoy religious liberty. He held a claim against the government, bequeathed to him by his father Admiral Penn, and succeeded in obtaining from Charles II., in lieu of payment, a grant of the territory now known as Pennsylvania.* His charter was confirmed in 1681, and in the October of the following year he took possession of his province. He went to England in 1684, and during his stay there, was thrown into prison by William of Orange on account of his attachment to the dethroned king James H. He was for the same reason deprived of the administration of the affairs of his province, but succeeded in obtaining the restoration of his proprietary rights in 1694. On his

---

* Penn, in a letter written in 1681, says, that the province was named Pennsylvania in honor of his father the Admiral by Charles II. He adds, " I chose New Wales, being a hilly country, and when the secretary, a Welshman, refused to call it New Wales I proposed Sylvania and they added Penn to it, though I much opposed them and went to the king to have it struck out." Spencer, vol. i., p. 130.

return here in 1699 he was accompanied by James Logan *
a native of Lurgan, Armagh Co., Ireland, whom he appointed
his Secretary, and who afterward became Chief Justice and
President of the Council, in which latter capacity he governed the province from 1736 to 1738.

The liberal principles of the founder of Pennsylvania,
and the assurances of civil and religious liberty, which he
held out to all, as an inducement to settle in his province,
attracted towards it favorable attention from many quarters
and especially from Ireland, where he was so well known
and so highly regarded, by the great majority of the people,
because of his attachment to the cause of the sovereign for
whom they had fought, as well as on account of the injuries
he had suffered at the hands of William. The confiscation
by the latter's greedy Parliament in 1692, of almost the last
acre left in possession of the Catholics, and the Penal laws
and formal violation of the Treaty of Limerick in 1695, induced many of those who professed the ancient Faith, to
seek a new home beyond the Atlantic, in a colony distant
from England, where land was to be had cheaply and
where religious toleration was promised. Before long,
too, the Irish of other denominations were made to feel

---

* Logan was born in 1674. He learned Greek, Latin, and partially
Hebrew before he was thirteen years old. At nineteen he had become
acquainted with French, Italian and Spanish as well as mathematics, in
which last especially he showed great ability. At different periods he
filled the positions of Provincial Secretary, Commissioner of Property
and Receiver General, Mayor of Philadelphia, Recorder of the City, and
President Judge of Common Pleas, besides the offices mentioned above.
He was a great friend of the Indians, and the celebrated Mingo chief
Logan—whose famous speech has been preserved by Jefferson—was so
named by his father Shikellimus, because of the latter's admiration
for the distinguished Irishman. Logan died in 1751, leaving his large
collection of books to form a public library. He has been well called
" the friend of man, the friend of peace, and the friend of science "

the effects of English jealousy and prejudice, as well as to suffer through the ingratitude of the "Deliverer," who, having become ruler of Ireland, mainly through their efforts, repaid their services to him, in his characteristic manner, by the destruction of their most important and flourishing industry, the woolen manufacture. In June, 1698, the English lords presented an address to William, stating that the growing manufacture of cloth in Ireland invited his subjects of England to settle there, and requesting his interference to prevent its growth. Later in the same month the Commons made a similar request, and in reply the "glorious, pious and immortal" object of so much veneration, among some of the descendants of those he sought to ruin, showed his appreciation of Irish Protestant devotion, by saying, " I will do all that in me lies to discourage the woolen manufacture in Ireland," * and for once at least he kept his word. A "law" was speedily passed prohibiting the export of wool, yarn, and new or old drapery from Ireland to any other country except England, on pain of forfeiting the ship and cargo, and five hundred pounds for every offence. "The permission to export the woolen manufactures of Ireland to England was merely illusive, the duties on importation into the latter country being tantamount to a prohibition." † Other restrictive enactments followed and the result was, the almost complete ruin of the once flourishing Irish industry. Large numbers of those who had been engaged in it sought new homes in the colonies, and especially in Pennsylvania. Stewart † tells us that " The destruction of the woolen manufactures of Ireland compelled a multitude of the Episcopalian Protestants to desert the country " and Lord Fitzwilliam declares that these British laws against

---

* Newenham, p. 103.   † Ibid.
‡ History of Armagh.

Irish industry drove " 100,000 operatives " away from their Native Land.

The Catholic Irish became so numerous in Philadelphia within a few years after the events above mentioned, that their assembling for the purpose of fulfilling their religious duties, attracted the attention and aroused the evil passions of some over-zealous bigots, who promptly informed the British government of these proceedings and no doubt demanded that a stop should be put to them. The " officers of the crown " were only too ready to hearken to the malicious fanatics, and reproached Penn because of the toleration extended to the adherents of the proscribed Faith in his province. He became alarmed and wrote to Logan in 1708, " There is a complaint against your government that you suffer public Mass in a scandalous manner. Pray send me the matter of fact, for ill use is made of it against us here." *

After the accession of George, the Elector of Hanover, to the throne of England, the feeling of bitterness against the Irish Catholics became so rampant, that they were spoken of in all the debates of Parliament as " the common enemy," and even those who sympathized with their deplorable condition were styled " enemies of the constitution " and looked on with suspicion. They emigrated about this time in considerable numbers to Pennsylvania, and settled generally near the Maryland border. By an ordinance of 1720, the Irish located in Lancaster county were exempted from rents, " in consideration of their being a frontier people forming a kind of cordon of defence if needful." † Between 1720 and 1730 an extraordinary emigration from Ireland to America took place,‡ particularly during the three

---

* Watson's Annals of Philadelphia. † Watson.

‡ Potter's *American Monthly* for March, 1875, says : " A very large emigration from the North of Ireland to Pennsylvania took place between the years 1720 and 1730. They at once pushed to the frontier of Chester

last years of that period. In 1727 the Irish Catholics found themselves bereft of the last remnant of their liberties; they were deprived of the elective franchise, which was not restored to them until after the French Revolution. This outrage seems to have been the principal cause of the exodus by which it was followed, though at the same time there was a scarcity of corn in Ireland which led to riots at Cork and Limerick. In 1728 Stewart * tells us there was "a considerable emigration from the North to America," which Primate Boulter, the head of the English faction, and certain dissenting ministers in vain endeavored to prevent. In 1729 Logan complains the payment of the tax of twenty shillings a head imposed on every "servant" arriving in the Province, was evaded in the case of the arrival from Dublin of a ship "with one hundred Papists and convicts." He adds, "It looks as if Ireland is to send all its inhabitants hither, for last week not less than six ships arrived and every day two or three arrive also. The common fear is that if they thus continue to come they will make themselves proprietors of the Province." † From December, 1728, to December, 1729, 5,655 Irish emigrants landed at Philadelphia.‡ During the same period 267 English and Welsh, 243 Palatines (Germans) and 43 Scotch arrived, the Irish being more than ten times as numerous as all the others taken together. In 1730 Logan complained that the

---

County, and settled along Chiogues, Alungo, Swatara and Paxtong Creeks, in the township of Donegal. They were a brave and hardy race." The following are some of the names mentioned by the *Monthly:* Davenport, Cartridge, Baily, Harris, Burt, Galbraith, Croghan, Lowery, McGinty, &c., &c. "The two latter," says the *Monthly,* "traveled Kentucky both ways, and explored it before Gist made his appearance south of the Ohio."

* History of Armagh.
† Watson.
‡ Holmes' Annals of America.

Irish had possessed themselves of the whole of Conestoge manor of 15,000 acres, alleging that "it was against the laws of God and nature that so much land should be idle while so many Christians wanted it to labor on and to raise their bread." * His successor, as secretary to the proprietaries, Richard Peters, a few years later sought to dispossess these settlers, and to measure the land, but they resisted, broke the surveyor's chain and compelled the sheriff and his posse to retire. They afterwards, however, made engagements for leases.† Gordon says, writing in 1806, "Emigration, which has since increased, was observed in Primate Boulter's time of office, (1724 to 1742), to draw over 3,000 people annually from Ulster." ‡ In 1735 the action of the so-called Irish Parliament in abolishing tithes of agistment or pasturage, and thereby throwing an additional heavy burden on the tillers of the soil, led to a great increase in the number of emigrants to America.§ There can be no doubt that the enormous growth of the population of Pennsylvania, from 20,000 in 1701 to 250,000 in 1749,‖ was mainly owing to the vast multitudes of Irish immigrants who found their way to the province during the period.

The cruelties and exactions of the rack-renting landlords of Ireland, and especially of the Marquis of Donegal, provoked an agrarian insurrection there in 1771, the suppression of which by the British government after a hard struggle, led multitudes of the people to emigrate to America. Of these the province founded by Penn received a considerable proportion. Spencer says on this subject, after referring to the great numbers of Irish immigrants who arrived here in 1771 and 1772, "Within the first fortnight of August, 1773, there arrived at Philadelphia three thousand five hundred

---

* Watson.   † Ibid.   ‡ History of Ireland.
§ Ibid.   ‖ Compendium of the seventh census.

emigrants from Ireland, and from the same document which has recorded this circumstance, it appears that vessels were arriving every month, freighted with emigrants from Holland, Germany, and especially from Ireland and the Highlands of Scotland." *

"Redemptioner" was the appellation given to an immigrant who, having been unable to pay for his passage, undertook to work during a stipulated time for the party advancing the necessary funds. Some of these became wealthy and rose to distinguished positions.† More than one of the

---

* History of the United States, vol. i., 306.

† Watson says, "Some of these turned out frugal and industrious and became in time part of our wealthy citizens. In one case a servant was found to be a lord and returned home to inherit his estate. The general facts are to the following effect: Arthur Annesley (Lord Altham) married a daughter of the Duke of Buckingham, by whom he had a son. In the next year the parents had some difference which terminated in a separation. The father took exclusive possession of the child and manifested much fondness for him until the death of his wife, when his affections were alienated from his offspring by a lady who aspired to become his second spouse. She succeeded in having the boy placed at a school in Dublin, and soon after, Lord Altham dying, his brother, who wished to possess the estate and title, caused the youth to be enticed on board an American vessel which sailed from Dublin in April, 1728. He was landed at Philadelphia, being then in his thirteenth year, sold as a redemptioner, and actually served out twelve years in hard labor until an accident, in the year 1740, brought him to such acquaintance as led to his return home. It happened that two Irishmen, John and William Broders, travelling the Lancaster road, stopped at the house where young Annesly was in service. During a conversation with him they learned that he was a native of Wexford, where they also belonged, and finally discovering who he was, they volunteered to go back to Ireland and testify to the fact of his existence and whereabouts, and they kept their promise. The young man secured a passage home, and succeeded in obtaining a verdict against his treacherous uncle, but the latter appealed to the House of Lords, and while the case was pending there, the young redemptioner died. His life formed the groundwork for the popular nov-

Signers of the Declaration is said to have come to America
as a redemptioner, and among the rest George Taylor of
Pennsylvania, who at an early age, while studying medicine
with a physician of his native town in Ireland, became tired
of the profession, ran away from home and obtained a passage to Philadelphia on the terms above referred to. Many
of his countrymen came over under similar conditions.
Those able and willing to work were wanted here to till the
soil, and immense numbers of young Irishmen availed
themselves of the opportunities presented to them of escap-
ing from the deplorable situation in which they were placed
at home through British misrule, by consenting to labor for
a limited time in order to repay the cost of their passage
hither. The comparatively prosperous condition of England
rendered her people far less willing to leave their own country, and kept emigration from it within narrow limits.
Another very large class of emigrants from Ireland were
styled " servants." * The Penal laws enforced their " inflicted banishment to a colony and service therein as a penalty for the crime of practising many of the duties of the

---

els, " Roderick Random" and " Florence McCarthy."—*Annals of Philadelphia.*

* " In 1741 public information is given to merchants and captains that
Augustus Gun of Cork, bellman, has power from the mayor there to
procure servants for America for many years past." *Annals of Philadelphia.*

Watson says, "In some cases the severity of British laws pushed off
young men of good abilities for very small offences. I have knowledge
of two or three among us, even within my memory, who rose to riches
and credit here and have left fine families. One great man, before my
time, had been sold in Maryland as an offender in Ireland. While serving his master as a common servant, he showed much ability unexpectedly in managing for him an important lawsuit, for which he instantly made
him free. He then came to Philadelphia and amassed a great fortune
in landed estate, now of great value among his heirs." *Annals.*

Catholic religion, and the persons transported under those laws were known as Irish servants." *

As early as 1686 Penn in a letter to his steward speaks of an old priest then living at Philadelphia. In the year named, mass was celebrated in a wooden building on the northwest corner of Front and Walnut Streets in that city.† A chapel stood on the road leading from Nicetown to Frankfort in 1729, connected with the house of Miss Elizabeth McGawley, an Irish lady who had brought over a number of tenants and had settled in that place. Watson says, " It may be a question whether this chapel may not have been there before Miss McGawley settled there, even from the earliest origin of the city, and adds "that it was put there for Catholics because their religion, however agreeable to Penn's tolerant spirit, was not so to most Protestants then in power." ‡ The writer named also speaks of a house on the southeast corner of Chestnut and Second Streets, having been " built for a Papal chapel before 1736," but adds that " the people opposed its being so used in so public a place." In 1734 Governor Gordon " informed the Council that a house (St. Joseph's Chapel) had been erected for the open celebration of mass contrary to the statutes of William the Third. The Council advised him to consult his superiors

---

* Bishop England, Works, vol. iii.
† Life and Times of Archbishop Carroll, *Cath. Magazine,* 1845.
‡ Watson's *Annals,* vol. ii., 453.
In a note Watson says, " Near the place (one eighth of a mile off) is a stone enclosure in which is a large tombstone of marble, inscribed with a cross and the name 'John Michael Brown, Ob. 15 Dec., A. D. 1750. R. I. P.' He was a priest." DeCourcy, in his Catholic Church in the U. S., adds that this " did not escape the fury of the fanatics who in 1844 set fire to two of the Catholic Churches of Philadelphia. The gravestone was broken by these miscreants, who sought to glut on the memorial of the dead their hatred of the living."

at home, and in the meantime they judged them (the Catholics) protected by the charter which allowed liberty of conscience." * The chapel referred to was built by Father Greaton, who had been sent from Maryland to Philadelphia in 1730. He was assisted for some time in the performance of his arduous duties by Father Henry Neale, who died there in 1748.† St. Mary's was built in 1763. From an early period in the history of Pennsylvania there were larger Catholic congregations at Lancaster, Goshenhoppen and Conewago, mainly composed of Irish, who had been driven from their native land by the violation of the Treaty of Limerick and the barbarous penal laws to seek a new home in America, but whose children were to have the satisfaction of avenging the wrongs done their fathers by overthrowing here the despotism which had oppressed them. The Irish "Pennsylvania Line" paid its share of "the deep debt so long due."

---

* Watson.

† De Courcy's *Catholic Church in the U. S.*, translated and enlarged by John Gilmary Shea.

CHAPTER V.

ABOUT the beginning of the seventeenth century, many members of the Puritan sect, known as Independents or Brownists, took refuge in Holland from one of the religious persecutions, of which England had almost constantly been the theatre since Henry the Eighth sent More and Fisher to the scaffold. In a few years the number of the exiles increased considerably, and influenced by the favorable reports which reached them of the prosperity of the colony of New Netherland, (now New York,) they became desirous of settling there, and asked permission of the Dutch Government to do so.* Their request was, however, refused, and they next sought and obtained permission from the Virginia Company to settle upon a part of its territory, and proceeded to England to complete arrangements for their voyage. After various delays and disappointments they finally set sail from Plymouth, intending to land near the Hudson river, but, according to some writers, through the treachery of the captain of their vessel, who was bribed by the Dutch, they were carried further north, and at length landed from the *Mayflower* to the number of one hundred and one on Plymouth Rock, December 21, 1620. The severe hardships which they encountered caused great loss of life among them, so that within three months one half of their number perished, and notwithstanding fresh accessions of immi-

---

* Brodhead's *History of the State of New York.*

grants the population of the settlement at the end of ten years did not amount to three hundred.

In 1628 the colony of Massachusetts Bay was founded, and two years later about one thousand immigrants began a settlement at Boston. Sickness, however, prevailed among them to such an extent that, within six months, more than two hundred of those poor people died, and many of the rest became disheartened and returned to England, spreading there alarming reports of difficulties and hardships encountered, which greatly tended to check emigration to the new colonies. The intolerant spirit displayed by the settlers was also calculated to prevent intending emigrants from desiring to locate among them. In 1631 they passed a law which declared that " no man should be admitted to the freedom of the body politic, but such as were members of the churches within the limits of the same," and the effect of this enactment will be understood from the fact that " in consequence of the difficulties attendant on becoming a member of one of the churches, not one fourth of the adult population were ever church members." * Settlements were commenced at Dover and Portsmouth, New Hampshire, in 1623, which were joined to Massachusetts in 1641, and remained a part of that province for thirty-nine years, when the former district was constituted a separate colony Connecticut was settled in 1636, and in the same year Roger Williams, banished from Massachusetts, founded Providence, Rhode Island.†

---

* Spencer, vol. i.

† Williams is represented as one who favored " soul liberty," but he appears to have had a " fantastical scruple," according to Spencer, " as to the red cross in the English colors, which cross, being a relic of popery and abomination, he got Endicott, the commander at Salem to cut out from the national flag." Moreover, although the charter of Rhode Island, ratified by Chas. II., in 1662, provides that no person

The bitter contest between Charles I. and his Parliament put a stop to emigration to New England for a considerable time.*   Its population in 1647 did not exceed twenty thousand.†   At the close of the Confederate War in Ireland, in 1652, it was found that the utter extirpation of the Irish people, which Clarendon tells us had been intended by the Cromwellians, "was still very difficult."   It was therefore determined to expatriate as many as possible, and to crowd the remnant into the province of Connaught.   Nearly forty thousand men, the greater part of whom had seen military service, were "permitted," however, to enter the service of foreign States, before this decision was made public.

The deserted lands of the other three provinces were then ordered to be divided among Cromwell's followers and friends, including some of the New England colonists, whose affairs were not in a prosperous condition.   Prendergast says of this project: "Ireland was now, like an empty hive, prepared to receive its new swarm.   One of the earliest efforts of the government towards replanting the parts reserved to themselves, was to turn toward the lately expatriated English in America.   In the early part of the year 1651, when the country, by their own description to the

---

within the said colony shall be molested, punished, disquieted or called in question for any differences of opinion in matters of religion," yet the laws of the colony as first printed expressly excluded Catholics from the privilege of voting at elections or filling offices under the government.

* "Now that the fountain began to be dried, and the stream turned another way, and many that intended to have followed their neighbors and friends into a land not sown, hoping by the turn of the times and the great changes that were then afoot to enjoy that, at their own doors and homes, which the others had travelled so far to seek abroad; there happened a total cessation of any passengers coming over; yea, rather, as at the turn of a tide, many came back, with the help of the same stream or sea that carried them thither." Hubbard.

† Spencer.

Council of State, was a scene of unparalleled waste and ruin, the Commissioners of Ireland affectionately urged Mr. Harrison, then a minister of the gospel in New England, to come over to Ireland, which he would find experimentally, was a comfortable seed-plot (so they said) for his labors. Mr. Harrison was unable to come; but proposals were made in 1655 for the planting of the town of Sligo, and lands thereabouts, with families from New England, and lands on the mile line, together with the two little islands called Oyster Island and Coney Island, were leased for one year from 10th of April, 1655, for the use of English families from New England in America.

" In 1656, several families arriving from New England at Limerick had the excise of tobacco, brought with them for the use of themselves and families, remitted; and other families in May and July of that year, who had come over from the same colony, were received as tenants of State lands near Garristown, in the County of Dublin, about fifteen miles north of the capital." *

Large multitudes of women and children, however, still remained in Ireland, after the slaughter and expatriation of their natural protectors, and it was determined to get rid of them by transportation to America. The commissioners appointed by Cromwell to report on the condition of Ireland in 1652, urged among other measures " that Irish women as being too numerous now * * * be sold to merchants and transported to Virginia, New England, Jamaica or other countries." Their advice was adopted. Immense numbers of people of both sexes and all ages were so treated. According to Bruodin † over one hundred thousand of the Irish race were thus swept from their native soil.

---

* History of the Cromwellian Settlement in Ireland.
† *Propuguaculum.* (*Pragæ* anno 1669.)

Dr. Lingard says that a letter in his possession, written in 1656, gives the number of those victims of English hate, carried away up to that year to America, at sixty thousand.* Prendergast gives the following details:

" Just as the King of Spain sent over his agents to treat with the government for the Irish swordsmen, the merchants of Bristol had agents treating with it for men, women and girls to be sent to the sugar plantations in the West Indies *and to New England.* The Commissioners of Ireland gave them orders upon the governors of garrisons to deliver to them prisoners of war; upon masters of work-houses for the destitute in their care, ' who were of an age to labor, or if women who were marriageable, and not past breeding,' and gave directions to all in authority to seize those who had no visible means of livelihood, and deliver them to these agents of the British merchants, in execution of which latter order, Ireland must have exhibited scenes in every part like the slave hunts in Africa. How many girls of gentle birth must have been caught and hurried to the private prisons of these men-catchers, none can tell. But at last, the evil became too shocking and notorious, particularly when these dealers in Irish flesh began to seize the daughters and children of the English themselves, and to force them on board their slave ships; then, indeed, the orders, at the end of four years, were revoked. Messrs. Sellick and Leader, Mr. Robert Yeoman, M. Joseph Lawrence and others, all of Bristol, were active agents. As one instance out of many: —Captain John Vernon was employed by the Commissioners for Ireland into England, and contracted in their behalf with Mr. Daniel Sellick and Mr. Leader, under his hand, bearing date 14th of September, 1653, to supply them with 250 women of the Irish nation, above twelve years and

---

* *History of England,* vol. x., p. 336.

under the age of forty-five; also 300 men above twelve years of age and under fifty, to be found in the country within twenty miles of Cork, Youghal, and Kinsale, Waterford and Wexford, *to transport them into New England.*'' *

That people brought from their native land under such circumstances left but few traces upon the records of New England, will excite no surprise. But it cannot be doubted that they greatly contributed to the increase of its population. The number of Irish, transported to the British colonies in America, from 1651 to 1660, exceeded the total number of their inhabitants at that period, a fact which ought not to be lost sight of by those who undertake to estimate the strength of the Celtic element in this nation. They were poor: cut off from their old associations: deprived of the means of practising the duties of their religion: and in most cases regarded with prejudice by those among whom they were thrown: their children, consequently, in a generation or two, lost pride in preserving the memory of their origin, and took no interest in preserving the traditions of their ancestors.

An incident which occurred in 1676, however, illustrates the kindly feeling of the Irish people toward the New England settlers. At that time, in consequence of the havoc wrought by King Philip and his allies, the colonists suffered from famine. When the news of their distress reached Ireland a ship freighted with supplies of all kinds, to the value of nearly one thousand pounds or five thousand dollars,† was sent from Dublin to Boston, the proceeds of which were divided among one hundred and sixteen destitute families of the latter city.

A few years later a scene of a different character was wit-

---

* *Cromwellian Settlement in Ireland.*
† Chief Justice Daly states the amount as above.

nessed there. In 1688, "the last year of the administration of Andros in Masachussetts," says Bancroft, "the
daughter of John Goodwin, a child of thirteen years,
charged a laundress with having stolen linen from the
family. Glover, the mother of the laundress, a friendless
immigrant almost ignorant of English, like a true woman
with a mother's heart, rebuked the false accusation. Immediately the girl to secure revenge became bewitched.
The infection spread. Three others of the family, the
youngest a boy of less than five years old, soon succeeded
in equally arresting public attention * * * Cotton Mather
went to pray by the side of one of them, and lo ! the child
lost her hearing till prayer was over. What was to be done ?
The four ministers of Boston and the one of Charlestown
assembled in Goodwin's house and spent a whole day in
fasting and prayer. In consequence the youngest child, the
little one of five years, was delivered. But if the ministers
could thus by prayer "deliver" a possessed child, there
must have been a witch. The honor of the ministers required a prosecution of the affair, and the magistrate, William Stoughton, being one, with 'vigor,' which the united
ministers commended as just, made a discovery of the
wicked 'instrument of the devil.' The culprit was evidently an Irishwoman of a strange tongue. Goodwin, who
made the complaint, had no proof that could have done her
any hurt, but the 'old hag' whom some thought 'crazed in
her intellectuals,' was bewildered and made strange answers,
which were taken as confessions, sometimes in her excitement using her native dialect. * * * It was plain the
prisoner was a Catholic; she had never learned the Lord's
Prayer in English; she could repeat the Pater Noster flu-
ently enough, but not quite correctly; so the ministers and
Goodwin's family had the satisfaction of getting her con-

demned and executed as a witch." * "The girl," adds the
historian, who knew herself to be a deceiver, had no remorse,
and it never occurred to the ministers that vanity and love
of power had blinded their judgment.†

The number of Irish and their immediate descendants at
this period was considerable, and it was soon largely
augmented by the great immigration from Ireland which followed the successful efforts of William of Orange and his
Parliament for the destruction of the Irish woolen manufacture.   Lord Bellamont, an Irish peer of agreeable manners and very popular with all parties, though a bigot like
the rest of his class, was Governor of Massachusetts from
1699 to 1701, when he suddenly died.   It was he who in
1700 caused the arrest of the famous pirate Captain Kidd,
and sent him to England to be tried and executed.   About
the year 1718, "a large body of immigrants arrived from
Londonderry, bringing with them the manufacture of linen
and the implements used in Ireland.   The matter was
earnestly taken up by the people of Boston, and it was decided to establish a spinning school there.   Those immigrants likewise introduced the general use of the potato." ‡

Among the "redemptioners" who landed in Massachusetts in 1723 was John Sullivan of Killarney, Kerry county,
or, as some assert, of Limerick, the father of Major-General
Sullivan, who, on December 16, 1774, struck the first blow
in the Revolutionary struggle, by capturing Fort William
and Mary, near Portsmouth, N. H., and carrying off the
artillery and ammunition stored there.   There was considerable jealousy manifested about this time at the large
influx of Irish into New England.   The General Court of
Massachusetts, in 1720, warned certain families recently

---

* *History of the United States*, vol. iii.
† Bancroft.   ‡ *Landmarks of Boston*, Drake.

arrived from Ireland who had presumed to make a settlement, to move off within the space of seven months, threatening, in case of non-compliance, that the offenders should
" be prosecuted by the attorney-general by writs of trespass
and ejectment." In 1725 a meeting held at Haverhill, to
begin the settlement of Concord, decided that " no aliena-
tion of any lot should be made without the consent of the
community," the object of this regulation being the exclu-
sion of Irish settlers, " against whom a strong national
prejudice existed, heightened perhaps by zeal in differing
religious opinions." * But these unfriendly manifestations
were disregarded, and the people against whom they were
directed continued to arrive and settle and spread in the inhospitable territory.

In 1737 the Irish element in Boston, had become so numerous that at a meeting of its principal members held on St. Patrick's Day of that year, it was decided to form a national and
benevolent organization to be known as the Charitable Irish
Society, and to be composed of men of Irish birth or extraction. This was the first association of the kind established on
the continent of America, the pioneer in the path of Irish
American progress, and it still flourishes in undiminished
vigor, old in years but young in spirit, like the nation whose
name it bears, and which has such right good reason to be
proud of it. It has given gallant soldiers and general officers
of distinguished merit to the Republic not only in the first
struggle against British despotism, but in later conflicts, and
especially in that for the preservation of the Union, and gives
to-day promise of a future as brilliant as its past has been
glorious.

One defect in the original constitution of the society may
be noted here, though perhaps it might seem ungenerous to

---

* *Hist. Coll. of N. H.*

allude to a matter of the kind when more than a century has elapsed since its removal. One of the rules declared that the managers or officers of the organization should be Protestants. The bitter spirit of the British constitution, and the blighting influence of British penal laws, made themselves then felt, even among the warm-hearted sons of Ireland who engaged in a work of benevolence and patriotism. But the obnoxious clause was soon stricken out, and thenceforth Irishmen of all creeds stood upon an equal footing as members of the association.

The names of the twenty-six original members of the Society are as follows:—Robert Duncan, Andrew Knox, Nathaniel Walsh, Joseph St. Lawrence, Daniel McFall, Edward Allen, William Drummond, William Freeland. Daniel Gibbs, John Noble, Adam Boyd, William Stewart, Daniel Neal, James Mayes, Samuel Moor, Philip Mortimer, James Egart, George Glen, Peter Pelham, John Little, Archibald Thomas, Edward Alderchurch, James Clark, John Clark, Thomas Bennett and Patrick Walker.

The meetings were continued uninterruptedly until 1775, after which date none were held until 1784, a proof that the members "were not idle spectators of the great and successful effort made by America for its independence. * * * When heart and hand and blood were required in the cause of liberty they contributed their share most cheerfully, and when the cause had triumphed and they rested from their labors, one of the first acts of the society on resuming its meetings and intercourse was to congratulate each other on the success which had attended their efforts." §

Among the many names of Revolutionary patriots which a glance at the records of the Charitable Irish Society reveals, may be mentioned those of Major-General Henry

---

* President Boyd's Centennial Address, St. Patrick's Day, 1837.

Knox, Brig-Gen. Simon Elliot, Capts. Ash, Callahan, Dalton, Dunn, Fletcher, Howard, Leslie, Malcolm, McNeil, McClure, McCordey, Mackay, Magee, and others. Capt. Malcolm died early in the struggle, and his tombstone in Copps Hill burying ground served King George's soldiers for a target, upon which the mark of the bullets are yet to be seen. Rev. John Moorhead, first pastor of the Old Presbyterian Meeting House, who left Ireland in 1730 and became a member of the Society in 1739, was an energetic patriot. The Daughters of Liberty, previous to the Revolution, used to meet at his house, where they were treated with the greatest kindness. "The founders of his congregation were Irish Presbyterians, and their first house of worship was a barn which sufficed until they were able, in 1744, to build a neat wooden edifice.* It was in this church that the State Convention met in 1788, to ratify the Federal Constitution.

Peter Pelham, an original member of the Society, is the first Boston engraver of whom mention is made. He was also a painter of some reputation. Having married the widow of Copley, a tobacconist, he taught the rudiments of art to her son, J. S. Copley,† who afterward went to England where he acquired great reputation as a painter, and became the father of Lord Lyndhurst, so well known for his denunciation of the Irish as "aliens in blood, language and religion."

In 1719 Londonderry in New Hampshire was colonized "by one hundred Irish families who introduced the spinning wheel and the culture of flax and potatoes."‡ They rapidly increased in numbers. "In process of time the descendants of the Londonderry settlers spread over Wind-

---

* Drake's *Landmarks of Boston*, p. 263.   † *Landmarks of Boston.*
‡ Marmion's *Maritime Poets of Ireland.*

ham, Chester, Litchfield, Manchester, Bedford, Goffstown, New Boston, Antrim, Peterborough and Ackworth, in New Hampshire, and Barnet in Vermont. They were also the first settlers of many towns in Massachusetts, Maine and Nova Scotia." [*] About 1738, according to Spencer, " The manfuacture of linen was considerably increased by the coming of Irish emigrants.[†] At the same period the town of Dublin, N. H., was founded and named after the Irish capital. In the petition for incorporation it is described as " a tract of land commonly called and known by the name of Dublin (or Monadnock). When it was first called by the name of Dublin does not appear." [‡] Irish immigrants in large numbers continued for a long time to seek a home in this quarter, and when the tocsin of Revolution sounded, their children followed Stark, Reed and Poor, to fight under the standard of liberty.

In 1723 a colony of Irish arrived in Maine, and gave the name of Belfast to the first settlement which they founded. Others of their nationality following in their footsteps located in the vicinity of Bangor and Kittery, where Whipple, one of the Irish-American Signers of the Declaration, was born in 1730, and Machias, where Maurice O'Brien, of Cork, reared up the five sturdy sons, who at the dawn of the Revolution won for the young Republic its first naval victory.

Among the arrivals here, in the year 1726, was the father of Matthew Thornton and his family, who settled in Connecticut. The future Signer, however, after some years, having studied medicine, removed to New Hampshire. Matthew Lyon was among the Redemptioners who came over in 1759. He was first assigned to one Bacon of Woodbury, who afterwards transferred him to Hugh Hannah,

---

[*] Barstow's *New Hampshire.* [†] Spencer, vol. i., p. 214.
[‡] *History of Dublin, N. H.*

of Litchfield, for two stags.   Other Irish immigrants settled about this time at Saybrook and other towns in Connecticut. In 1729 Berkeley, Anglican Bishop of Cloyne, came over and settled near Newport, R. I., where he waited for three years expecting that the English government would send on money voted him by the Parliament, to enable him to carry out a project of converting the "savage Americans to Christianity." He waited in vain, however, and at the end of the period named returned to Ireland, after having given his farm of ninety acres, and "the finest collection of books that ever came at one time into America," to Yale College.

NEW YORK AND NEW JERSEY.

Henry Hudson, a famous explorer in the service of the Dutch East India Company, in 1609 sailed up the river which bears his name, but which had been previously discovered by some Spanish navigators. He ascended the river as far as Albany, and returning soon after called in at Dartmouth, England, where his ship and himself were seized and held for eight months. At the end of that time the ship was allowed to finish her voyage to Holland, but Hudson was still not permitted to depart, and was soon sent out on another exploring expedition, from which, however, he never returned. The Dutch, on receiving the reports of the discoveries made by their officer, despatched vessels to open a trade with the Indians, caused forts to be erected at several points, and named their newly-acquired territory New Netherlands, and its principal post New Amsterdam, (now New York). The English, not satisfied with their already very large possessions on this side of the ocean, wished to own the whole continent, and manifested annoyance and anger at the progress of the Dutch. So bitter was their feeling that when Minuet, the Director General of

the new colony, was driven by stress of weather, while returning home in 1632, to take shelter in Plymouth, the
English officials detained him, and affected to look upon
him as an intruder on their territory. Wrangling continued
between the English and Dutch colonists until 1664, when
a body of British troops seized upon New Netherlands,
which was thenceforth called, except during a very brief
interval, New York, in honor of the Duke of York, afterwards James II.

There were, at least, a few Irish at an early period in this
colony. Father Jogues, the noble Jesuit missionary, says in
a letter written in 1642, that he found a young Irishman,
whose confession he heard, on the Island of Manhattan. In
1653 Father Poncet administered the Sacraments of Penance
and Holy Communion to two Catholics, presumably Irish,
whom he met at Fort Orange (Albany). In 1683 Thomas
Dongan, Earl of Limerick, an Irish Catholic, was appointed
governor of the colony, to succeed Sir Edmund Andros.
In October of that year he convened the first Legislative
Assembly ever held in New York. Like Lord Baltimore
he was opposed to religious persecution, and the first act
passed by the Assembly declared that " no person or persons
who profess faith in God by Jesus Christ, shall at any time
be any ways molested, punished or disquieted; but that all
and every such person or persons may from time to time
and at all times, freely have and fully enjoy his or their
judgments or consciences, in matters of religion, throughout
all the province." This body also provided for the election
of its members every three years. A short time after the
Governor gave charters to the cities of New York and
Albany.

Governor Dongan favored immigration. In a letter to
the Lord President he says, " It will be very necessary to
send over men to build those forts. * * * My Lord,

there are people enough in Ireland who had pretences to
estates there, and are of no advantage to the country, yet
may live here very happy. I do not doubt, if his majesty
think fit to employ my nephew, he will bring over as many
as the King will find convenient to send, who will be no
charge after they are landed."* A Catholic college was

---

* *N. Y. Hist. Doc.*, vol. i. 256.

Thomas Dongan was the son of Sir John Dongan, an Irish baronet,
and was born in 1634. He had eight brothers and three sisters. At
the close of the Confederate War he joined the French army, but in 1677,
Charles II. issued an order recalling all British subjects in foreign service and he returned home. In 1683 as, above stated, he was made Governor of New York. The Charter of charters and privileges, adopted
under his direction in 1683, decreed that there should be no taxes imposed except by act of the Governor and Assembly. In 1687, the Declaration of Indulgence was promulgated, which authorized public worship by any sect and abolished all religious qualifications for office.
At the close of his services as Governor "he was offered a regiment
and the rank of Major-General by King James, but he refused, and retired to his county seat on Long Island." When the news of the change
reached New York, Leisler seized the fort and pretended that the
partisans of King James had formed a plot to seize the province. Dongan, charged with being a Papist, was hunted about from place to place,
and writs issued for his apprehension. After lying in the bay for a
fortnight, waiting to sail for England, stress of weather compelled his
return. He escaped to Rhode Island and reached England in 1691.
Dongan found his brother, the Earl of Limerick, an exile, and the family estates confiscated. His brother died in 1698 and he became Earl of
Limerick. An Act of Parliament was passed in 1702 recognizing his
claim to the family estates, but he could only redeem them on payment
of incumbrances placed on them by the Dutch general to whom they
were given, and in 1714 he states that, after paying his brother's debts
and his own, he had little left for his support. In December, 1715, the
last Earl of Limerick of his race died peacefully in London. On his
tombstone, at St. Pancras, is the inscription: "The Right Hon. Thos.
Dongan, Earl of Limerick, died Dec. 14, 1715, aged 81 years. *Re-
quiescat in pace.* Amen." Hon. James W. Gerard, says: "He was
a man of experience in war and politics, and filled the public duties of

founded on Manhattan Island at this time, and three priests were stationed there. But on the accession of the Prince of Orange to the English throne, bigotry again grew rampant. Leisler, a merchant of New York, usurped the government, and addressed a letter to William justifying his act. He at the same time caused statements to be published, in which was affirmed the need of protecting "the security of the Protestant religion," and it was added that "the Papists on Staten Island did threaten to cut inhabitants' throats and to come and burn the city;" that a certain individual "had arms in his house for fifty men; that eighty or a hundred men were coming from Boston and other places who were hunted away, and that there were several of them Irish and Papists; that a good part of the soldiers

---

his difficult post with activity and wisdom. He was considerate and moderate in his government—just and tolerant—and his personal character was that of an upright and courteous gentleman. Hinckley, of Plymouth, a zealous Puritan, declares that, "he was of a noble, praiseworthy mind and spirit, taking care that all the people in each town do their duty in maintaining the minister of the place though himself of a different opinion of their way," and Dominie Silgus wrote to the *classis* at Amsterdam, that Gov. Dongan was "a man of knowledge, politeness, and friendliness."

We trace "the footsteps of the Celt" at Albany at an early period of its history. It was taken by Capt. Manning, acting under the order of Lord Lovelace, in 1664. The Dutch retook it in 1673, and among the soldiers then found in it were Capt. John Manning, Sergts. Patrick Dowdall and John Fitzgerald, and Lewis Collins and Thomas Quinn. There were only fifty soldiers in all. That there were Irishmen in the province prior to that time cannot be proved from the absence of Irish names in the records, for the Dutch so modified the orthography, that no linguist could trace them. As, for instance, in the ancient records of this County it will be found that in the year 1657 a conveyance was made to Jan Andriesse (the Irishman at Katskill). Certainly without the addition, nobody would ever suspect his nationality.

Hon. H. Reiley's Address at Bi-Centennial celebration, July 22, 1886.

in the fort already were Papists," etc.* William did not
reply to the letter of his would-be friend, but sent Col.
Slaughter out as governor, who tried and hanged Leisler
and his son-in-law as rebels and traitors.   The Assembly,
called together in 1691, passed a resolution declaring all laws
passed by the late Assembly null and void.   This of course
destroyed the effect of Dongan's " Charter of Liberty."
A " Bill of Rights " was then passed, by which Catholics
were deprived of the sacred right of liberty of conscience.
This precious pronouncement declared " Nothing herein
mentioned or contained shall extend to give liberty for any
persons of the Romish religion to exercise their manner of
worship contrary to the laws and statutes of their majesties'
kingdom of England." †   In 1697 this was repealed, or
rather one much more severe was substituted for it.   By
this last " law " every priest, etc., remaining in or coming
into the province after November, 1700, should be " deemed
and accounted an incendiary and disturber of the public
peace and safety, and an enemy to the true Christian religion, and should be adjudged to suffer perpetual imprisonment."   In case of escape and capture he was
to undergo death, and those guilty of giving him shelter
were to pay a fine of $1,000 and to stand three days in the
pillory.   In 1701 another enactment was made by which
" Papists and Popish recusants were prohibited from voting
for members of Assembly, or any office whatever from
thenceforth and forever ! " ‡

The natural result followed.   We are told that the cry of
" the Church in danger " was often heard on elections and
other occasions, in New York at this time.   A man did

---

* N. Y. Hist. Doc., vol. iii.
† Journal of Legislative Council of New York.
‡ Hist. Cath. Church in New York.

not dare avow himself a Catholic—it was odious.   A chapel
would then have been pulled down.*

In 1741, when New York City contained from twelve to
twenty thousand† inhabitants, a pretended plot was detected
which led to the judicial murder of a larger number of people,
including one who is believed by most writers to have been
a Catholic priest, John Ury.   Several fires had broken
out in different places within a short time, and the rumor
was started that they had been caused by negroes, who
formed at that period almost one-sixth of the population.
Many persons were arrested, and tried for alleged complicity
in this supposed plot, two white men and eighteen
negroes were hanged, fourteen of the latter burned, and
seventy-one transported and sold, chiefly in the West Indies.
From the reports of these proceedings which have reached
us it is evident that New York contained a number of
Catholics, and that the old superstitious dread of what was
called "Popery," by the fanatical and ignorant, still exercised
a demoralizing influence over the minds of many.

Many settlements throughout New York State were
founded by Irish immigrants, at a comparatively early period.
New Windsor, the oldest town in Orange county, was first
settled in 1731 by Irish immigrants ‡ at the head of whom
was Charles Clinton,   father of   General James Clinton,

---

* Hist. Cath. Church in New York.

† Hist. Cath. Church in New York says 12,000 ; O'Kane Murray,
20,000.

‡ McKenzie's Remarkable Irishmen ; History of Orange County,
etc.   Near the old church of Fort Herkimer, or Mohawk, about four miles
west of Little Falls, Herkimer county, is to be seen a large brown sand-
stone slab, placed there by the Provincial government, on which is the following inscription: "Here reposeth the body of John Ring, Esq., of the
kingdom of Ireland * * * * who departed this life the 20th day of September, 1755, in the 30th year of his age."—Lossing.

and of Governor George Clinton of Revolutionary fame, and
grandfather of Dewitt Clinton. The eastern portion of
Montgomery county was also settled by Irish immigrants,
and the Irish, we are told, "continued to keep up the
emigration to various localities in the county, and contributed quite their proportion to the general mass of population and labor of settling a new country.

Sir W. Johnson, a native of Meath, came here in 1734
to take charge of large tracts of land in the Mohawk valley
which had been granted to or purchased by his uncle. He
offered considerable encouragement to settlers, particularly
those of his own nationality, and a large number of Irish
soon found their way to that part of the State. Those whom
Johnson engaged to assist him were, like himself, Irish.
Lafferty, his secretary, was a good lawyer and attended to his
legal business; his overseer was named Flood; his physician,
Daily, and the first teacher of the school which he erected
at Johnstown, Wall. He learned the Indian language
and gained the friendship of the savages by honest trading
and civil treatment. To some extent he conformed to their
manners also, and took the sister of Brant, the Mohawk
chief, as his wife. His popularity with the Six Nations was
so great that he was able to restrain them from joining the
French in the war which closed in 1748. He died in 1774.

Among the earliest settlers in Newburgh were the families of Wauch, Sly, McCollum, Denniston, Wear, Burnet,
Batie, Crowell and others, all from Ireland. Cherry Valley was in great part peopled by offshoots from the Irish
colony of Londonderry, N. H., and many others of the
first settlements in New York State were begun by Irishmen. At Wilemantown, we are told, "there was an early
settlement made by Henry Wileman, a free and noble-
hearted Irishman, who owned a patent of 300,000 acres,
granted in 1709."

The Irish came in great numbers to New York as to other States, just before the Revolution.   In *Rivington's Gazette* of Aug. 4, 1774, appears the following item:—

"Yesterday arrived the *Needham*, Captain Cheevers, with 300 passengers from Newry, the times of servants of both sexes to be disposed of to pay for their passage."

New Jersey began at an early period to receive consider-able accessions to its population from Ireland.   Thomas Sharp, a Dublin Quaker, who came over about 1680, and settled in Newtown, has left an account of the emigration of his party, in which he says: "Let it be remembered that, it having wrought upon ye minds of some friends that dwelt in Ireland, and a pressure being laid upon them for some years, from which they could not remove until they gave up to leave their friends and relatives there, with their com-fortable subsistence, to transport themselves and families into this wilderness.   In order, thereto, they sent from Dublin, in Ireland, to one Thomas Lunkin, a Friend in London, commander of a punk, who came and made his agreement to transport them into New Jersey.   But while the ship lay at Dublin, Thomas Lunkin, getting sick, re-mained behind, and put the command under his mate, John Daggar, who set sail the 19th, 9th month (two months) following, where they were well entertained at the house of the Thompsons, who had before gone from Ireland in 1677.   These had attained a good living by their industry. From there we went to Salem, where were several houses that were vacant of persons who had left the town to settle in the country.   In these we resided for the winter, which proved to be moderate.   At Wickacoa (Philadelphia) we purchased a boat of the Swansons, and so went to Burlington, to the commissioners, of whom we obtained a warrant of survey from the then surveyor-general, Daniel Seeds,

Then, after some considerable search to and fro in what was then called the third of Irish tenth, we at last pitched upon the place then called Newtown, which was before the settlement of Philadelphia. In the spring of 1682 we all removed from Salem, together with Robert Zane, who had before come with the Thompsons from Ireland, and was also expecting us. So we began then our settlement; and though we were at times pretty hard bestead, having all our provisions, as far as Salem, to fetch by water, yet, through the mercy of God, we were preserved in health and from any extreme difficulty. A meeting was immediately set up at the house of Mark Newby, and in a short time it grew and increased, into which Mr. Cooper and family, that lived at the Poynte, resorted. We had then zeal and fervency of spirit, although we had some dread of the Indians as a salvage people, nevertheless, ye Lord turned them to be serviceable to us, and to be very loving and kinde. Let, then, the rising generation consider that the settlement of this country was directed upon an impulse, by the spirit of God's people, not so much for their ease and tranquillity as for their posterity, and that the wilderness, being planted with a good seed, might grow and increase. But should not these purposes of the good husbandman come to pass, then they themselves shall suffer loss. These facts I have thought good thus to leave behind, as one having had knowledge of these things from the beginning.''*

---

* Appendix to Watson's Annals of Philadelphia,

CHAPTER VI.

THE IRISH IN THE SOUTH.

THE first permanent settlement in Virginia was begun at Jamestown in 1607. For many years the emigrants had great difficulties to contend with, and the reports of their privations were calculated to retard emigration to the colony. James the First, in 1619, sent there one hundred convicts taken out of the prisons and sold for a term of years, and this practice, we are told, was continued up to the reign of George III. It need not be supposed that, in the great majority of cases, the men then sent to Virginia were criminals of the ordinary type. Obstinate peasants who resisted the inclosure of commons, and often political offenders, formed a considerable proportion of those who were transported to the colony. In the year above mentioned the treasurer of the London company to which the territory had been granted, shipped to Virginia a number of young women who became the wives of the colonists on payment to the company of one hundred pounds of tobacco for each of them.

In 1652 Cromwell's commissioners appointed to report on the condition of Ireland, advised that "Irish women as being too numerous now * * * be sold to merchants and transported to Virginia, New England, Jamaica, or other countries." The suggestion was acted on, and the number of women and children transported from Ireland to the West Indies and the colonies named, exceeded the entire white population of those territories at that period.

It may be remarked here that this atrocious system of seizing and transporting the Irish to America did not, as is
generally supposed, terminate with the restoration of
Charles II. In 1699 Father Garganel, S. J., superior of
the Island of Martinique, asked for one or two Irish Fathers
for that and the neighboring islands, which were "full of
Irish;" for he continues, "every year ship loads of men, boys,
and girls, partly crimped, partly carried off by main force
for purposes of slave trade, are conveyed by the English
from Ireland."*

In course of time many of those who had been transported

---

* Lenehan's History of Limerick. The following extract is from the
work just quoted of the numbers, and the terrible situation of the expatriated Irish in those Islands. In 1652 "twenty-five thousand Irishmen,
sold as slaves in Saint Kitt's and the adjoining islands, petitioned for a
priest. Through the Admiral du Poenry the petition was placed in
Father Hartegan's hands. He was a Limerick Jesuit. He volunteered
himself and disappeared from our view. As he spoke Irish, English,
and French, he was very fit for that mission, which was always supplied
with Irish Jesuits from Limerick for more than a hundred years afterwards. It is thought that Father Hartegan assumed the name of De
Stritch, to avoid giving umbrage to the English, for, in the year 1650,
according to letters written five years after the petition, an Irish Father
De Stritch was welcomed and blessed by the Irish of Saint Kitt's, heard
the confessions of three thousand of them, then went disguised as a
timber merchant to Montserrat, employed numbers of Irish as wood-
cutters, revealed his real character to them, and spent the mornings administering the sacraments, and the day in hewing wood, to throw dust
in the eyes of the English. Meanwhile the heretics, jealous of the
religious consolations of the Catholics of Saint Kitt's, treated them with
great cruelty, transported one hundred and fifty of the most fervent and
respectable to Crab Island, where they left them to die of starvation.
This blow fell heavy on the heart of poor Father De Stritch. He got
together as many of the Irish of Saint Kitt's as he could, and passed
with them to the French island of Guadaloupe, where he lived a long
time with them, now and then going in disguise to help the Irish of the
neighboring isles."

to the West Indies in this manner found their way to the colonies on the continent, in search of greater freedom and a more healthful climate. They were enabled to do so without much difficulty, owing to the fact that many of their countrymen had managed, notwithstanding all the obstacles in their way, to engage in the trade carried on by the people of New England and the other provinces with those of Barbadoes and the adjacent islands. Many Irishmen commanded vessels engaged in this trade and not a few soon became owners themselves.

In 1690 an Irish trader named Doherty from Virginia visited the Cherokees and afterwards lived among them for a number of years.* Like many others of his countrymen he was among the earliest pioneers of civilization in the then unknown West. The first Presbyterian minister regularly settled in Virginia was a native of Donagor, Antrim county, named Craig, born in 1709 who emigrated to America at an early age.† In 1693 "Thomas Neale obtained a patent for establishing a post in the colonies at rates proportioned to those of the English post-office."‡ Under the government of William Gouch, who assumed the duties of office in 1727, Virginia received large accesions of Irish emigrants. Those who had received grants of frontier lands, especially Hite, Beverly and Burden, "sent out advertisements to meet the emigrants as they landed on the Delaware, and also as they were about to leave their native land, offering favorable terms to actual settlers; and soon after Hite removed his farm to Opecquon. The Irish immediately from Ireland began to rear habitations around him and his sons-in-law, Bowman and Christian, and near to Stephens and McKay. Samuel

---

* Ramsay's Annals of Tennessee.　　† Foote's Sketches of Virginia.
‡ Spencer, vol. i.

Glass took his residence at the head spring of the Opecquon, having purchased from Hite 16,000 acres. A son-in-law, Becket, was seated between Mr. Glass and North Mountain. His son David took his residence a little below his father, at Cherry Mead. His son Robert was placed a little further down, at Long Meadows. * * * Next down the creek was Joseph Colovin and his family. Then came John Wilson and the Marquis family, with whom he was connected. Next were the McAuleys, and then William Hoge. Adjoining these, to the south, were the Allen family, a part of whom speedily removed to Front Royal. The McGill family now occupy their position there. A little beyond the village lived Robert Wilson; his residence remains to this day. A little down the stream lived James Vance, son-in-law of Sam Glass, and ancestor of a numerous race—most of whom are to be found west of the Alleghanies. Those were all as early as 1736, or, '37.(*) * * * There is a limestone pyramid which tells us it was reared to the memory of Samuel Glass and Mary Gamble, his wife, who came from Banbridge, County Down, Ireland, and were among the early settlers, taking their abode on the Opecquon in 1736."

"Among others who came to Virginia about this time (1736) was an Irish girl named Polly Mulhollin. On her arrival she was hired to James Bell, to pay her passage, and with whom she remained during the period her servitude was to continue. At its expiration she attired herself in the habit of a man, and with hunting-shirt and moccasins, went into Burden's grant for the purpose of making improvements and acquiring a title to land. Here she erected thirty cabins, by virtue of which she held one hundred acres adjoining each. When Benjamin Burden,

---

* Foote's Sketches of Virginia, edition of 1855.

the younger, came on to make deeds to those who held cabin rights, he was astonished to see so many of the name of Mulhollin. Investigation led to the discovery of the mystery, to the great mirth of the other claimants. She resumed her Christian name and familiar dress, and many of her respectable descendants still reside within the limits of Burden's grant.''*

The counties of Patrick and Rockbridge were settled chiefly by Irish at the beginning of the eighteenth century. The McDowells, Breckenridges, McDuffies, McGruders, were among the first pioneers of the district. In 1750–54, we are told that the population of Virginia grew "every day" more numerous through the influx of Irish emigrants, who took up ground in the remote counties of that province as well as in North Carolina and Maryland. Jefferson speaks of the Irish who "had gotten possession of the valley between the Blue Ridge and the North Mountain forming a barrier which none could venture to leap" at this period.† Mitchell tells us that the migration of Protestant dissenters from Ireland, which commenced in Lord Carteret's time (1731), afterwards took large proportions, and Western Virginia, Pennsylvania, North Carolina and Georgia were in a great measure peopled by those emigrants.‡ Among the new arrivals from Ireland at this period were Philip Embury or Emory and Barbara Hock, who, it is said, "laid the foundation of the Methodist Church both in the United States and Canada."§

John Campbell, the great ancestor of the Campbells of Holston, came from Ireland to America, with a family of five grown sons and several daughters, in the year 1726. About the year 1730 he removed to what was then Orange,

---

* Historical Collections of Virginia.   † Jefferson, Op. vi., 485.
‡ History of Ireland.   § Hon. John Kelly, Early Irish Settlers.

afterwards Augusta county, where he resided until his
death, and where his numerous descendants lived for many
years.   Patrick had a son Charles, and he a son William,
who was the General William Campbell of the Revolution,
David, the youngest son of John, married May Hamilton,
and had a family of thirteen children, seven sons and six
daughters, the youngest of whom was nineteen years old
when they removed to Holston.   In 1765 John, the oldest
son of David Campbell, in company of Dr. Thomas Walker,
explored the western wilderness, and purchased for his
father and himself an ancient survey, near the headwaters
of the Holston.

"The first settlers on the Shenandoah were, like those of
Opecquon, from Ireland.   John Lewis came from Ireland
by way of Portugal, to which he first fled after a bloody
encounter with an oppressive landholder, of whom Lewis
was lessee.   Lewis brought his wife, Mary, with him.   He
had four sons: three of them, Thomas, Andrew, and
William, born in Ireland, and Charles, the child of his old
age, born a few months after settlement in their mountain
home.   Attended by his family and a band of about thirty
of his faithful tenantry, he arrived in Virginia, and fixed
their residence amid the till then unbroken forests of West
Augusta.   John Lewis' settlement was a few miles below
the site of the town of Staunton, on the banks of the
stream which still bears his name.   Charles was the hero of
many a gallant exploit, which is still treasured in the memories of the descendants of the border riflemen, and there
are few families among the Alleghanies where the name
and deeds of Charles Lewis are not familiar as household
words.   Thomas Lewis, though less efficient during the
Indian wars than his brethren, was a man of learning and
sound judgment, and represented the county of Augusta
for many years in the House of Burgesses; was a member

of the convention which ratified the Constitution of the
United States and formed the Constitution of Virginia, and
afterwards sat for the county of Rockingham in the House
of Delegates of Virginia. In 1765 he was in the House of
Burgessess, and voted for Patrick Henry's celebrated
resolutions. Thomas Lewis had four sons who actively
participated in the war of the Revolution; the youngest of
whom, Thomas, bore an ensign's commission when only
fourteen years of age. Andrew Lewis, the second son of
John Lewis, was the General Lewis who commanded at
the battle of Point Pleasant. Willliam Lewis, the third son,
was an active participator in the border wars, and was an
officer of the Revolutionary army, in which one of his sons
was killed, and another maimed for life.''*

Among others may be mentioned Col. James Patton, who
came from Donegal about 1750 and obtained "from the
Governor of Virginia a grant of 120,000 acres of land,"
upon which a large number of his countrymen settled.†

In the latter part of December, 1743, the inhabitants of
Timber Ridge were assembled at McDowell's house, on the
road from Staunton to Lexington, to resist one of the
murderous incursions of the Indians from Ohio, who would
not yield the valley of the Shenandoah to the whites, but
with their lives. McDowell had rallied his neighbors; but,
poorly skilled in savage warfare, the company fell into an
ambush, at the junction of the North River and the James,
and at one fire, McDowell and eight of his companions fell
dead. "The Indians fled precipitately, in consequence
probably of the unusual extent of their murderous success.
The alarmed population gathered in the field of slaughter,
thought more of the dead than of pursuing the savages,
whom they supposed far on their way to the West, took the

---

* Hist. Call. of Virginia. † Foote's Sketches of Virginia.

nine bloody corpses on horseback and laid them side by
side, near McDowell's dwelling, while they prepared their
graves in overwhelming distress. Though mourning the
loss of their leading men, and unacquainted with military
maneuvers on the frontiers, no one talked of abandoning
possessions for which so high a price of blood was given
in time of profound peace. In their sadness the women
were brave. Burying their dead with the solemnity of
Christian rites, while the murderers escaped beyond the
mountains, men and women resolved to sow their fields,
build their church, and lay their bodies in Timber Ridge.
The burial place of these men is to be seen in a brick
inclosure on the west side of the road near the Red House,
or Maryland Tavern, the residence of McDowell. Entering the iron gate, and inclining to the left, about fifteen
paces, there is to be seen a rough, unhewn limestone, about
two feet in height, on which, in rude letters by an unknown
and unpracticed hand, is the following inscription, next in
age to the Irish school-master's wife in the graveyard of
Opecquon:*

HERE LYES THE BODY OF
JOHN MackDOWELL,
Deced. December, 1743.

"Let us pause a few moments at this rough, low, time-
worn stone, in the very center of the graves, the first, with
an inscription, reared in the valley of Virginia, to mark
the resting-place of an emigrant. You will scarcely read
the inscription on one side or decipher the letters on the
other. The stone crumbled under the unskillful hands of
the husband, who brought it from that eminence yonder
in the west, and, in the absence of a proper artist, inscribed

* Foote's Sketches of Virginia.

the letters himself, to be a memorial to his young and lovely wife.   Tradition says he was the schoolmaster.

(*On one Side.*)	(*On the Other.*)
JOHN WILSON	
INTERRED HERE	FROM
THE BODIES OF HIS 2	IRLAND
CHILDREN & WIFE	Ju l y Vith, **1737.**
Ye MOTHER MARY MARCUS,	Coty ARGMA
who Dyed Agst.	g H
THE 4th 1742,	S
Aged 22 years	

"On the side on which Ireland is chiseled, the pebbles in the stone or his unsteady hand made large indentures and rendered the inscription almost illegible.   Here the stone has stood, a monument of affection, and marks the grave of the early departed, while the graves of more than a century have passed away."*

THE CAROLINAS AND GEORGIA.

In 1663 Charles II. granted to Lord Clarendon and others the territory lying between the thirty-first and thirty-sixth degrees of north latitude and extending from the Atlantic to the Pacific.   Locke devised an eleborate system of government for the infant colony, which, as Spencer says, only "affords a singular proof of how little practical value are theoretical attempts to arrange and regulate satisfactorily the position and claims of the governors and the governed."†
It was not difficult to find men willing to become palatines, landgraves, caciques, or barons, as Locke's arrangement contemplated; but intending emigrants did not care to become their serfs or subjects, and so the scheme fell to the ground.

In 1716, the Yemassee Indians attempted to extirpate

---

* Foote's Sketches of Virginia.   † History of the U. S., vol. i.

the white settlers, but they were defeated and their lands
confiscated.   In order to strengthen their frontiers against
further attacks, the Assembly offered the vacant lands on
the most favorable conditions to those who would occupy
them.   This induced five hundred Irish families to come
over and settle down in the district, but soon after their
arrival the proprietaries infamously broke through the
arrangement made by the Assembly and deprived these
emigrants of their lands.   Many of the Irish settlers, it is
said, perished, and the rest moved further north.   The
proprietors were however soon punished for their greed
and treachery; the people entered into an association for
common defence against them, and selected Col. Moore, the
former governor, to take charge of affairs.   Finally their
charter was declared forfeited and they were obliged to
accept £22,000 in lieu of their claims upon the province.*
"In 1737 multitudes of laborers and husbandmen in Ireland,
unable to procure a comfortable subsistence for their families
in their native land, embarked for Carolina.   The first
colony of Irish receiving a grant of lands near the Santee
river formed a settlement which was called Williamsburgh."†   It should be mentioned that Carolina was
divided into two distinct governments in 1729, known as
North and South Carolina.

"In 1739 the landlords of Ireland, armed with despotic
power under acts framed and passed by themselves, rigorously exercised it against their defenceless tenantry and
compelled them in thousands to leave their native land and
seek an asylum in America.   An Irish colony was planted
this year in the Carolinas, and extensive tracts of land of
assigned it."‡   Spencer says that such numbers left the

* Spencer, vol. i.   † Ibid.

‡ Marmion.

North of Ireland at this time for the Carolinas that "the depopulation of whole districts was threatened."*

In 1745 a large number of Irish immigrants settled in North Carolina, "along the Cape Fear and its tributaries and in the fertile domain between the Yadkin and Catawba."† About this period the fathers of Jackson, Calhoun and Pickens settled in the Carolinas, and brought with them that hatred of British despotism which they transmitted undiluted to their sons. Ramsay, the historian of South Carolina says on this subject: "Of all other countries none has furnished the province with so many inhabitants as Ireland. Scarce a ship sailed *from any of its ports* for Charleston that was not *crowded* with men women and children."‡

Georgia was the last settled of the thirteen colonies. In 1733 one hundred and sixteen persons, headed by Oglethorpe, began a settlement at Savannah. Into this colony also there came a considerable number of Irish, who did good service afterwards for the cause of American liberty.§

---

* Hist. of U. S., vol. i.

† Lossing

‡ History of South Carolina.

§ At the first public meeting of the Sons of Liberty held in Savannah, July 14, 1774, John Glenn was chairman, and amongst those present were S. Farley, J. Bryan, W. Gibbons, J. Winn, E. Butler and several others bearing Irish names.

CHAPTER VII.

IMMENSE IRISH IMMIGRATION JUST BEFORE THE REVOLU-
TION. MULTITUDES OF EVICTED TENANTS COME
OVER AND FIGHT FOR AMERICAN LIBERTY.

WHEN George II. saw the flower of his army reel and
break before the headlong onset of the Irish Brigade at
Fontenoy, he cried out in his despair, "Cursed be the laws
which deprived me of such subjects." His ill-starred grandson, the third of the "fools and oppressors" who bore his
name, had still greater reason to execrate the infamous system which drove myriads of maddened Irish across the Atlantic, when he learned that Washington had triumphed over
his mercenary hordes, and that of the army which followed
the patriot chief to final victory, fully one half was composed
of those whom British "law," and landlord greed and hate,
had deprived of even the humble shelter of a cabin's roof
upon the soil of Ireland. The Pennsylvania Line, the Riflemen of Stark and Morgan, and the fierce Maryland troopers
who charged with Moylan—all these and tens of thousands
besides of America's defenders remembered "British faith"
as well as their kindred who a generation before had driven
the bloody Cumberland from the hardest fought field of
France. The important effects which the British penal laws,
and landlord system in Ireland, produced on the destinies of
America have not hitherto received adequate consideration.
There are however ample grounds for asserting that to those
combined evils, the thirteen colonies were indebted for from

a third to a half of their population at the commencement of the Revolution.

Of the Irish half of the Continental army, a large proportion was composed of evicted Irish tenants, who, driven from their homes, especially in 1771 and the two following years, and unsuccessful in their resistance to British "law," fled to America, to escape the prison and the scaffold, and there became the most determined enemies of the tyrannical government which had oppressed and persecuted them. The proofs which can be given of this most important but too frequently ignored fact are numerous and conclusive. Rev. Mr. Gordon, a Protestant clergyman says:* "In the government of Lord Townshend a part of Ulster began to be disturbed by an insurrection which, originating from a local cause yet a severe grievance, was much more extensive and of longer duration than that of the 'Hearts of Oak' (an agrarian organization which existed a short time previous). An estate in the County Antrim, a part of the vast possessions of an absentee landlord, the Marquis of Donegal, was proposed, where its leases had expired, to be set only to those who could pay large fines, and the agent of the marquis was said to have exacted extravagant fees on his own account also. Numbers of the former tenants, neither able to pay the fines, nor the rents demanded by those who on payment of fines and fees took leases over them, were dispossessed of their tenements and left without the means of subsistence. Rendered thus desperate they maimed the cattle of those who had taken their lands, committed also other outrages and to express a firmness of resolution styled themselves 'Hearts of Steel.' To rescue one of their number confined on a charge of felony in Belfast, some thousands of peasants, who neither before

---

* History of Ireland, vol. ii., 257.

nor after took any part in the insurrection, marched with the
Steelmen into the town and demanded the prisoner from
the military guard, the officers of which were fortunately
persuaded by a respectable physician to his liberation in
order to prevent the ruinous consequences of a dreadful
battle.   The association of the Steelmen extended into the
neighboring counties, augmented by distressed or discontented peasantry, who were not affected immediately by the
original grievance.   By the exertions of the military, some
were taken and tried at Carrickfergus.   As they were acquitted from the supposed partiality of the witnesses and jury
an Act of Parliament was passed in March, 1772, ordering
their trials to be held in counties different from those in
which their offences were committed.   Some, in consequence, were carried to Dublin, but were there, from prejudices entertained against a law so unconstitutional, acquitted.   In the December of 1773, during the administration
of Earl Harcourt, the obnoxious act was repealed.   From a
sense of the evil consequences of disorders, insurgents tried
in their respective counties were now condemned and executed.   The insurrection was totally quelled, but its effects
were long baneful.   So great and wide was the discontent
that many thousands emigrated from those parts of Ulster to
the American settlements, where they soon appeared in arms
against the British Government, and contributed powerfully
by their zeal and valor to the separation of the American
colonies from the Empire of Great Britain."

Several other writers give a similar account of this "land
war," its causes and consequences.*   Marmion, speaking of

* Taylor says: "The rapacity of the agent of an absentee nobleman,
the Marquis of Donegal, produced a fierce agrarian insurrection in the
county of Antrim, which soon extended over the greater part of Ulster.
The insurgents named themselves *Hearts of Steel*, to show the firmness
of their resolution.   They determined not to pay the extravagant rents

it, says: "The effects of this agrarian insurrection, which extended to the adjoining counties (from Antrim), seriously affected the welfare of the province of Ulster and was instrumental in extending liberty to the whole human race. Thousands of men, driven from their holdings, dissatisfied with the country, and expressing the deepest resentment against the Irish landlords, emigrated to America. Arriving there at a critical moment and actuated by their wrongs, they joined the armies of Washington, then contending for Independence, and contributed by their numbers as well as by their courage and conduct to separate the United States from the British Crown. The emigration to America during the years 1771, 1772 and 1773, from the north of Ireland exceeded all former precedent. The emigrants were chiefly farmers and manufacturers who, by converting their property into specie, which they took with them abroad, it was calculated deprived Ulster of one-fourth of its circulating medium, which then consisted altogether of specie, and also

---

and fines demanded by the landlords and their agents, and to destroy the cattle and houses of any tenants who should take the land 'over their heads.' By the exertions of the military, several of the Steel-men were arrested and brought to trial at Carrickfergus; but they were acquitted, from the supposed partiality of the witnesses and the juries. The Irish aristocracy, enraged at being disappointed of the expected vengeance on their revolted vassals, passed a law, that trials for insurrectionary offences should be held in counties different from those in which the crimes had been committed. Some of the insurgents were, in consequence, brought to trial in Dublin; but the juries, disgusted at such an arbitrary and unconstitutional proceeding, acquitted the prisoners without hesitation. This infamous law was repealed during the administration of Lord Harcourt, and the juries in the disturbed districts were at the same time induced to do their duty with firmness. After several of the insurgents had been convicted and executed, the disturbances were suppressed; but an immense number of the Ulster Protestants sought refuge from the rapacity of their landlords in the wilds of America."—History of Ireland, Harpers, New York.

a portion equal thereto of the most valuable part of its population.*   He adds that from Belfast there sailed in the
three years named thirty ships filled with emigrants. from
Londonderry thirty-six, and from Newry twenty-two, and
estimates the number of their passengers at over twenty-five
thousand.†

At this period, and in fact for a considerable time before,
emigration to America on a corresponding scale took place
from the other three provinces of Ireland.   This was caused
not only by the landlord exactions which had compelled so
many of the Protestant population of Ulster to abandon
their native land, but also by the privations and persecutions to which the Catholics were subjected through the
operation of the Penal laws.   The overburdened and exasperated people were driven by the instinct of self-preservation to organize for mutual protection, and the association
known as the Whiteboys was formed in 1762 to check evils
which had become intolerable.

Writers and speakers of the period sufficiently account
for the existence of this organization by the facts which they
relate.   According to one authority the landlords of Munster "let their lands to cotters far above their value, and, to
lighten their burden, allowed commonage to their tenants
by way of recompense; afterwards, in despite of all equity,
contrary to all compacts, the landlords inclosed these commons and precluded their unhappy tenants from the only
means of making their bargains tolerable."‡   Another writer
says, "Thrown by law upon the miserable tillers of the soil
for support, the majority of the (Anglican) clergy employed
a class of men called tithe proctors to collect revenues: and

---

* History of the Maritime Ports of Ireland, p. 333.
† History of the Maritime Ports of Ireland.
‡ McGee, History of Ireland.

never was there a greater scourge inflicted on an unfortunate country. Their exactions, their cruelties, their oppressions would furnish material for volumes; and would even
then convey but a faint image of the intolerable misery they
occasioned. The Irish law of tithe was far more severe
than the English: it armed the parson with greater powers,
it took from the farmer every means of defence against
illegal overcharges. If the Irish (Anglican) clergy and
their proctors had been angels they must have been cor-
rupted by the system: but they were not even the best of
men, and they used their tremendous power to its fullest extent. The oppressions of the landlords and the tithe
mongers produced their natural effect. The peasants,
driven to despair, broke out in agrarian insurrections which
soon became formidable. There was not a man in Ireland
ignorant of the cause of these disturbances, but the rulers of
the land were neither willing to acknowledge their tyranny
nor inclined to cease from their rapacity. They adopted
the usual favorite remedy of (Anglo-) Irish legislators, and
passed a sanguinary code of laws to which no country in
Europe can furnish a parallel.''* ''Acts were passed,'' says
Arthur Young ''for the punishment of the Whiteboys, which
seemed calculated for the meridian of Barbary,'' and which
tended ''more to raise than to quell an insurrection.''† Some
members of the corrupt and cruel Anglo-Irish Parliament
were found manly enough to protest against those legalized
crimes. Lucius O'Brien, member for Clare, denounced
them in the Irish House of Commons, and added, ''It has
been said that to prevent opposition to such demands we
should put in force our penal laws against those that have
opposed them already, but no penal law, however sanguinary
in itself and however rigorously executed, will subdue the

---

* Taylor's History of Ireland.   † Tour in Ireland.

natives of a free country into a tame and patient acquiescence
in what must appear to be the most flagitious injustice and
the most cruel oppression.   The insurrections against which
we are so eager to carry out the terrors of the law are no
more than branches of which the shameful negligence of
our clergy and the defects in our institutions are the root.*
Those who endeavored to befriend the people were persecuted and punished with extreme severity.   Because of his
well-known sympathy with them, Father Nicholas Sheehy was
executed on an absurd charge after a mock trial at Clonmel
in 1765.   Five years later Edmund Burke, the faithful advocate of the rights of America, was accused of having "sent
his brother Richard, Recorder of Bristol and a relative, Mr.
Nagle, on a mission through Munster, to levy money on
the Popish body for the use of the Whiteboys."   Burke had
in fact started a subscription to defend the members of the
organization when on trial, but he was able to baffle the
malice of his enemies and escape evil consequences, although
others, accused of the same offence, including the Bishop of
Cloyne, Right Rev. Dr. McKenna, Robert Keating, and
other Catholics, were arrested on account of it.

The Whiteboys spread themselves all over Munster,
leveled the hedges and fences of those who had inclosed
the commons, dug up the land of greedy graziers who preferred to fatten cattle upon it rather than allow human beings
to enjoy its fruits, and performed many other acts which
indicated their sentiments more distinctly and emphatically
than the most eloquent orators could perhaps have done.
But a large force of regular troops was dispatched to the disturbed districts by the Government, under the command of
the Marquis of Drogheda, and after considerable effort and
much bloodshed and cruelty it succeeded in suppressing the

---

* Irish Parliamentary Debates.

outbreak. Those who had been engaged in it, and many
others, obnoxious to the landlord faction, were forced to flee
the country. From Galway, Limerick, Cork, Waterford
and Wexford they escaped to America to find shelter and,
before long, an opportunity of avenging themselves upon the
despotism which had refused to allow them to live in peace
in their native land. The Moylans, Barry, and tens of
thousands of their countrymen, who left Ireland in these
days, had ere long the satisfaction of driving from American
soil those who had compelled them to abandon their own.
The Presbyterians and other dissenters of Ulster, precluded
by the Test Act from aspiring to political or municipal offices,
were in this respect almost as harshly dealt with as the
Catholics: all suffered alike from the landlord and other exactions already alluded to, and the vast numbers of all creeds
who were forced to leave their homes met here upon a
common ground and made common cause against the common enemy.

Spencer, speaking of the influx of emigrants here at this
time, says, "No complete memorial has been transmitted of
the particulars of the emigrations that took place from Europe to America at this period, but (from the few illustrative
facts that are actually preserved) they seem to have been
amazingly copious. In the years 1771 and 1772, the number
of emigrants to America from Ireland alone amounted to
seventeen thousand three hundred and fifty. Almost all
of them emigrated at their own charge; a great majority of
them consisted of persons employed in the linen manufacture, or farmers possessed of some property which they
converted into money and carried with them. As most of
the emigrants, and particularly those from Ireland and Scotland, were personally discontented with their treatment in
Europe, their accession to the colonial population, it might
reasonably be supposed, had no tendency to diminish or

counteract the hostile sentiments towards Britain which were daily gathering force in America." ⁰*

With all these facts borne in mind the acknowledgment that half the Revolutionary army was Irish—wrung from the reluctant lips of the Tory, Galloway, when examined before the English Parliamentary Committee, ought to excite no surprise.

---

* Hist. of the U. S., vol. i

CHAPTER VIII.

By the treaty of Paris, signed in 1763, the supremacy of England over the whole of this continent, east of the Mississippi, was acknowledged by France. The most brilliant event of the war then closed was the victory which Wolfe—the great grandson of one of the Irish confederates who defended Limerick against Ireton—won with his life-blood over Montcalm on the Plains of Abraham. The whole-sale expulsion of the Acadians from their homes early in the contest showed that the spirit of Cromwell still swayed England's councils and that her rulers were still as remorse-less and conscienceless as ever towards those whom they hated or feared. The result of the struggle was in a great measure owing to the efforts of the colonists who had displayed the highest bravery and the greatest generosity in aiding the power which was so soon to become their own malignant oppressor and enemy. Success made the English overbearing and arrogant. Far from being grate-ful for the assistance given them, they only regarded with jealousy the growing strength of those from whom they had received it. In order to make the Americans feel their inferiority it was resolved by the British government to quarter a large body of troops upon them; and to swell the English revenues, it was decided that duties should be imposed by the London Parliament upon sugar and other commodities imported into the colonies. This policy

naturally excited indignation amongst those against whom
it was directed, but their protests and remonstrances only
rendered the British oligarchy more determined to persist
in wrong-doing.

In 1765 the Stamp Act was passed in the House of
Commons by a vote of two hundred and forty-five to forty-
nine—there was no opposition at all in the House of Lords.
One of the ministers, adding insult to injury, asked "Will
these Americans, children planted by our care, nourished
by our indulgence till they are grown to a degree of
strength and opulence, and protected by our arms—will
they grudge to contribute their mite to relieve us from the
heavy weight of this burden which we lie under?" To the
great majority of those who listened to him, his argument
appeared unanswerable, but not to all. There were a few
Irish in that assembly, and one of them, Col. Isaac Barre,
stood up to defend "these Americans." "They planted by
your care?" he said. "No, your oppressions planted them
in America. They fled from your tyranny to a then uncul-
tivated and inhospitable land where   *   *   *   they met all
hardships with pleasure compared with those they had
suffered in their own country from the hands of those who
should have been their friends.

"They nourished by your indulgence! They grew by
your neglect of them. As soon as you began to 'care' for
them, that 'care' was exercised in sending persons to rule
them who were   *   *   *   instructed to spy out their
liberties, to misrepresent their actions and to prey upon
them, men whose behavior has caused the blood of those
Sons of Liberty to recoil within them—men promoted to
the highest seats of justice; some of whom, to my own
knowledge, were glad by going to a foreign country to
escape being brought to the bar of a court of justice in
their own.

"They protected by your arms! Those *Sons of Liberty*
have nobly taken up arms in your defence * * * and
believe me—remember I this day told you so—that same
spirit of freedom which actuated that people at first, will
accompany them still; but—prudence forbids me to explain
myself further." Speaking in a place where the truth
was so rarely heard; in the presence and under the power
of the unscruplous and unprincipled enemies of the American
people, and of all disposed to be their friends, he refrained
from saying all that he felt, and expressing fully his antici-
pations. But his meaning was well understood even then,
and the correctness of his opinions proved before many
years had passed away.

On the same night on which he spoke, Franklin, then in
London, wrote to his Irish friend, Charles Thomson, of
Philadelphia—afterwards Secretary of Congress—"The
sun of liberty is set, the Americans must light the lamps
of industry and economy." But the sturdy Celt replied
"Be assured that we shall light torches of a very different
sort," and they did—torches whose flame consumed the
rotten fabric of British despotism, and illumined the world
with the radiance of freedom.

When the news of the passage of the Stamp Act reached
America, the Virginia Assembly was in session, and Patrick
Henry, then a member of that body, in moving resolutions
denying its validity, said "Cæsar had his Brutus, Charles
I. his Cromwell, and George III.—"

"Treason!" shouted the speaker. "Treason," echoed
the Tories and Loyalists, but the great orator, rising to a
loftier altitude and fixing on the speaker an eye of the most
determined fire, finished his sentence with the firmest
emphasis*—"and George III.—may profit by their example!

---

* Wirt's Life of Patrick Henry.

If this be treason, sir, make the most of it." The resolutions were carried.

What the English are so fond of calling "outrages," when committed by Americans or Irish, promptly followed. The houses of obnoxious officials were attacked and in some cases torn down, their effigies hanged, beheaded, and burned; bells were tolled, mock funeral processions paraded the streets, and the precious stamps, from the sale of which such an increase of England's revenue was expected, were seized and consigned to the flames in many places. Moreover, British goods were boycotted, and British merchants and manufacturers made to feel how unprofitable was their exultation over America's assumed weakness. Associations were formed which adopted the name first applied by the Irish member of Parliament to the American patriots—Sons of Liberty—and which bound themselves "to march with the utmost expedition, at their own cost, and with their whole force, to the relief of those who should be in danger from the Stamp Act, or its promoters, or abettors."

These indications of national spirit produced considerable effect upon the English mind. A change in the British Ministry took place in a short time, and on February 22, 1766, General Conway brought in a bill for the repeal of the Stamp Act. Pitt, who had before strongly advocated its annulment, though he maintained other English pretensions equally absurd,* aided, and the measure was carried;

---

* "Let the Stamp Act," he said, "be repealed absolutely, totally and immediately. At the same time let the sovereign authority of this country over the Colonies be asserted in as strong terms as can be devised, and be made to extend to every point of legislation whatsoever, that we may bind their trade, confine their manufactures and exercise any power whatever except that of taking their money out of their pockets without their consent."—British Parliamentary Debates.

It would appear to be as unjustifiable to "bind their trade and confine their manufactures" as "to take money out of their pockets."

but an English Ministry never knew how to make a concession gracefully, and that in power at the time spoken of, insisted on the previous passage of an act which declared that "Parliament had, and of right ought to have, power to bind the colonies in all cases whatsoever."

The Americans were glad at the repeal of the obnoxious Act, but their satisfaction was short-lived. In the year following (1767) a bill was passed in the British Parliament imposing a duty on tea imported into America as well as on paints, paper, glass and lead. This had the effect of renewing the excitement, which was soon increased by the sending over of two regiments of British troops to Boston, and by a subsequent address to George III. from the English Lords and Commons, praying that he would order the Governor of Massachusetts to send to England for trial all who might be guilty of treason.

The presence and conduct of the British soldiers in Boston created disgust and irritation, and on March 5, 1770, a collision occurred between a body of those mercenaries—the 29th regulars—and a number of citizens, which resulted in the killing of five of the latter by their enemies. One at least of the murdered men was an Irishman named Patrick Carr. That there were many of his countrymen among the crowd who on the occasion referred to shouted, "Down with the bloody backs" was well known. John Adams, who defended the soldiers when brought to trial for their attack on the people, said in his address on their behalf, that the "mob" was in part made up of "Irish Teagues." This outrage, known as the "Boston massacre," still further exasperated the colonists against the British and made a deep impression throughout the entire country.

About this time the people of North Carolina, harassed by exorbitant taxes, and the exaction of greedy British officials, were engaged in a struggle with the latter for

their rights.   In 1767, an association known as "The Regulators," or "Sons of Liberty," had been formed, to obtain
the removal of abuses.   This body becoming very powerful
and making its influence felt in various ways, the Governor,
Tryon, treacherously arrested some of its leading members,
and ordered the organization to be disbanded.   The severe
punishment, however, inflicted after a mock trial on those
who were seized, excited such indignation in the public
mind that the British official, in order to appease it, felt
compelled to issue a proclamation, granting a general
pardon to all the Regulators, except thirteen.   Among
those "outlaws" were John O'Neill, Malachi Tyke, and
several others, whose names indicate their Irish origin.
William Butler and Samuel Divinny are mentioned as
leaders of the organization in 1770, and as endeavoring to
secure a fair trial for some of their fellow members, who
had been arrested.   The Governor, however, determined to
crush the Regulators, and for this purpose he assembled at
Newbern, early in 1771, a large body of militia, with which
and several pieces of artillery he moved towards the
Allamance river, where the "malcontents" were encamped.
In the conflict which ensued the latter were defeated, mainly
in consequence of the fall of their principal leader, Captain
Montgomery, a brave young Irish American who commanded a company of "Mountain Boys" and who was killed
early in the engagement by a discharge from the British
artillery.   The proportion of Irish among the Regulators
was very considerable.   Their most trusted adviser and friend
was the Rev. David Caldwell, an Irish Presbyterian clergyman, and a relative of Samuel Caldwell of Philadelphia, one
of the original members of the Friendly Sons of St. Patrick
of that city.   This minister had great influence over the
people of his congregation and those living in the district.
He sympathized with their struggles against oppression,

but being aware of their unprepared condition had hastened
to the scene of conflict, and riding between the two hostile
bodies, urged his own people to go home quietly.   He
then went to the British Governor, and obtained from him
a pledge that he would abstain from bloodshed, but this
notwithstanding, that official ordered his troops to fire upon
the people, and when the contest was over caused many of
them who had been taken prisoners to be executed.   He
afterwards traversed the adjacent country, burning houses,
destroying crops, and compelling the inhabitants to take the
oath of allegiance to the English king.

Some writers speak of this fight on the Allamance as
"the first battle of our war for independence,"* but this is
claiming too much for it.   Lossing himself, whose words
have been just quoted, says that the resistance of the
Regulators, "arose from oppressions more personal and real
than those which aroused the people of New England.   It
was not wholly the abbstract idea of freedom for which
they contended, their strife consisted of efforts to rid themselves of actual burdens.   * * * While the Regulators'
movement planted deep the seeds of resistance to tyranny,
the result of the battle on the Allamance was disastrous in
its subsequent effects.   The people from whom Tryon
wrung an oath of allegiance were conscientious, and held a
vow in deep reverence.   Nothing could make them swerve
from the line of duty; and when the hostilities of the Revolution fully commenced, hundreds whose sympathies were
with the patriots felt bound by that oath to remain passive."†
A little further on, when speaking of events which occurred
three years later, this historian tells us that Governor
Martin—Tryon's successor—in his efforts to secure allies
in the struggle against the people, "dispatched messengers

---

* Lossing.   †Field Book of the Revolution, vol. ii., 372.

to the Highlanders at Cross Creek, upon whose loyalty he relied; and others were sent into the more westerly districts to promise the Regulators exemption from the punishments to which they were still liable for past misdeeds if they would assist the king's government against its opposers. These promises had great effect, and, strange as it may seem, many of the Regulators were active Loyalists."*

It will be evident that the acts of the Regulators were not looked upon by the British officials in the same light as those of the "rebels." The first named resisted extortion and spoliation like the Irish farmers, Scotch crofters, and Welsh dissenters of the present day; but this movement did not, necessarily, involve an attempt to overthrow the British government, and to establish an independent Republic.

This subject is dwelt on here because some writers have affected to regard the conflict on the Allamance as the first blow for Independence; with a view to eclipsing the exploit of Sullivan at Fort William and Mary, near Portsmouth, N. H., in December, 1774, which is justly entitled to the distinction of being considered as such, according to the opinion of the highest authorities,† and which is therefore recalled with peculiar and pardonable pride by men of the race from which the hero of the achievement sprang. But were it otherwise, Irish Americans could still feel proud that the "principal leader"‡ of the Regulators at the battle of the Allamance was one of their own blood— Captain Montgomery—whose fall, like that of his heroic namesake at Quebec, was the main cause why his followers failed to win a victory on the occasion.

---

* Field Book of the Revolution, vol. ii., 374.
† Appleton's Cyclopedia.   Peabody's Life of Gen. Sullivan.
‡ Lossing.

When the famous "Tea Party" was given in Boston on the night of December 16, 1773, several Irishmen were among the "invited guests." Gen. Henry Knox was a member of the committee of twenty-five which kept guard over the three Indiamen, to prevent their cargoes from being landed, and Thomas Moore, Capt. Samuel Howard, of the Charitable Irish Society, and others of their nationality were among the "Mohawks" who boarded the vessels and flung the tea into the harbor.

CHAPTER IX.

IRELAND'S SYMPATHY WITH AMERICA.

It may not be considered improper to refer here to the sympathy manifested in Ireland for the American patriots at the period of the Revolution. Franklin, writing from London to Samuel Cooper in April, 1769, affirms, "All Ireland is strongly in favor of the American cause. They have reason to sympathize with us. I send you four pamphlets written in Ireland, or by Irish gentlemen here, in which you will find some excellent well-said things."*

Three years later he visited Ireland, accompanied by an English member of Parliament named Jackson and was most warmly received. In a letter to William Franklin he says: "At Dublin we saw and were entertained by both parties, the courtiers and the patriots. The latter treated me with particular respect. We were admitted to sit among the members of the Commons House: Mr. Jackson as member of the British Parliament and I as member of some Parliament in America. The speaker proposed it in my behalf, with some very obliging expressions of respect for my character, and was answered by the House with a unanimous aye of consent, when two members came out to me, led me in between them and placed me honorably and commodiously. I hope our assemblies will not fall short of them in this politeness if any Irish member should happen to be in

* Life of Franklin, written by himself, edited by Bigelow.

our country."*   As it was a standing rule of the House to
admit members of the English Parliament to sit, though of
course not to vote among its members, the privilege accorded
to his fellow traveler was nothing unusual, but the honor
shown him was exceptional, and proved a desire on the part
of the Irish Parliament to manifest its feeling towards his
country, no less than its regard for himself.   Franklin's wish
that the courtesy extended to him in Dublin should be reci-
procated here, was fulfilled when Mr. Parnell visited this
country a few years since, and was honored with the privilege
of addressing the House of Representatives while in session.†

---

* Life of Franklin.

† Extract from Congressional Record of Jan. 15, 1880.

"Speaker Randall laid before the House the following :—

"WASHINGTON, D. C., Jan. 13, 1880.

"MR. SPEAKER—The undersigned, on behalf of the Clan-na-Gael Association, present their compliments, and have the honor, through you, to
earnestly and respectfully solicit the illustrious body over whose deliberations you preside to confer upon the undersigned and the Irish patriotic
organization they represent the distinguished honor of accepting this invitation to be present at the delivery of an address on the present suffering in Ireland by Charles Stewart Parnell on the 2d of February next,
and in such place in Washington as will best suit the convenience of the
honorable House of Representatives.

"The lively sympathy with the suffering people of Ireland so recently
and cordially manifested by the House of Representatives, and the deep-
seated love of justice which inspires their deliberations, encourage the
undersigned to entertain the hope that the occasion referred to will be
honored by the presence of the House.

"We have the honor to remain, most respectfully, your obedient servants,   "ED. O'MEAGHER CONDON,
                                            "RICARD O'S. BURKE,
                                            "Committee on Invitations.

"To the Hon. Samuel J. Randall,
        " Speaker of the House of Representatives.

"Ex-Gov. Thos. L. Young of Ohio immediately followed the reading

Elsewhere he says of "the principal patriots:" "I found them disposed to be friends of America, in which I endeavored to confirm them, with the expectation that our growing weight might in time be thrown into their scale. * * * There are many brave spirits among them."

What a contrast is there between the respect shown to the great American philosopher and patriot by the Irish Parliament and the indignity with which he was treated when before the English Privy Council? In presence of the latter body, Wedderburne, the solicitor-general, accused him of becoming improperly possessed of private letters belonging to others, and said:* "Nothing will acquit Dr. Franklin of

---

of the above by submitting this resolution, which was read, considered and agreed to.

"*Resolved by the House of Representatives,* That the invitation extended to this body to hear the address of Hon. Mr. Parnell, to be delivered in this city on the evening of February 2, on the distressed condition of Ireland, be accepted.

"Mr. Cox, of New York, then said—I propose the following resolution, to follow that of the gentleman from Ohio :

"The clerk read as follows :—

"In response to the invitation just presented and accepted, requesting the House to agree to take part in the ceremonies to be observed in the reception of Mr. Charles Stewart Parnell, *a representative of the Irish people*, for the delivery of an address on Irish affairs, and because of the great interest which the people of the United States take in the condition of Ireland, with which this country is so closely allied by many historic and kindred ties : Therefore,

"*Be it resolved,* That the Hall of this House be granted for the above purposes on the 2d day of February next, and that the House meet on that day and time to take part in said ceremonies."

After some discussion this resolution was also adopted, and, in compliance therewith, C. S. Parnell addressed the House while in session on the evening of February 2d. The speaker called the House to order and introduced Mr. Parnell, at the conclusion of whose speech the body adjourned on motion of M. P. O'Connor of South Carolina.

* Life of Franklin, vol. ii., 102.

the charge of obtaining them by fraudulent or corrupt means for the most malignant of purposes: unless he stole them from the person who stole them. I hope, my lords, you will mark and brand the man for the honor of this country, of Europe, and of mankind. * * * Into what companies will he hereafter go with an unembarrassed face, or the honest intrepidity of virtue. Men will watch him with a jealous eye: they will hide their papers from him and lock up their escritoires. He will henceforth esteem it a libel to be called a man of letters—*homo trium literarum.** And for this cowardly and disgusting conduct Wedderburne was made a peer. We are told, too, that "At the sallies of his sarcastic wit all the members of the council, the president himself (Lord Gower) not excepted, frequently laughed outright."†

That the American patriots recognized and appreciated the kindly feeling of Ireland towards them and their cause is clearly shown by the address of the Continental Congress of 1775 to the Irish people, which speaks as follows:—

"ADDRESS OF CONGRESS TO THE PEOPLE OF IRELAND.

"PHILADELPHIA, May 10, 1775.

"Friends and Fellow-subjects. As the important contest into which we have been driven has now become interesting to every European State, and particularly affects the members of the British Empire, we feel it our duty address you on the subject. We are desirous (as is natural to injured innocence) of possessing the good opinion of the virtuous and humane. *We are peculiarly desirous of furnishing you with a true state of our motives and objects*, the better to enable you to judge of our conduct with accuracy, and deter-

---

* A man of three letters—"*fur*," a thief.
† Life of Franklin, vol. ii., p. 205.

mine the merits on the controversy with impartiality and precision.

"Attempts have been made under cover of Parliamentary authority to seize Americans and carry them to Britain to be tried for offences committed in the colonies. Ancient charters have no longer remained sacred—that of Massachusetts Bay was violated, and their form of government essentially mutilated and transformed. On pretence of punishing a violation of some private property, committed by some few individuals, the populous and flourishing town of Boston was surrounded by fleets and armies, its trade destroyed, its port blocked up, and 30,000 citizens subjected to all the miseries attending so sudden a convulsion in their commercial metropolis. And to remove every obstacle to the rigorous execution of this system of oppression an Act of Parliament was passed calculated to indemnify those who might, in the prosecution of it, imbrue their hands in the blood of the inhabitants.

"A Congress consisting of Deputies from twelve United Colonies assembled. They, in the most respectful terms solicited a redress of their grievances. They also agreed to suspend all trade with Britain, Ireland and the West Indies, hoping by this peaceful mode of opposition to obtain that justice from the British Ministry which had been so long sought in vain. And here permit us to assure you that it was with the utmost reluctance that we could prevail upon ourselves to cease our commercial connection with your island.

"Your Parliament had done us no wrong. You HAD EVER BEEN FRIENDLY TO THE RIGHTS OF MANKIND, and we acknowledge with pleasure and gratitude that THE IRISH NATION HAS PRODUCED PATRIOTS WHO HAVE NOBLY DISTINGUISHED THEMSELVES IN THE CAUSE OF HUMANITY AND AMERICA. On the other hand, we were not ignorant that the labors and manufactures of Ireland, like those of the silk-worm, were of little moment to herself, *but served only to give luxu. y to those who neither toil nor spin.*

"We perceived that if we continued our commerce with you our agreement not to import from Britain would be fruitless, and we were therefore compelled to adopt a measure to which nothing but absolute necessity would have ever reconciled us. It gave us, however, some consolation to reflect that, should it occasion much distress, the fertile regions of America would afford you a safe asylum from poverty and in time from oppression also—an asylum in which many thousands of your countrymen have found hospitality, peace and affluence, and become united with others by all the ties of consanguinity, mutual interest and affection.

"The more fully to evince their respect for authority, the unhappy people of Boston were requested by Congress to submit with patience to their fate, and all Americans united in a resolution to abstain from every species of violence. During this period that devoted town suffered unspeakably, and its inhabitants were insulted and their property violated. Still relying on the justice of the English king and nation they permitted a few regiments to take possession of their town, to surround it with fortifications, and to cut off intercourse between them and their friends in the country.

"With anxious expectation did all America wait the event of her appeal for justice. All America laments its fate. Their ruler was deaf to their complaints, and vain were all attempts to impress him with a sense of the sufferings of his American subjects: of the cruelty of their taskmasters and of the many plagues which impended over his dominions. Instead of directions for a candid inquiry into our grievance, insult was added to oppression and our long forbearance was rewarded with the imputation of cowardice. Our trade with foreign States was prohibited, and an Act of Parliament passed to prevent us from fishing even on our own shores.   Our peaceable assemblies, for the purpose of consulting with respect to the common safety, were declared seditious; and our assertion of the very rights which placed the crown of Britain on the heads of three successive princes of the house of Hanover, styled rebellion.   Orders were given to reinforce the troops in America.   The wild and barbarous savages of the wilderness were solicited by gifts to take up the hatchet against us, and instigated to deluge our settlements with the blood of innocent and defenceless women and chlldren.   The whole country was moreover alarmed with the horrors of domestic insurrection—refinements of cruelty, at which the people of Britain must blush; refinements which admit not of being even recited without horror, or practiced without infamy.   We should be happy were these dark machinations the mere suggestions of suspicion.   We are sorry to declare that we are possessed of the most authentic and indubitable evidences of their reality.

*   *   *   *   *   *   *

"Despairing of driving the colonists to resistance by any other means than actual hostility, a detachment of the army at Boston marched into the country in all the array of war and, unprovoked, fired upon and killed several of the inhabitants.   The neighboring farmers suddenly assembled and repelled this attack.   From this time all communication between town and country was interrupted.   The citizens petitioned the general for permission to leave the town, and he promised, on surrendering their arms, to permit them to depart, with their other effects.   They accordingly surrendered their arms, and the general violated his faith.   Under various pretences, passports were delayed and denied, and many thousands are at this day confined in the town in the utmost wretchedness and want. The lame, the blind and the sick have indeed been turned out into the neighboring fields, and some, eluding the vigilance of the sentries, have escaped from the town by swimming to the adjacent shore.

"The war having been thus begun on the part of Gen. Gage's troops, we are compelled to behold thousands of our countrymen imprisoned, and men women and children involved in promiscuous and unmerited misery. When we find all faith at an end, and sacred treaties turned into tricks of state; when we perceive our friends and kinsmen massacred, our habitations plundered, our houses in flames and their once happy inhabitants fed only by the hand of charity, who can blame us for endeavoring to restrain the progress of desolation? Who can censure our repelling the attack of such a barbarous band? Who in such circumstances would not obey the great, the universal, the divine law of self-preservation? Though vilified as wan ing spirit we determined to behave like men; though insulted and abused we wished for reconciliation; though defamed as seditious we were ready to obey the laws.

"But we forbear to trouble you with a tedious detail of the various and fruitless offers and applications we have repeatedly made, not for pensions, for wealth, or for honors, but for the humble boon of being permitted to possess that degree of liberty to which God and the Constitution have given us an undoubted right.

"Blessed with an indissoluble Union, with a variety of internal resources, and with a firm reliance on the justice of the Supreme Disposer of all human affairs, we have no doubt of rising superior to all the machinations of evil and abandoned ministers. We already anticipate the golden period when Liberty, with all the gentle arts of peace and humanity, sh ll establish her mild dominion in this Western

World, and erect eternal monuments to the memory of those virtuous patriots and martyrs who shall have fought, bled and served in her cause.

"Accept our most grateful acknowledgments for the friendly disposition you have *always* shown towards us. We know that *you* are not without your grievances. We sympathize with you in your distress, and are pleased to find that the design of subjugating us has persuaded the Administration to dispense to Ireland some vagrant rays of ministerial sunshine. Even the tender mercies of [the British] Government have long been cruel towards you. In the rich pastures of Ireland many hungry parasites have fed and grown strong to labor for its destruction. We hope the patient abiding of the meek may not always be forgotten, and God grant that the iniquitous schemes of extirpating liberty may soon be defeated. But we should be wanting to ourselves, and should be perfidious to posterity, should we submit with folded arms to military butchery and deprivations, to ratify the lordly ambition or sate the avarice of a British ministry. In defence of our persons and properties, under actual violation, we have taken up arms. When that violence shall be removed, and hostilities cease on the part of the aggressors, they shall cease on our part also.

"For the achievement of this happy event we confide in the good offices of our sympathizers beyond the Atlantic. Of their friendly dispositions we do not yet despair, aware as they must be, that they have nothing more to expect from the same common enemy, than the humble favor of being last devoured." *

This appeal intensified the sympathy of those to whom it was addressed for their friends and kindred beyond the Atlantic. "Meetings were

---

* Journal of Congress of 1775.

held in many parts of Ireland to cheer the Americans."* Soon after the debates in Parliament "went very little short of formally justifying the American Revolution."† Some writers have indeed sought to create a different impression, but in their endeavor to do so, they have strangely misrepresented or perhaps misapprehended the real significance of the incident upon which they relied to support their views. It may be as well to set at rest here any doubts that may have arisen on this question. Lossing says: "The (English) king wrote an autograph letter to the States General of Holland, soliciting them to dispose of their Scotch brigade for service against the Americans. The request was nobly refused. A message was sent to the Parliament of Ireland requesting a supply of troops; that body complied by voting four thousand men, for the American service. They servilely agreed to send men to butcher their brethren and kinsmen, for a consideration; while the noble Hollanders with a voice of rebuke dissented, and refused to allow their soldiers to fight the strugglers for freedom, though strangers to them in blood and language."‡ It is hard to conceive how a writer of ability and research could consider himself justified in speaking in this manner. His words are calculated to deceive. The inference to be drawn from them is, that of two legislative bodies, each equally at liberty to grant or deny the proffered request of the English king, one boldly refused compliance while the other basely yielded assent, and did so for a "consideration." It is not questioned that the Hollanders have often displayed a love of liberty which does them honor. At the same time it should be remembered that they went, under William of Orange, "to fight the strugglers for freedom" in Ireland, who merely wished to exercise

* Mooney's History of Ireland, p. 831.
† Mitchel's History of Ireland, 118.
‡ Field Book of the Revolution, vol. i., 588.

the same right which they and the English claimed for themselves—that of choosing their own ruler.   The existence,
moreover, to-day of Belgium as an independent State, and
the remembrance of the struggles through which her people won their freedom, serve to show that the House
of Orange can oppress and provoke resistance as well as the
House of Brunswick, and that the Hollanders have not always hesitated to fight against even "their brethren and
kinsmen" on behalf of tyranny.   Holland was a free nation.
The English king had no more right to demand troops
from it in order to suppress revolt in the Colonies than had
the President of the United States to ask England for
soldiers to assist in subduing the Confederates during our
late troubles.   The Hollanders did well in refusing the request of George III., but they could not have done otherwise without lowering themselves to the level of the petty
despots who sold their unfortunate subjects like slaves to
fight for the enslavement of the Americans.

With the Irish the case was altogether different.   They
were not free, nor had they a Representative body to
even voice their sentiments.   Ireland was, like America,
subject to England.   The so-called Irish Parliament
did not at all represent the Irish people, more
than five-sixths of whom—being Catholics—were ineligible
to a seat in it and even prohibited from casting a
vote at the election of its members.   Half the remaining
sixth, the Presbyterians, Methodists and other "dissenters"
from the Anglican Church were, by the operation of the
Test Act, almost as much excluded from political privileges,
power, or position—including the right to sit in the Legislature—as the adherents of the Ancient Faith.   The alleged
Parliament of Ireland did not, however, represent even the
small fraction of the population still unaccounted for.   Over
three-fourths of its members were practically *appointed* by the

English Lord Lieutenant and about a score of Anglo-Irish peers, and less than a fourth owed their seats to the voters of the skeleton constituencies, to whom was restricted the election franchise. Barrington says: "The Earl of Ely nominated nine members to the House of Commons. The Earl of Shannon nominated seven, and above twenty other members of the House of Lords nominated and elected members for the House of Commons. Many individuals openly sold their patronage for money to the best bidders; others returned members at the nomination of the viceroy or his secretary: and it appeared that the number of representatives elected freely by the people upon constitutional principles did not compose one-fourth of the House of Commons."* There is still more to be added. By the "Law of Poynings" passed in the Irish "Parliament" in the reign of the English king Henry VII., that body deprived itself of the right to originate any bill whatever. "Before any statute could be finally discussed, it was previously to be submitted to the Lord Lieutenant of Ireland and his Privy Council for their consideration, who might, at their pleasure, reject it or transmit it to England. If the latter course were adopted, the British Attorney-General and Privy Council were invested with power, either to suppress it altogether or model it at their own will, and then return it to Ireland with *permission* to the Irish Parliament to pass it into a law; but without any alteration, though it frequently returned from England so changed as to retain hardly a trace of its original features or a point of its original object."† Long after, in the sixth year following the accession of George I. to the British throne, the English Parliament passed a "iaw" by which it assumed the power "to bind Ireland by every

---

* Rise and Fall of the Irish Nation.
† Ibid.

British statute in which she should be expressly designated."*

It must now be evident that the mass of the Irish people
cannot in any way be held responsible for the acts of their
pretended Parliament, composed of the elements and con-
trolled by the authority and influences just indicated. It
had no sympathy with those whom it affected to represent and
for whom it assumed to speak. By its penal enactments, its
wanton and offensive exclusiveness, and its abject subserv-
ience to England, it earned the hatred of the people, and was
forced to provide for the support of an army to keep them
in subjection. When in 1775 it was asked, more as a matter
of form than of necessity, to signify its consent to the transfer to America, in order to sustain English supremacy and
strengthen the loyalists—of four thousand of these troops,
for whose maintenance it taxed the Irish people, the request
was complied with. Not, however, without vigorous opposition and strong expressions of sympathy with the American
patriots, from those who did not owe their positions to the
favor of British officials.

When the matter was first hinted at in the royal address
at the opening of Parliament, Yelverton justified the action
of the Americans, and said that "No slavery could be more
perfect than where men were taxed without being represented. The Ministry had cut off the rights of thirteen
colonies at once. Ireland would be the next victim. When
liberty had but one neck, that too would be lopped off at
one stroke."

Hatch asserted that the dispute was not between Ireland
and the Colonies but between them and Britain. "If the
resistance of the Americans, to those who would take their

---

* Rise and Fall of the Irish Nation.

liberties from them, were deemed rebellion, all honest men would be rebels.''

Wilson solemnly declared "that no reward the king could give, would be able to satisfy his conscience if he voted for the measure.''

Hussey Burgh was opposed to taxing the Americans without their consent, and "would not vote for a single sword" against them. "Gentlemen,'' he said, "might argue against taxing Ireland also, but should thirty thousand English swords enforce that doctrine, eloquence would be a weak defence against them.'' Bushe was opposed to the project, for he felt that if "they agreed to it the next step would be to tax Ireland in the British House of Commons.

Daly, in speaking against the scheme, affirmed that the English "might well permit Ireland to have a Parliament while its members made themselves tools to fleece the public.''

Ponsonby said: "If troops are sent abroad without our consent we are not made parties to the quarrel. If we give consent we take part against America, but to do this would be unjust.'' Newenham expressed the belief that "though America might be conquered, the spirit of liberty there could never be subdued.''

Ogle boldly declared that "they would not be intimidated by threats. They would not send men to cut the throats of the Americans. While the Irish Parliament would do all that was absurd they would, no doubt, have a Parliament just as the Romans had a Senate in the times of the Emperors, to give sanction to Imperial edicts. If men must be sent to America let them send foreign mercenaries.'' The elder Fitzgibbon, Connolly, and others, also strongly opposed the proposition;* but the nominees of the viceroy

---

* Irish Parliamentary Reports.

and his allies were too strong, and they carried their point, with the concession, however, that Ireland was not be called on to pay or support those "armed negotiators" while engaged, along with twenty-five thousand armed American Tories*—in an effort to prevent the Colonies from separating from Britain. It may be stated here—in order to show how merely formal was the request made by the British Minister, to the so-called Irish Parliament for its consent to the departure of the troops alluded to—that Lord North, although he had only asked for four thousand of the men stationed in Ireland, sent orders to embark eight of the regiments there, which made up much more than the number requested. When he offered to replace the troops sent away by an equal number of Hessians, to be maintained at the expense of England alone, his proposition was promptly declined. This was the only return proffered for the compliance of the Irish Parliament with the request of the British Ministry, so that Lossing's assertion that the former consented to the latter's wishes, "for a consideration," is as groundless as his comparison of the course pursued by a subject body with that of an independent one is unfair.

Froude speaks of what he calls a "petition of the Catholics in Ireland" in 1775; the signers of which assert that they regard with "abhorrence" the "unnatural rebellion" in America; that their loyalty "is, and always was, as the dial to the sun true though not shone upon," and that they know "these sentiments to be those also of their fellow Roman Catholic subjctes." This precious paper is signed by Lords Fingal, Trimleston and a few others. It is addressed to the Secretary of the Lord Lieutenant, who is asked to represent the views contained in it to his superior officer, and to request the latter, if he think proper, to lay

---

* Sabine.

them before the English king.* There were no doubt a
few Tories among the old Catholic aristocracy of Ireland,
who were as anxious as those of the same stripe here to
show their loyalty to George III. But this paper, in as far
as it pretended to represent the sentiments of the mass of the
Irish Catholics, was much further from the truth than the
address of the American Tories to the king in which it was
declared that "quite as many if not more Americans" had
joined his armies as had fought against him.† Froude's
argument in the case, however, as in almost all others, con-
futes itself. Speaking of the Catholic Irish at this period
he says: "The friends of the Americans in Ireland were their
worst foes, who but for England would have put the penal
laws in force against them,"‡ which is equivalent to saying
that Grattan and his patriotic colleagues were anxious to
enforce the penal laws.§   Comment is needless.

----

* English in Ireland.   At the time of the "veto" agitation in Ireland
(1808–14) when the people indignantly protested against allowing the
rulers of England a negative upon the appointment of Catholic Bishops,
Lord Fingal tried to get up a petition in favor of the scheme.   His paper received four signatures, all like himself lords.   So much for his influence and for the weight to be attached to what he might say.   The
petition of which Froude speaks was equally valueless.

† Sabine.

‡ English in Ireland, vol. ii., p. 174.

§ Grattan, during a debate, which occurred a few years later gave Flood
a terrible scoring for his conduct in consenting to the transfer of troops
from Ireland to America in 1775.   Affecting—in order not to offend
against Parliamentary courtesy—to speak of an imaginary individual, he
said: "With regard to the liberties of America, which were inseparable
from ours, I will suppose this gentleman to have been an enemy decided
and unreserved : and that he voted against her liberty and voted, moreover, for an address to send four thousand troops to cut the throats of the
Americans that he called those butchers' armed negotiators : and stood
with a metaphor in his mouth and a bribe in his pocket a champion

It may not be out of place here to allude to some evidences of the feeling of indignation with which the Irish people regarded the sending of troops to America. When the regiments required for the odious service were designated, Lord Effingham, who held a commission in one of them, sent his resignation to the English Secretary of War, and frankly stated his reasons for taking this step. To manifest its appreciation of his patriotism, the City of Dublin, at the ensuing midsummer quarter assembly, voted him its thanks and eulogized him for having "refused to draw his sword against the lives and liberties of his fellow-subjects in America." Soon after, the Guild of Merchants of the Irish Capital presented an address of thanks to the peers who had voted against the measure, and "in opposition to a weak and wicked administration protested against the American Restraining Bills."* This address and the replies of the lords to whom it had been presented, open declarations of sympathy with America, were at once published in the journals throughout the country, and produced a profound impression, even in England.

Froude speaks of the Catholic gentry and clergy of Ireland coming forward with an offer of a subscription in aid of the British government during its contest with America. He bases his assertion on the alleged petition to the Secretary of the Lord Lieutenant, before referred to, but as that only speaks of an intention never carried out "to raise a fund for encouraging recruits for H. M.'s service," on the part of the few insignificant and uninfluential individuals who signed it; and as the paper itself, moreover, was not thought worthy of a reply by those to whom it was addressed, and was never even made public until the

---

against the rights of America, the only hope of Ireland and the only refuge of the liberties of mankind."—Select Speeches of Grattan, p. 104.

* Mitchel's History of Ireland. 118.

author of the historical romance called the "English in Ireland" saw fit to set it forth, the charge cannot be deemed deserving of serious notice.

The subjects above referred to may not, at first sight, seem to require consideration in these pages. But when it is remembered that they are spoken of, and sometimes misrepresented by, writers of American history, it will not appear improper to have attempted here briefly the correction of erroneous impressions with regard to them, and the removal of prejudices which those impressions are calculated to excite among those who have not heard both sides of the question at issue.

The Irish people were, with exceptions far fewer than were to be found in America itself, enthusiastic friends of American liberty. In Britain the case was quite a different. "In England," says Spencer, "there was a general sentiment in favor of compelling the colonists to submission.* Chatham said, in the English House of Lords, in 1775: "There is scarcely a man in our streets, though so poor as scarcely to be able to get his daily bread, but thinks he is the legislator of America. '*Our American subjects*' is a common phrase in the mouths of the lowest order of our citizens."†

Taylor says: "The war for the subjugation of the Americans was at first decidedly popular in England. From the habit of using the phrase '*our* colonies,' there was not an English peasant who did not regard the colonists as rebels against himself, and as enemies to some fancied authority and power which he deemed the privilege of every Englishman by his birth-right."‡ Addresses and petitions "glow-

---

* History of the U. S., vol. i., 328.
† Chatham's Speeches.
‡ History of Ireland vol. ii., 238.

ing with loyalty to the king and indignation against the rebels,'' from London and the provincial towns, were poured in upon ''his majesty'' and his advisers. The House of Lords was like ''a seething caldron of impotent rage,'' and the cry of ''*Delenda est Carthago*'' was raised in the House of Commons when the news of the Boston ''Tea Party'' reached that body. In Scotland the feeling towards America was not much less heated, and the manner in which it was manifested excited the strong indignation of the American patriots and especially of Jefferson and Franklin.* On the other hand, the sympathy felt by the people of Ireland for their trans-Atlantic brethren was so strong that when a regiment was ordered from there to fight for British despotism in America, ''every man in it had to be shipped on board tied and bound;''† and, hope-

---

* In the original draft of the Declaration of Independence Jefferson denounces, in the clause beginning with the words ''Nor have we been wanting in attention to our British brethren''—those who permit the sending over of ''Scotch and foreign mercenaries to invade and destroy'' the people. The word *Scotch* was struck out at the request of Dr. Witherspoon, of New Jersey, one of the Signers, a native of Scotland.— Lossing, ii., 74.

Franklin, in a letter to Hartley, speaking of the American prisoners of war in England, says that a subscription raised there for the purpose of affording them some relief, would ''have an excellent effect in favor of Englishmen,'' and adds, ''The Scotch subscriptions for raising troops to destroy us, though amounting to much greater sums, will not do their nation half so much good.''—Life of Franklin, vol. ii.

The active part taken also by large numbers of Scotch here, against the patriots, no doubt excited considerable indignation towards them. But it must not be forgotten that two of the Signers, Witherspoon and Wilson, were Scotchmen, and that Mercer, Stirling, and others of that nationality, proved themselves worthy descendants of those who had, under Bruce and Wallace, fought against English tyranny.

† Arthur Lee, Letter to Washington.

less of help from that quarter, the British government turned to the petty princelings of Hesse Cassel, Hesse Brunswick and Waldeck, and purchased from them seventeen thousand troops for its hateful service, while France and Europe looked on with indignation, and Frederic the Great denounced "the scandalous man-traffic of his neighbors."*

---

* Lossing, vol. ii., 347.

CHAPTER X.

THE FIRST ACT OF WAR. SULLIVAN'S CAPTURE OF FORT
WILLIAM AND MARY—LEXINGTON AND CONCORD—FIRST
AMERICAN NAVAL VICTORY—O'BRIEN AT MACHIAS.

WHEN the first Continental Congress, which met at Phila·
delphia on September 5, 1774, adjourned, after a session of
fifty-one days, many of its members returned home impressed with the conviction that England would recognize
the rights of America only when compelled by force.
Some of the delegates resolved to lose no time in endeavoring to prepare for the conflict which they felt to be at hand.
Among these was John Sullivan, one of the representatives
from New Hampshire, who, on December 11, 1774, along
with John Langdon, afterwards Governor of that State, and
a company of citizens from Portsmouth, N. H., surprised
Fort William and Mary at Newcastle, made prisoners of the
soldiers who guarded it, and carried off the military stores
which it contained, consisting of a hundred barrels of gun-
power, fifteen pieces of artillery, and a considerable supply
of arms. These munitions of war proved a valuable
acquisition to the men who, half a year later, fought on
Bunker Hill. This exploit is regarded, and justly, by the
best authorities, as the first act of war waged by the colonists against England. Peabody says:—

"This affair may appear in itself of no great moment;
but it assumes another aspect when we consider the
time at which it occurred. *It was the first act, which could
be regarded as one of open and direct hostility, committed by*

a military force against the Royal Government. It was con-
summated by the seizure of the king's property, and the
disarming and imprisoning of his soldiers; *and this, too, at
a time when the universal language held in public was that of
peace, and anticipated reconciliation:* and, if the course of
events had been otherwise than it was, it is difficult to
see how those concerned in it could have screened themselves from the penalties of treason. It was not until four
months afterwards that the first blood was shed at Lexington; and later still that an enterprise, in character not dis-
similar, was executed, under the command of Patrick
Henry, in Virginia."*

The same view is taken of this enterprise in *Appleton's
Cyclopædia,* and by various other authorities.

Some writers, however, speak of the conflict at Alamance
Creek, N. C., before alluded to, which took place in May,
1771, as the "first battle of the war for independence."
But that affair had no direct connection with the Revolution.
Its influence did not reach, much less enter into, the
War of Independence. It had simply *a local effect.* Alamance Creek had even less to do with the Revolution than
did the "Boston Massacre," which occurred on March 5,
1770. These events, like the Boston "Tea Party," were
isolated actions, which the American historian should note,
not as the beginning of the war, but as tokens of ill-feeling
that had existed in the colonies anterior to the war. The country slept for years after these local storms. But Sullivan's
exploit was quite different in its character. His surprise
of Fort William and Mary was a premeditated thing. It
was undertaken by a man who had the war in sight, and
who was determined to hasten and urge it on. It was a
purely military enterprise. The cannon and other war ma-

---

* Life of General Sullivan in Sparks Library of American Biography.

terial captured at that fort did first service at Bunker Hill.
The hero of the affair became a major-general in the Rev-
olutionary army.   His act entered into and influenced the
War of Independence.   It was the first link in the chain.
It was, in fact, the first blow in the War of Independence.*

---

* John Sullivan was born in Berwick, Maine, on the 17th of February,
1740.   His father came to America about the year 1723, from Kerry, or,
as some say, Limerick, Ireland, and lived to see his two sons—James, the
governor of Massachusetts, and John, become distinguished among their
fellow-countrymen ; dying at the patriarchal age of one hundred and
five.   The earlier years of General Sullivan were passed in laborious work
on his father's farm ; but on arriving at manhood he applied himself to
the study of law, and after a time opened an office for its practice in the
village of Durham, New Hampshire.   When the first Continental Congress assembled, he was chosen a delegate to that body; and after his return, as stated above, projected and carried out successfully the capture of
Fort William and Mary.

On the organization of the Continental army, in 1775, Sullivan was
appointed one of its eight brigadier-generals, and in the year following,
a major-general.   He superseded Arnold in command of the American
army in Canada in 1776.   When General Greene fell sick on Long Island,
the command of his division devolved on Sullivan who was taken prisoner
in the battle fought there in August, 1776.   He was soon exchanged,
however, and once more in active service.   When General Charles Lee
was surprised and carried off by a British detachment in New Jersey,
Sullivan succeeded to the command of his division, and rendered good
service in the battles of Brandywine and Germantown.   In the winter
following, he was transferred to the command of the army in Rhode
Island, where, after considerable maneuvering, he, in conjunction with
D'Estaing, who was at the time in command of the French fleet, laid
siege to Newport, Rhode Island, then in possession of the English.   Instead, however, of coming to the aid of Sullivan, D'Estaing sailed for
Boston, and left him under the necessity of raising the siege, and retreating before the enemy.   On the 29th of August, he paused in his retreat and gave the British battle, which had the effect of preventing them
from pursuing him further.

In the summer of 1779, he assumed the command of an expedition
against the Indians, in the State of New York, in which he was, after

Early in 1775, the people of Massachusetts began to prepare for war. Large quantities of ammunition and arms were secretly removed from Boston, and stored at Concord and other points. Gage, who was at the head of over three thousand five hundred troops in the city of

---

some time, joined by General Clinton. Marching upon the savages he found them encamped in immense numbers at Newton, between the Tioga river and the south end of Seneca lake, and under command of the celebrated Brandt and other tory leaders. Before the first of September, they were either slain, taken prisoners, or scattered and driven away. Soon after this, Sullivan, becoming disgusted at the manner in which he was treated by the Board of War, resigned his commission and retired to his farm in New Hampshire. He was soon after elected to Congress, where he served until 1786, when he was chosen President of New Hampshire. He held this office until 1789, when he was appointed district judge, filling that office until his death, which took place January 23, 1795, at the age of fifty-four years.

James Sullivan, brother of the general, born in 1744, was elected to Congress from Massachusetts in 1788. He became attorney-general of that State in 1790, and while in that position projected the Middlesex Canal, and wrote the "History of the District of Maine" which the Legislature ordered to be published. He was elected Governor of Massachusetts in 1807, and re-elected in 1808, in which year he died. His son, Hon. William Sullivan, was an eminent jurist and scholar and wrote many valuable works. He was a member of the Legislature of Massachusetts for nearly twenty-six years, and died in 1839.

The mother of General Sullivan was a woman of great energy and spirit. There is a story told of a visit which she paid to her distinguished son when he was Governor of New Hampshire and had as a guest his brother John. The servant, not knowing her, replied that she could not see the Governor—he was engaged. "But I must see him," said the old lady. "Then, madam, you will please to wait in the anteroom." "Tell your master," said she, sweeping out of the hall, "that the mother of two of the greatest men in America will not wait in any one's anteroom." The Governor having called his servant, on hearing the report said to his brother—"James, let us run after her ; it's my mother, for certain." Accordingly the two governors sallied out, and soon overtook and made their peace with the indignant, but easily mollified lady.

the Tea Party, resolved to destroy the war material of the patriots, and on the night of the 18th of April sent eight hundred British regulars, under the command of Smith and Pitcairn, to Concord, to seize the military stores there. These were under the charge of Colonel James Barrett, an Irish-American officer, who had held a commission in the Provincial army during the French war. He was advanced in years, but at the urgent solicitation of his fellow-citizens, who told him that they only required instruction and advice, not active service, from him, he took command of a regiment. Information was given to the people along the road to Concord, by Paul Revere and William Dawes, of the British movement, and about a hundred American militia assembled at Lexington, six miles from the town just named. On seeing these, Pitcairn rode up to them, shouting, "Disperse, you villains! lay down your arms! Why don't you disperse, you rebels?" They did not obey, and some shots were fired at them without orders by the regulars, which were promptly returned, when Pitcairn gave the order to his troops to fire, and before they ceased eight Americans were dead or dying, while their comrades fell back and dispersed. The British, emboldened by their success, then pushed on to Concord, where they saw several hundred militia under Colonel Barrett assembled at some distance while the rest of the citizens were engaged in carrying off to a place of safety the much sought after military stores. Among those busied in this duty, mention is made of Hugh Cargil, a native of Ballyshannon, who, along with a man named Bullock, rendered good service that day by saving the town records from destruction, at great risk to himself. The British succeeded in destroying a portion of the war material which was still left at Concord. Some shots were exchanged, too, with fatal effect between them and the Americans, but the militia and people assembling at this

time in great numbers the regulars retreated rapidly towards
Lexington. They were pursued and fired into all along
the route. When they reached the last named town, a
reinforcement of nearly a thousand men, sent to their aid
from Boston, met them, but the retreat was soon continued,
when the firing from the militia was renewed, and before
the British reached Charlestown they had lost two hundred and seventy-three of their number, including killed,
wounded, and missing, while the loss of the " rebels " only
amounted to one hundred and three. The main body of the
redcoats camped that night on Bunker Hill, and the next
day they returned to their quarters in Boston.

The Provincial Congress was at once summoned to assemble. It met at Watertown, seven miles from Boston, on
April 22, and decided to send a report of the events of the
19th to Arthur Lee, its agent in London. The dispatch
bearer was instructed "to make for Dublin or any other
good port in Ireland and from thence cross to Scotland or
England," and hasten to his destination. He arrived eleven
days before Gage's dispatches reached the British Ministers,
and King George learned first from American sources how
his troops had been beaten by those they had endeavored
to trample on.

" THE LEXINGTON OF THE SEAS."

The manner in which the patriots had dealt with the
marauding expedition to Concord, excited great enthusiasm
everywhere throughout the colonies, and filled the minds
of the British with mortification and bitterness. They
sent their ships to commit depredations along the New
England coasts, hoping by such acts to revenge themselves for their defeat. But here again they met with a
well-merited disaster. One of their armed vessels, the

Margaretta, put into Machias Bay, Maine, early in May. Among the townsmen was Maurice O'Brien, a native of Cork, who had five stalwart sons, all eager like himself to show their hatred of British tyranny and do their part in aiding the cause of American liberty. These with a number of their fellow citizens determined to capture the English ship, and on May 11th they went on board a sloop lying in the harbor, and bore down on the *Margaretta.* The latter hoisted her sails and scudded from the bay; but she was soon overhauled and boarded, when a fierce conflict ensued, which terminated, after about twenty men on each side had fallen, in favor of the Americans.

This was the *first naval fight* of the Revolution, and Jeremiah O'Brien was the victorious commander. Two British cruisers, the *Diligence* and the *Tapnaguish,* were at once dispatched to lay Machias in ashes, but they also were met and captured by O'Brien, his brothers and comrades. The young hero immediately sailed, with his prizes and prisoners, for Watertown, Mass., where the Provincial Congress was in session, and received the thanks of that body and a captain's commission. But the British were not yet satisfied. They sent from Halifax a squadron, including a frigate, a twenty-gun corvette, a brig of sixteen guns, and several armed schooners, to crush the weak American fleet; but O'Brien, aided by Colonel Foster, was once more triumphant, and beat them off after a hard struggle. They then sent a strong body of land forces against Machias, but " after the second day's march from Passamaquoddy the British troops returned to Halifax, despairing of effecting a passage through the woods," or perhaps, hopeless of accomplishing their purpose when confronted by those who had already conquered their fellow mercenaries three times at sea. We are told that Maurice O'Brien, old as he was, could hardly be restrained from joining his gallant sons, in their daring enterprises against the British.

Cooper, says speaking of the exploit at Machias: " This affair was the Lexington of the Seas; for, like that cele-brated conflict, it was the rising of the people against a regular force—was characterized by a long chase, a bloody struggle and a victory. It was also *the first blow* struck on the water after the war of the American Revolution had actually commenced."*

Three of the O'Briens, Jeremiah, John, and William, continued in the naval service of the Republic until the close of the war. Jeremiah was appointed to the command of the *The Liberty*, and his brother William served under him as lieutenant. "For two years this vessel and another did good service on the northern coast, affording protection to American navigation, after which they were laid up."†
Jeremiah, with others, then fitted out a twenty-gun letter-of-marque, called the *Hannibal*, manned by one hundred and thirty men. She took several prizes; but at length fall-ing in with two British frigates, she was overhauled af-ter a chase of forty-eight hours and captured. O'Brien was first confined in the *Jersey* prison-ship, otherwise known as the "Hell," at the Wallabout, where the Brooklyn Navy Yard now is. At the end of about six months he was sent to Mill Prison, England, whence he succeeded in effecting his escape about a year later. He retired after the war to Brunswick, Maine, where, at the age of over fourscore, he furnished the details of his brave achievements to a genera-tion which had shamefully forgotten him and them.‡

John O'Brien was more fortunate than his gallant bro-ther. From a journal kept by him the following extracts

---

* Cooper's Naval History.   † Portland Eclectic. 1851.
        ‡ Historical Collection of Maine.

are taken: "On June 9, 1779, he sailed in the armed
schooner *Hibernia.* On June 21th he took an English brig,
and sent her in. On June 25, he had an engagement with
a ship of seventeen guns, from three till five o'clock P. M.,
when a frigate came up and the *Hibernia* was compelled to leave her anticipated prize and was pursued by the
frigate till midnight. O'Brien had three men killed and
several wounded in this fight. On July 7 he took a
schooner, and sent her to Newburyport. On the day following, in company with Captain Leach of Salem, he took
a ship carrying thirteen four-pounders; a few hours after, a
brig, and then a schooner laden with molasses. On July
11 he took a hermaphrodite brig in ballast, and then chased
and captured another which just hove in sight. He adds
that if Captain Leach and he had not parted in the fog they
could have taken the whole fleet. Captain John O'Brien
was engaged in a large number of battles and enterprises of
various kinds against the British, but was never taken.*

No trace is found, after the capture of the *Hannibal,* of
Lieutenant William O'Brien. He was most probably
among the eleven thousand victims of British cruelty, whose
corpses were buried, or flung on the shores of the Wallabout.

Among the events of the Revolution the conflict at
Machias Bay should ever be regarded as entitled to a conspicuous place. When the poet descants, or the orator di-
lates, upon the glories of the past, it should not be left un-
mentioned. The canvas of the painter should reproduce
the scene; and upon the shore from which first England's
red ensign was seen to sink before American manhood, a
fitting monument should rise in honor of the brave men
who compelled British tyranny to yield up the supremacy
of the seas to those she had sought to treat as slaves.

---

* Coffin's Newburyport.

Premonitory shocks of the great political earthquake, which was to make totter and fall the whole fabric of British power from the Lakes to the Gulf, were felt about this time throughout all the Colonies. The second Continental Congress—that which addressed the people of Ireland—met at Philadelphia on May 10th, 1775, at ten o'clock. Six hours before, Ethan Allen had summoned Ticonderoga to surrender, and when asked by what authority he made the demand, replied, " In the name of the Great Jehovah and the Continental Congress." The fort was yielded up to him without bloodshed, and two days later Crown Point also fell into his hands.

At Savannah a number of the Sons of Liberty, on the same day that O'Brien won his victory over the British at Machias, broke open the military magazine, took out the powder, sent some to Beaufort, South Carolina, and hid what was left in convenient receptacles. This organization contained a large proportion of Irish Americans, as may be seen from the list of names of a committee appointed a short time previous to draft resolutions declaring hostility to British oppression. John Glenn was the chairman, and amongst the members were Jonathan Bryan, Samuel Farley, William Gibbons, John Winn, E. Butler, and others, of Irish origin.

A convention met in May at Charlotte, Mecklenburg county, North Carolina, to express an opinion on the situation. Large numbers of Irish had settled in the district, and there were many Irish Americans among the delegates. Included in the number were Richard Barry, Neil Morrison, Benjamin Tatton, John Flenekin (or Flannigan), W. Kennon, John Ford, R. Irwin, Matthew McClure, John Queary, L. Wilson, and others, the majority being evidently of northern Irish stock. While this body was in session the **news of the fights** at Lexington and Concord reached

Charlotte, and produced a sensation in the minds of those assembled and all in the district. On May 31 the convention adopted what is known as the Mecklenburg *Declaration of Independence*, in which it is declared:

" (1) That all commissions, civil and military, heretofore granted by the crown to be exercised in these Colonies, are null and void.

" (2) That the Provincial Congress of each province, under the direction of the great Continental Congress, is invested with all legislative and executive powers within their respective provinces, and that no other legislative or executive power does or can exist at this time in any of those Colonies.

*   *   *   *   *   *   *

" (4) That the inhabitants of this county do meet on a certain day appointed by the committee, and, having formed themselves into nine companies, do choose a colonel and other military officers, who shall hold and exercise their several powers by virtue of the choice, and *independent of the crown of Great Britain* and former Constitution of this province."

The eighteenth clause of *the Declaration* decrees " That whatever person shall hereafter receive a commission from the crown, or attempt to exercise any such commission heretofore received, shall be deemed an enemy to the country."

CHAPTER XI.

BUNKER HILL—SIEGE OF BOSTON—QUEBEC—EMBASSY TO CANADA.

On the day following the battle of Lexington the Committee of Safety of Massachusetts issued a circular to the towns in that province, urging them to " hasten and encourage by all possible means the enlistment of men to form an army,"and to send them forward at once. "Our all," continued the appeal, "is at stake. Death and devastation are the certain consequences of delay, every moment is infinitely precious, an hour lost may deluge your country in blood and entail perpetual slavery upon the few of your posterity who may survive the carnage."* Another circular was sent to the other New England colonies on April 26, asking for as many troops as could be spared to march forthwith to the assistance of Massachusetts. The response was prompt. Companies and regiments were hurriedly organized and sent on to the rendezvous at Cambridge, and soon it was estimated that over twenty thousand men were assembled at that point. Artemas Ward was appointed commander-in-chief, but for some time there was considerable confusion among the hastily collected patriots, as the officers were not regularly commissioned, nor the men mus· tered in.

The New Hampshire troops, among whom Irish-Ameri-

---

* Journals of Provincial Congress, p. 518.

cans formed a large proportion,* came toget_er at Medford on April 26, and the field officers decided that Colonel

---

* The following are the names of one company raised in Bedford, and from it the reader may form an estimate of the number of Irish recruited in New Hampshire for the Revolutionary forces. They were part of the force stationed at the rail-fence on Bunker Hill, who twice drove back the redcoats with the bayonet, and saved the main body of the patriots from total annihilation. The names are found in the Hist. Coll. of N. H., vol. i., p., 291:—

Colonel Daniel Moore,	Major John Goffe,
Capt. T. McLaughlin,	Lieut. John Patten,
John Patten, senior,	Sam. Patten,
James Patten,	Robert Patten,
John Gault,	Isaac Riddle,
John Riddle,	A. Martin,
James Martin,	Stephen Goffe,
Hugh Horton,	Burns Chandler
Samuel Moore,	Samuel Barr,
John Callahan (killed),	James Moore,
Ira Greer,	Wm. Parker,
John McAllister,	John Griffer,
Robert Victorey,	Daniel Larkin,
James Paterson,	John O'Neill,
George Hogg,	W. Gilmore,
James Houston,	John Ross,
Stephen March,	John Tyrrel,
Patrick O'Fling	C. Johnston,
John Gardnie,	Robert Corn,
Jones Cutting,	John Hiller,
Barnet McCla,	Luke Gardner,
R. Dalrymple,	Sam. Patterson,
Solomon Hemp,	John Dorr (killed),
William Houston,	Zac. Chandler,
Valentine Sullivan,	John Steel,
Robert Morrel,	Patrick O'Murphy,
David Riddle,	Eben Sullivan,

and eighteen others, making a total of seventy-one Irishmen who belonged to one New Hampshire company at the battle of Bunker Hill.

John Stark should take command until the decision of the Provincial Congress was made known. That body, on May 20, voted to raise two thousand men, who were to be formed into three regiments, of which Stark, Reed and Poor, were made colonels, with Folsom as brigadier-general. The latter, however, did not reach Cambridge until June 20, three days after Bunker Hill. Poor's battalion did not arrive at the camp until the battle was over, but Stark and Reed, with their regiments, hurried forward in time to participate in the memorable conflict.*

No military operations of importance took place until the seventeenth of June, though several skirmishes occurred, which resulted generally in favor of the Americans. On June 12, General Gage, who commanded the British, issued a proclamation couched in the boastful and offensive terms usually employed by the military and civil authorities of Britain. "Whereas," he began, "the infatuated multitudes who have long suffered themselves to be conducted by certain well-known incendiaries and traitors in a fatal progression of crimes against the constitutional authority of the state, have at length proceeded to avowed rebellion, and the good effects which were expected to arise from the patience and lenity of the king's government have been often frustrated, and are now rendered hopeless by the influence of the same evil counsels, it only remains for those who are intrusted with the supreme rule, as well for the punishment of the guilty as the protection of the well-affected, to prove that they do not bear the sword in vain." He then declared martial law, denounced those who had assembled in arms and their abettors as "rebels and traitors," and offered pardon to those who would "stand distinct and separate from the parricides of the constitution," excepting, how-

---

* Siege of Boston, p. 99.

ever, John Hancock and Samuel Adams, whose offences were, as he chose to fancy, "of too flagitious a nature to admit of any other consideration than that of condign punishment." People at a distance, who understood little or nothing of the question at issue, might, on reading this precious document, be led to imagine that the American patriots had been guilty of atrocious crimes, just as some few simple and easily deluded persons are imposed on by British proclamations and "royal" speeches at the present day with regard to the efforts of the people of Ireland to assert their rights. But the American Sons of Liberty were no more impressed by Gage's pompous pronunciamento than Irish Nationalists have been by similar productions, and its only effect was to embitter them still more and make them eager for an opportunity to avenge his insults and show their contempt for his threats.

The British, having received considerable reinforcements, and rendered still more confident in their own ability to overcome the colonists by the arrival of Generals Howe, Clinton and Burgoyne, determined to advance their lines and take possession of Dorchester Heights. The night of June 18 was the time fixed for this undertaking, but information of the proposed movement was soon conveyed to the American camp, and the patriots decided to anticipate their enemies, and to fortify and hold Bunker Hill, if possible. Detachments from several regiments, amounting in all to about twelve hundred men, were accordingly sent to the point mentioned on the night of the sixteenth to throw up works; but the officers in command, on arriving at the spot, concluded that another position, nearer Boston and known as Breed's Hill, would suit their purpose better, and accordingly they entrenched there. At early dawn on the seventeenth, the British were surprised and provoked at seeing the work which had been accomplished so successfully

during the night by their enemies, and they resolved upon
an attack. It was made in the afternoon. Nearly four
thousand English regulars were twice driven back, by little
over half their number of untrained Americans. But the ammunition of the patriots soon became exhausted, and when
the British, strongly reinforced, advanced a third time to
the assault, aided by a heavy artillery fire, no means were
left of offering them an effective resistance, and General
Prescott gave his men the order to retreat, which was reluctantly obeyed. During the engagement the New Hampshire
regiments of Stark and Reed, very largely composed of
Irish-Americans, were posted on Bunker Hill, and, aided by
some Connecticut and Massachusetts troops, "maintained
their ground with great firmness and intrepidity and successfully resisted every attempt to turn their flank.* This
line indeed was nobly defended. The force here did a great
service, for it saved the main body, who were retreating,
in disorder from the redoubt, from being cut off by the
enemy."† And when it was useless to continue the conflict longer, the men who composed it "gave ground, but
with more regularity than could have been expected of
troops who had not been long under discipline, and many
of whom had never before seen an engagement."‡ Stark's
regiment lost sixty in killed and wounded, a greater loss
than was sustained by any other regiment except Prescott's.

When his troops were about to encounter the British, the
Irish-American veteran addressed them in a brief but fiery
speech, which was responded to with cheers. Major Andrew
McClary, of this regiment, was killed after the conflict was
ended, and his loss was deeply regretted. "He was nearly
six feet and a half in height and of an athletic frame. Dur-

---

*Siege of Boston, p. 151. † Committee of Safety's Account.
‡ Siege of Boston, p. 193.

ing the action he fought with great bravery and amidst the
roar of artillery his stentorian voice was heard animating
the men and inspiring them with his own energy.   After
the action was over he rode to Medford to procure bandages
for the wounded; and on his return went with a few of
his comrades to reconnoiter the British, then on Bunker Hill.
As he was on his way to rejoin his men a shot from a
frigate lying in the harbor passed through his body.   He
leaped a few feet from the ground, pitched forward, and fell
dead on his face.   He was carried to Medford and interred
with the honors of war."*   Another distinguished officer
who fell on the 17th was Major Willard Moore, of Doolit-
tle's regiment, who, owing to the absence of his colonel and
lieut.-colonel, took command himself and displayed great
courage and skill.   The depositions speak in glowing
terms of his good qualities.   He was a firm patriot and a
chivalrous soldier.   On the second attack he received a
ball in the thigh, and while his men were carrying him to
the rear, another ball went through his body.   He called
for water, but none could be obtained nearer than the Neck.
He lingered until the time of the retreat, when, feeling his
wounds to be mortal, he requested his attendants to lay him
down, leave him, and take care of themselves, and died a
soldier's death.   He was from Paxton; took a prominent
part in the Worcester convention of January, 1774; was
chosen captain of the minute-men a year later, and on the
Lexington alarm immediately marched for Cambridge.†
The death of Warren was however the severest blow which the
cause of America and freedom received that day.   He had
performed his duties as President of the Provincial Congress
at Watertown on June 6th, and passed the night there.   On
the morning of the battle he hastened to Cambridge, where

---

* Siege of Boston, p. 186.   † Ibid., p. 178.

through illness he was compelled to lie down and rest.
When however he became aware that the British were about
to attack the works on Breed's Hill, he could not be restrained from proceeding at once to the post of danger. When he
arrived at the redoubt, he was received with enthusiastic
cheers by the men and was tendered the command by
Prescott. He however declined promptly the proffered
honor, although he had been elected major-general a few
days before, and said that he had only come to encourage
a good cause. "He displayed great bravery throughout
the conflict and was among the last to leave the redoubt.
Falling back slowly and reluctantly he had retired but a
few rods when a ball struck him in his forehead, and he
sank lifeless to the ground. His body lay on the field until
the next day, when it was recognized by acquaintances who
came out from Boston to view the scene, and buried where
he fell. After the evacuation of Boston by the British, the
remains were disinterred and transferred to King's Chapel,
whence they subsequently removed to St. Paul's Church.
General Howe said that the death of Warren was equal to
the loss of five hundred men.*

Colonel Nixon, while fighting "with great gallantry at the
head of his regiment," and bravely supported by his captains,
Gleason, Moore, McFarland, McCobb, and others, was
severely wounded and carried off the field. Among the
thirty prisoners taken by the British, several of whom it is to
be presumed were wounded when captured, judging from
the fact that twenty were reported dead before the following September, the names of Daniel McGrath, Lawrence

---

* At Irish National Festivals it was usual to couple the names of Warren and Montgomery. For instance, at the St. Patrick's Day festival of
the Hibernian Society of Savannah, 1824, the sixth toast was "*Warren
and Montgomery*—offerings made by Ireland upon the altar erected to
Liberty in America."—Works of Bishop England, vol. v., p. 58.

Sullivan, and others of Irish origin, appear in the list published in the journals of the month named. Henry Knox (afterwards General and Chief of Artillery) participated in the action as a volunteer, and displayed the utmost bravery and coolness.

On June 15, two days before the battle of Bunker Hill, Congress resolved to choose a general " to command all the Continental forces raised or to be raised for the defence of American liberty." Washington was elected by a unanimous vote, and officially notified to that effect by Hancock on June 17. Four days later, he set out for Cambridge, where he arrived on July 2, accompanied by Joseph Reed as his aid and secretary. He found himself at the head of about fourteen thousand men, fit for duty, while the English in Boston had nearly twelve thousand effective men on land, and a considerable naval force besides.

By an act passed June 17, 1775, Congress authorized the raising of a corps of riflemen, to the number of eight hundred, and a few days latter two additional companies were voted from Pennsylvania. Recruiting proceeded so rapidly that one company under Daniel Morgan joined Washington at Cambridge on the 25th of July, and in less than two months a force of over fourteen hundred men, composed of the hardy frontiersmen and farmers of Virginia, Western Pennsylvania, and Maryland, arrived at the camp at Cambridge. These troops were mainly Irish-Americans. Their first Colonel, Thompson, was a native of Ireland, and a member of the Friendly Sons of St. Patrick of Philadelphia. Before the Revolution he resided at Pittsburgh. He was made a brigadier-general early in 1776, and, having joined General Sullivan in Canada, was made prisoner at Three Rivers. Edward Hand, formerly an officer of the Irish Brigade, was the lieut.-colonel. He succeeded General Thompson in command of the riflemen, was soon after raised to the rank of Brigadier-General and fought to the close of the war.

"These riflemen were the only purely distinctive body which the Revolution produced. In costume as in mode of fighting they were purely American. Their dress was a white or brown linen hunting shirt, ornamented with a fringe and secured by a belt of wampum, in which a knife and tomahawk were stuck. Their leggings and moccasins were ornamented in the Indian fashion with beads and brilliantly dyed porcupine quills. A round hat completed a costume which was simple, appropriate and pictur esque." * Upon their breasts they wore the motto, "LIB-ERTY OR DEATH." At a review "a company of them while on a quick advance fired at and hit objects seven inches in diameter at a distance of several hundred yards." † On account of their deadly aim they became objects of terror to the British. One of them, who was taken prisoner, was carried to England and gazed at and described as a remarkable curiosity. ‡

Their peculiar dress, manners and the Irish accent so prevalent among them, sometimes led to bantering on the part of their New England comrades, which on one occasion would have resulted in a serious riot, had it not been for the promptitude and vigor of Washington. A number of them were one day, in the winter of '75–'76, strolling about Cambridge, when some men of Glover's Massachusetts regiment began to criticise jocosely the peculiarities noted, and followed up their remarks with a shower of snowballs, which was promptly replied to. Both parties began to get excited, outsiders joined in the contest, and soon over a thousand men were engaged in a fight of alarming propor-

---

* Historic Fields and Mansions of Middlesex. † Ibid.
‡ Lossing.

tions.   Glover rushed in haste to Washington's headquarters and announced that his men were in a state of mutiny.
The General at once mounted his horse and, taking with him
the Hon. James Sullivan, brother of General Sullivan, rode
at full gallop to the scene of disturbance.   When arrived
there "he threw the bridle of his horse into his servant's
hands and rushing into the thickest of the fight seized two
of the contestants by the throat, keeping them at arm's
length, talking to and shaking them."*   His presence
and rebukes soon brought the men to their senses.   They
scattered in all directions and "in less than three minutes
none remained on the ground but the two he had col-
lared."†

On a previous occasion the good feeling, common sense
and wise foresight of Washington prevented a difficulty
of a similar character, and which might have led to more
serious consequences.   It had been the custom in Boston
and other parts of New England to celebrate what was
called Guy Fawkes Day (November 5), the anniversary of
the alleged Gunpowder Plot, by a parade in which an
effigy of the Pope was carried and afterwards burned.
Some among the New England troops at Cambridge proposed to celebrate the anniversary in 1775 in the usual
silly and offensive manner, and owing to the large proportion of Irish in the Continental army, there was great reason
to apprehend a serious difficulty, should an attempt be made
to carry out the project.   The matter coming to the ears of
the Commander-in-Chief, he forbade the proposed display,
characterized it as a ridiculous and childish custom, and expressed his surprise that there should be officers and men
in the army so devoid of common sense as not to see its impropriety, at a time too when the Colonies were endeavor-

---

* Trask, quoted by Irving in "Life of Washington."   † Irving.

ing to bring Canada into an alliance with themselves against
the common enemy.* His words had the desired effect,
the intended demonstration was abandoned, and peace was
preserved. The British, however, celebrated the day with
discharges of artillery, the last time they had an opportunity to do so in Boston.

Among the General officers appointed by Congress after
Washington had received his commission, were Montgomery
and Sullivan, and the latter within a short time superseded
Folsom in command of the New Hampshire troops composed
of the regiments of Stark, Reed and Poor. Nixon's regiment
was afterwards added to his command. Henry Knox, of
the Charitable Irish Society of Boston, was made Chief of
Artillery. † He brought from Crown Point and Ticon-

---

* Historic Fields, etc., of Middlesex.

† Major-General Henry Knox was born at Boston of Irish parents in
1750. When the Revolution commenced he was engaged in business as
a bookseller, in his native city, but he promptly sacrificed his personal
interests in his zeal for the national cause.

"The man," says Peterson, "who, of all others, stood first in Washington's affections was Henry Knox, commander of the artillery in the American army. The intellectual abilities of Knox were sound; but it was
his moral ones that were pre-eminently deserving of esteem, and in consideration of which Washington bestowed upon him the love and confidence of a brother. In every action where Washington appeared in person
Knox attended him: in every council of war he bore a part. His services
at the head of the ordnance were invaluable. He assumed command of
that branch of the army in the first year of the war, and continued at its
head until the close of the contest. At the battle of Monmouth the manner in which he handled his guns awakened the admiration of the enemy,
and, in fact, contributed more, perhaps, than anything else to repel the
last desperate assault. Greene had so high an opinion of Knox that
when Washington offered to the former the command of the Southern
army, he proposed Knox in his stead. * * * His first connection with
the artillery service occurred immediately after the battle of Lexington.
Knox had not been engaged in that struggle; but, a few days subsequently, he made his escape from Boston, and, joining his countrymen in

deroga, in the depth of the winter of 1775-'76, over frozen
lakes and a rough and snow-covered country, thirty-nine
guns, fourteen mortars and two howitzers—" a noble train
of artillery "—for service in the siege of Boston.

arms at Cambridge, offered to undertake the arduous task of transporting
from Ticonderoga and Canada, the heavy ordnance and military stores
captured there by the Americans.   The energetic spirit of the young
man, and the handsome manner in which he executed a task, abounding
with what some would have considered impossibilities, attracted the
special notice of Washington, and Knox, in consequence, was rewarded
with the command of this very artillery, most of which he employed with
good service in the siege of Boston.   Thus at the age of twenty-five he
occupied one of the most responsible positions in the army.   From this
period Knox remained with Washington, taking part in all the principal
battles fought by the commander-in-chief."

When Cornwallis surrendered at Yorktown, Knox was promoted to
the rank of major-general.   He was in command of the American troops
when they marched into New York, on its evacuation by the English,
November 25, 1783, halting for a few hours near where now stands the
armory of the Sixty-ninth regiment and then moving forward to take possession of Fort George, "amid the acclamations of thousands of eman-
cipated freemen and the roar of artillery upon the battery."   When, on
December 4, the principal officers of the army assembled at Fraunce's
Tavern to bid farewell to Washington, the latter entered the room
where they were all waiting, and, taking a glass of wine in his hand expressed the wish that their "latter days might be as prosperous and
happy as their former ones had been glorious and honorable."   Then,
having drunk, he said: "I cannot come to each of you to take my leave,
but shall be obliged to you if each will come and take me by the hand."
Knox, who stood next to him, grasped his hand and then "while the tears
flowed down the cheeks of each," the commander-in-chief embraced and
kissed him as he did afterwards the other officers.   Knox succeeded
Lincoln as Secretary of War under the old confederation, and in 1789, on
the organization of the Federal Government, he was chosen by Washington to fill the same position in his cabinet.   He resigned in 1794, and
went to live at Thomaston, Maine.   In 1798, when a foreign war seemed
imminent, he was appointed to an important command, but the trouble
passed over, and he was not called on for active service.

At the age of twenty-two years, in 1772, Knox joined the Charitable

Washington was anxious to drive the English from the city as soon as Knox had executed his mission. The majority of the American general officers, however, favored delay for various reasons, and the Commander-in-Chief reluctantly yielded to these representations. Smallpox meanwhile was rife in Boston, and a large number of persons suffering from it were sent out of the city by the British, evidently with a view of communicating the disease to the American army. At length, on March 4, 1776, the Revolutionary forces took possession of and fortified Dorchester Heights, which commanded the harbor. Preparations made by Howe for an attack on the American works were rendered useless by a storm which arose, and prevented the landing of reinforcements from the fleet, and he finally resolved to evacuate the city. On St. Patrick's Day the English troops, having plundered the stores and many of the dwellings, abandoned Boston and, embarking on board their fleet, set sail after a delay of some days in Nantasket Roads, accompanied by over one thousand American Tories, who preferred to a remain subjects of a foreign king, rather than become freemen in their native land. The following order of the day was issued by Washington on this day of triumph and glory for America:

" Head Quarters, 17th March, 1776.
" Parole, BOSTON, Countersign, ST. PATRICK."
" The regiments under marching orders to march to-morrow morning.
"Brigadier of the Day, General Sullivan.
" By His Excellency's Command."

Irish Society of Boston. His desire to mingle and be identified with men of Irish origin was further shown in 1782, when he became a member of the Friendly Sons of St. Patrick of Philadelphia. The Society of the Cincinnatti was formed at his suggestion. He died in 1806, at Thomaston, Maine.

About this time Stephen Moylan,* brother of the Right
Rev. Dr. Moylan, Catholic Bishop of Cork, and first President of the Friendly Sons of St. Patrick of Philadelphia, was
selected by Washington as one of his aids, and became, with
Joseph Reed,† one of the "military family" of the Com-

---

* Brigadier-General Stephen Moylan was born at Cork City, Ireland, in 1734. He was a brother of the Right Rev. Dr. Moylan,
Catholic bishop of the diocese. Coming to America he landed at Philadelphia when a young man, and became an ardent supporter of the
national cause. He was one of the first to respond to the call to arms
after the battle of Lexington, and when Washington had assumed command of the army at Cambridge, he chose Moylan as one of his aids,
and afterwards appointed him commissary-general. Anxious, however,
to be engaged as actively as possible, the young Irishman accepted the
command of a regiment of horse composed of Pennsylvania troops;
served at its head through the war, was engaged in nearly all the principal battles, and rose to the rank of brigadier-general.

His name stands first on the list of the original members of the
Friendly Sons of St. Patrick of Philadelphia, organized in 1771, and
his signature is the first attached to the rules. He was the first president of the society, and was one of the most active in its formation. He
was also its last president, being again elected to the office in 1796,
after an interval of twenty-two years. Moylan was a man of high
honor and respectability, and one of the original members of the Society
of the Cincinnatti. After the war he resided some years in Chester
county, where he was Prothonotary of the Court. He died at Philadelphia in 1811, and was interred in the burial-ground of St. Mary's
Church, South Fourth street. General Moylan had three brothers in
America, of whom two at least were in the military service of the Republic. One of them, John, was a quartermaster in the American army.
He was lost in the *Shilelah* on her voyage to France. Another
brother, Jasper, was a member of the legal profession, and in the enjoyment of an extensive practice. He belonged to the famous "First
Troop," and did good service when called on. A third brother was
named James. All four belonged to Friendly Sons of St. Patrick.

† Brigadier-General Joseph Reed was the son of an Irish settler in
New Jersey, and was born at Trenton in 1741, and his father soon afterwards moved to Philadelphia. Joseph graduated at Princeton in 1757.

mander-in-Chief. From this position he was soon after promoted to that of Commissary-General. But he longed for active service and, accepting a command in the Pennsylvania Line, fought with distinguished bravery throughout the war, rising to the rank of Brigadier-General, and always retaining the confidence and warm regard of his illustrious chief.

---

and then studied law with Richard Stockton, afterwards completing his legal education at the Temple, London. Soon after his return he became a member of the committee of correspondence of Philadelphia, and was chosen, in 1774, president of the first popular convention in Philadelphia. He, in 1775, accompanied Washington to Cambridge as his secretary and aid, and remained in that position during the whole of the campaign. Hs was made adjutant-general in the following year, and distinguished himself at the battles of Long Island, Princeton and Germantown. He was chosen a member of Congress in 1777, and was a member of that body in 1778, when the Earl of Carlisle, ex-Governor Johnston and Willlam Eden came from England as commissioners to endeavor to secure the return of the colonies to their cast-off allegiance. Finding their proposals rejected, the commissioners—according to the usual custom of English agents—endeavored to secure their ends by bribery, and a woman, the wife of a loyalist, was instructed to offer Reed " ten thousand pounds and the best post in the government " if he would betray his trust, or, as it was expressed, exert his influence, to settle the dispute. When the proposition was made to him by the temptress he at once indignantly replied: " I am not worth purchasing, but such as I am Britain is not rich enough to do it." The attempt on his integrity, and the noble answer with which he repelled it, soon became known, and Congress declared all correspondence with the commissioners to be at an end. Reed was chosen president of the council of Pennsylvania in October 1778, and continued in that position up to 1781, when he resumed his law practice. Like all men of firmness and straightforward honesty, he suffered much abuse from his political opponents, but when the clouds of party rancor passed away men recognized and were sorry for the injustice done him. He died March 4, 1785, at the age of forty–two. His youngest son, George W., commanded the *Vixen* in 1812, and died a prisoner in the hands of the English at Jamaica.

The proportion of Irish-Americans in the Revolutionary army at the siege of Boston cannot be accurately estimated, but all the evidence available goes to show that they formed nearly one-half of Washington's forces, and that they displayed a zeal and bravery worthy of their race and the cause in which they were engaged. An eminent writer says that "To this newly organized army of independence the Irish immigrants, who had been driven from their native homes by landlord oppression, flocked in great numbers, rightly concluding that by the overthrow of the British forces in America they were revenging themselves upon their late odious and relentless taskmasters; nor were there any in the American ranks more enthusiastic in the cause, brave in the highest degree, and abiding by the General until the cause of American Independence was finally triumphant."*

MONTGOMERY'S ATTACK ON QUEBEC.

In the autumn of 1775 Congress determined upon causing a vigorous effort to be made for the annexation of Canada. A force under Gen. Schuyler had already been sent, to enter that province by man of the Northern lakes; but, owing to the illness of the officer named, the command devolved upon Gen. Richard Montgomery.† Arnold was now ordered.

---

* Marmion. Maritime Ports of Ireland.

† Richard Montgomery was born at Raphoe, Donegal county, Ireland, December, 1737. His father represented Lifford in the Irish Parliament, and his brother afterwards sat for many years in that body as member for Donegal. Montgomery entered the British army at the age of eighteen, and served under Wolfe at the taking of Quebec in 1759. Having returned home, he in 1772 again came to America, and settled at Rhinebeck, on the Hudson, where he purchased a small estate. Soon afterwards he married a daughter of Robert Livingston. The union was a most happy one while it lasted, and the faithful wife, although she survived him half a century, ever cherished the memory of "her soldier" with unfading affection. When the Revolution broke

with eleven hundred men, to co-operate with the first named expedition and advance by another route on Quebec. His troops included ten companies of New England musketeers, and three of Morgan's Irish-American riflemen. Montgomery, with about two thousand men, laid siege to St, John's, which held out for a time, but he, having taken in the meanwhile the fort of Chambly, in which he found several pieces of artillery and a considerable quality of ammunition, was enabled to prosecute his task with so much vigor that the English garrison of St. John's surrendered on November 3.

Montgomery, while engaged in the siege, sent Colonel Ethan Allen into Canada for the purpose of inducing the people there to take up arms and aid the Americans. Al-

---

out, he, " with all the ardor of the people of his birthland," to use the words of Lossing, ranged himself on the side of the patriots. In April, 1775, he was selected as a delegate to the first Provincial Convention in New York, where he was distinguished for promptness of decision and soundness of judgment. In the autumn of the same year he was offered and accepted the appointment of Brigadier-General, and tore himself away from the home where he was so happy, saying: " The will of an oppressed people, compelled to choose between liberty and slavery, must be obeyed." When ordered to proceed on the expedition to Canada he was accompanied by his devoted wife as far as Saratoga, her apprehensions being soothed by his cheerfulness and assurances of success. Soon the chief command of the expedition devolved on him, and he moved forward rapidly, taking Fort St. John on November 3, Montreal on the 12th following, and effecting a junction with Arnold under the walls of Quebéc on December 5. The assault of the 31st would in all probability have been successful had he not fallen, but his death disheartened his men and caused them to abandon the attempt. The refusal at first of Sir Guy Carleton to allow the remains of America's first Irish general " the poor courtesy of a coffin " is mentioned in the *Massachusetts Historical Collections*, vol. i, p. 3—year 1792. His loss was deeply felt all over the country. Congress passed resolutions of condolence with his family in their bereavement, and expressive of its "grateful remem-

len succeeded in securing several hundred Canadian recruits, but on his return to camp, he was induced to attempt the capture of Montreal.   He was unsuccessful, was
made prisoner, threatened by the English General, Prescott,
with a halter at Tyburn, and afterwards put on board a British man-of-war, where he was handcuffed, and his limbs en-
cased in shackles to which a bar of iron eight feet long was
fastened.   He was then thrown into the hold of the ship,
with only a sailor's chest for his bed and seat, and kept in
this situation for five weeks, when he was sent to Quebec, and
transferred to another vessel.   Here he obtained a brief

---

brance, profound respect, and high veneration," for him and decided that
a monument should be erected to his memory.   This was placed in front
of St. Paul's Church, Broadway, New York, and upon it appears the following inscription :

This
Monument is Erected by Order of Congress,
25th of January, 1776,
To Transmit to Posterity a Grateful Remem-
brance of the Patriotic Conduct, Enter-
prise, and Perseverance of
MAJOR-GENERAL RICHARD MONTGOMERY,
Who, after a series of successes, amid the most dis-
couraging difficulties, FELL in the attack on
Quebec, 31st December, 1775.
Aged 37 years.

In the same enclosure stand the monuments of two other Irish
" rebels "—Emmet and McNeven—one on either side of that of the
hero who fell at Quebec.   Even in the London Parliament his character
was eulogized, not only by his countrymen Burke and Barre, but by
Chatham and Fox.   Lord North spoke of him as " *only* a brave, able,
humane and generous *rebel*," adding, " curse on his virtues, they have
undone his country ;" but Fox replied : " The name of ' rebel ' is no
mark of disgrace ; all the great asserters of liberty, the saviours of their
country, the benefactors of mankind in all ages have been called rebels."
Montgomery's widow, in 1818, finally succeeded in obtaining the remains
of her gallant husband.   They were disinterred at Quebec, conveyed to
New York, and deposited, with imposing ceremonies, beneath the mural
monument erected by order of Congress in front of St. Paul's.

respite from the brutal treatment to which he had been subjected, but on the approach of the American army he was
again handcuffed, placed on board an English war-ship and,
with thirty-three other American prisoners, sent to England.   They were all crowded in a single compartment, and
not allowed to leave it during the entire voyage, which lasted forty days.   When taken ashore at Falmouth, the prisoners were still kept in irons, and treated with extreme
harshness.   Allen was repeatedly threatened with execution
as a traitor, and the letters which he wrote to his friends
were intercepted.   At length the British Government
resolved to send the prisoners back to America; not, however,
as freemen, but probably as a preliminary to exchanging
them for Englishmen.   On the passage out the ship put in
to Cork, where the people showed the greatest possible sympathy for the brave and ill-treated Americans, and sought
to show them all possible kindness.   Poor Allen still wore,
through poverty, the same dress in which he had been captured, but the citizens of Cork supplied himself and his
comrades with new suits of clothes, and with as much
money as the English officers would permit.   The prisoners
were first brought to New York, whence they were transferred to Halifax and kept in a prison-ship there until scurvy
broke out among them owing to the bad food they received;
when, after great efforts to secure better treatment, they
were removed to the town jail.   After a time they were
again conveyed to New York, where Allen was allowed to
go on parole within certain narrow limits, and at length exchanged for a British colonel.

After the surrender of St. John's, Montgomery advanced
on Montreal, which the English commander, Carleton, abandoned to its fate and escaped by night down the river in a
canoe.   The Irish-American General entered the city on
November 12, and at once gained the good-will of the citi-

zens by engaging not to interfere with the free exercise of the Catholic religion, or with their laws or municipal government. Many of them in fact joined his forces, and to some extent made up for the loss caused by the withdrawal of some of those under him, who insisted on returning home because of the expiration of their term of enlistment. Montgomery then proceeded to Quebec and joined Arnold, who had reached the vicinity nearly three weeks before, at Point aux Trembles, about twenty miles from the city, on December 1. He gave Arnold's half-naked troops, new clothing, which he had the foresight to bring with him, and immediately after pushed on to his destination through huge drifts of snow and in the midst of a blinding storm of sleet. His whole force, including Arnold's command, now amounted to only nine hundred men. Nevertheless he commenced the siege of Quebec and continued it for three weeks; when, finding that his artillery was unfit to produce any serious effects upon the solid ramparts, that smallpox was carrying off nnmbers of his little force, and that many whose period of enlistment had nearly expired began to be discontented and anxious to turn homeward, he determined upon the bold and desperate course of attempting to carry the city by assault. It was decided that one detachment should make a series of feigned attacks upon the Upper Town, while Montgomery and Arnold, at the head of other bodies of troops, should move on the Lower Town from opposite directions, and, meeting at Mountain street, force a passage through Prescott Gate and up to the citadel.

In the gray dawn of the last morning of 1775, amid a raging snow storm, over huge masses of ice and through heavy drifts, Montgomery led his men along the route decided on. In his path stood a battery of three-pounders, in front of which was a stockade of strong posts, well fastened at top and bottom. The General sawed through some of these himself, until he had succeeded in clearing a passage for his troops, when, placing himself at their head, he cried out, "Men of New York, you will not fear to follow where your general leads," and rushed forward to capture the battery. Ere he reached it, however, a storm of grape swept through the column: he fell, and with him his aids, Mc Phun and Cheeseman, and several of the foremost soldiers. It is said that the Canadian militia who manned the battery abandoned their posts on the approach of the Americans, perhaps unwilling to fight against the latter, and that it was a New England sea-captain who applied a match to the gun whose discharge caused the death of Montgomery and his followers.* His troops, disheartened by the fall of their gallant chief, fell back hastily to Wolfe's Cove, and made no further effort to carry out the programme agreed on.

Arnold, while advancing at the head of his men from St. Roch's suburb, was wounded in the knee by a musket ball, and carried back to the hospital, where he learned of Montgomery's death. The command of his troops now devolved upon Morgan, who, after a hard struggle of over an hour, succeeded in driving the English from the first barrier at which they endeavored to check him, the deadly aim of his Irish-American riflemen causing great consternation among their antagonists. After this achievement he pushed on to the second barrier, which he succeeded, after a fierce conflict of over three hours' duration, in making himself master of. Just however as he was preparing to rush into the town, an English detachment, sent around by a circuitous route, attacked him in the rear; and, surrounded on all sides, hopeless of receiving help from any quarter, and deeply depressed by the announcement of Montgomery's death, he was forced to surrender. A portion of his force, however,

---

* "Hawkins' History of Quebec."

which he had left some distance in the rear, succeeded in
making its way back to the American camp.

When the conflict was ended the British sent out parties
to collect the dead and wounded. In the place where
Montgomery fell, they found thirteen bodies nearly buried
in the snow, besides an orderly sergeant, who died an hour
after he was discovered. The remains were taken to a
guard-house in the vicinity, where the body of the dead General was identified by one of the captured officers belonging
to Arnold's division. Carleton at first refused a coffin to the
corpse of his gallant foeman,* but Cramahe, the Lieut.-
Governor, who had known Montgomery years before, took
charge of the remains, and secured for them decent burial
within the walls surrounding a powder magazine, situated
near the ramparts facing St. Louis suburb. There they remained until 1818, when they were disinterred and removed
to New York, where they were deposited beneath the monument erected in honor of Montgomery in front of St. Paul's
Church on Broadway, by order of Congress. The bodies of Major McPhun and Capt. Cheeseman, the General's
aids, were, however, buried in their clothes, without coffins.

Arnold now succeeded to the command of the small
American forces before Quebec; and, retiring a few miles
from the city, entrenched himself as well as possible under
the circumstances. In April, 1776, General Wooster arrived
from Montreal, and, as he was the senior officer, superseded
Arnold. Gen. Thomas, who was appointed to fill Montgomery's place, arrived early in May, but in the meantime
the British had been strongly reinforced and the Americans
were compelled to retreat. Thomas died early in June, and
was succeeded by Sullivan, under whom was placed General
Thompson, a native of the North of Ireland and a member

---

* "Mass. Hist. Collection," vol. i., p. 3, year 1792.

of the Friendly Sons of St. Patrick of Philadelphia, who had been the first colonel of the rifle regiment. In a battle fought with an immensely superior force of British troops, at Three Rivers, towards the middle of June, Thompson was taken prisoner, as was also Colonel, afterwards General Irvine, another Irish officer of distinguished ability. Sullivan was afterwards forced to fall back before the numerous and well-equipped army of Burgoyne, and Canada was for the time preserved to the British Crown.

Early in 1776, Congress appointed commissioners to visit Canada, and try to induce the people of that province to make common cause with the American Revolutionists against England. Franklin, Charles Carroll and Samuel Chase, together with Father John Carroll, afterwards Archbishop of Baltimore — the " Jesuit rebel," as the English and their Tory allies here used to call him — were chosen for this purpose. The commissioners left New York on April 2, but did not reach Montreal until the 29th. Their labors, however, did not produce the desired result, and they soon returned. Their failure may be attributed partly to the feeling excited among the Canadians on hearing the expressions used by the Congress of 1774, when speaking of the Quebec Act—which established religious liberty in Canada—in an address to the people of Britain.* Another reason for their comparatively short

---

* The Continental Congress, in 1774, had resolved that the act of the London Parliament establishing the Catholic religion in the province of Quebec, was "an infringement and violation of the rights of the colonists." In its "Address to the People of Great Britain," in October, 1774, it affected to fear that the Canadians, "their numbers daily swelling with Catholic emigrants from Europe, might on occasion be fit instruments to reduce the ancient free Protestant colonies to the same state of slavery with themselves. Admit," continued the address, "that the ministry, by the power of Britain and the aid of our Catholic neighbors should be able to reduce us to a state of humiliation and

stay in Canada was that while they were at Montreal, a
messenger arrived from Quebec with the news that a
British fleet, with a large body of troops on board, had
reached that port, and had soon after attacked and defeated
the weakened American forces.   It was obviously necessary
to secure the sending of strong reinforcements by Congress to the assistance of its army in Canada, in order to put
it in a position to check the contemplated British advance
southward.   Franklin fell ill on the way home from Montreal, and was tenderly nursed by Father Carroll, speaking
of whose kindness the patriot philosopher says, in a letter:
"I find I grow daily more feeble, and think I could hardly
have got along so far but for Mr. Carroll's friendly assistance and tender care of me."*   He continued to
entertain through life the warmest regard for Dr. Carroll,
and showed his feeling in a special manner when the question of the appointment of a Bishop to preside over the
Church in the United States was under consideration by
the ecclesiastical authorities at Rome.

slavery; may not a ministry with the same armies enslave you? Remember the taxes from America, the wealth, and particularly the Catholics of this vast continent will then be in the power of your enemies, nor
will you have any reason to expect that after making slaves of us, many
among us should refuse to assist in reducing you to the same abject
state."   The British officials in Canada promptly circulated these addresses among the people, and thereby excited a strong feeling of indignation in their minds against those who had spoken of them in so offensive a manner.   When, therefore, the Congress of 1775 sent an address
to the people of Canada, it was coldly received, and when, in the following year, the embassy was sent to invite the Canadians to make common
cause with the other colonists, it failed of success, because they still felt
offended at the sentiments expressed by the Congress of '74 with regard
to themselves and their faith.

* Letter to the Commissioners in Canada, dated New York, May 27,
1776, in " Life of Franklin."

CHAP. XII.

THE expulsion of the British from Boston on St. Patrick's Day, 1776, gave intense satisfaction to the American patriots, and inspired them with confidence in the success of their cause. The announcement made soon after, that the mercenaries purchased in Northern Europe by the English king, were on their way to America, only exasperated the people. The popular feeling in favor of absolute independence grew stronger and more decided. On April 22, the convention of North Carolina empowered the delegates from that province in Congress "to concur with those in the other colonies in declaring independence." On the 15th of May the convention of Virginia unanimously instructed its delegates in Congress "to propose to that respectable body to declare the United Colonies free and independent States, absolved from all allegiance or dependence upon the Crown or Parliament of Great Britain."

The other colonies followed, more or less rapidly, the examples thus set them.

On June 7, Richard Henry Lee, of Virginia, offered a resolution in Congress, declaring "that the United Colonies are, and ought to be, free and independent States, that they are absolved from all allegiance to the British Crown, and that all political connection between them and Great Britain is, and ought to be totally dissolved." The discussion of the resolution was postponed to the following day, when it was debated in committee of the whole, and finally passed by a bare majority of the colonies, on the 10th. In order to secure greater, and, if possible, perfect unanimity, further action in Congress on the subject was postponed to the first of July, and meanwhile a committee was appointed, consisting of Jefferson, John Adams, Franklin, Sherman and Livingston, to prepare a Declaration of Independence. It was, however, written entirely by the first named. The resolution referred to above was, after having been reported from the committee of the whole on July 1st, passed on the day following, when the Declaration was brought for consideration, and after being debated and amended, was finally adopted, every colony voting for it on July 4th. The proceedings on that day are thus recorded in the "Journal of Congress," published by Captain John Dunlap, of the Friendly Sons of St. Patrick of Philadelphia, by order of the committee appointed to superintend the publication of this record.

"July 4th, 1776. Agreeably to the order of the day, the Congress resolved itself into a committee of the whole to take into further consideration the Declaration, and after some time the President resumed the chair, and William Harrison reported that the committee have agreed to a Declaration. The Declaration being read was agreed to by the colonies."*

It was two o'clock in the afternoon when the Secretary, Charles Thomson, of Maghera, Derry, rose to announce the final decision to Congress assembled in Independence Hall. It was a solemn moment, and as he concluded a deep silence overspread the whole assembly. A scene of a different kind was soon witnessed on the streets. The tidings had gone forth throughout the city that the final

---

* Journals of Congress, of July, 1776.

decision was to be made on that day. From an early hour in the morning thousands of citizens had gathered in the streets. Their faces wore an anxious look. The patriots had mustered their whole strength, hoping that their desires might be realized, yet fearing that they would not. The Tories—and they were numerous—gazed on the crowds with a malignant scowl upon their features. It had been announced that, should the Declaration of Independence be unanimously adopted, the old bell in the tower would ring out the tidings to the people. And from the hour that Congress convened the old bellman had sat in the steeple. On that bell was written: *"Proclaim liberty throughout all the land unto all the inhabitants thereof."* The bellman, too old and feeble to run down the stairs, had placed his boy at the door below to give him notice when the announcement should be made. But the hours passed slowly by, and no signal was given to the impatient watcher. Noon came, but it brought no relief to the thousands of beating hearts in the streets beneath. Men looked upon each other in doubt; their lips were silent, but the expression of their features told plainly of the feelings which agitated them. The old bellman had almost given up all hope of receiving the longed-for signal when suddenly he heard the clapping of hands below, and looking down saw the boy thus giving vent to his enthusiasm, while he shouted upward, almost wild with pent-up excitement, "Ring, ring." At once the sound of the bell was heard, the death-knell of British despotism and the birth-note of American Liberty, and a shout, loud and sudden as a thunder clap, pealed up from the vast multitude below. The other bells in the city caught up the glorious refrain, the guns joined in the chorus, and men, hurrying from all directions, shouted in the fullness of their joy and filled the city with their loud acclamations. That night, from the

Delaware to the Schuylkill, the bonfires blazed, the cannon pealed, and every *rebel* heart rejoiced, and held high carnival in the good old city of brotherly love.

THE DECLARATION

was only signed by John Hancock on the day of its adoption. It was ordered by Congress to be entered at length on the journals. It was ordered also to be engrossed on parchment for the delegates to sign it. On the second of August following, it was signed by the fifty-four delegates present; and by two others later, making the whole number fifty-six. On the 8th of July a grand demonstration took place in Philadelphia. Long before the event, an observatory had been erected near the Walnut street front of the State House by Rittenhouse, for astronomical purposes, and from this Captain John Nixon, of the Friendly Sons of St. Patrick, read the Declaration to a large concourse of spectators. Thousands from the surrounding country had gathered into the city, to participate in the rejoicings, and every artery of the city itself had sent forth its stream to swell the vast sea of people. Not a whispered word was spoken while the clerk was reading the Declaration, but as the son of the evicted Wexford farmer uttered the last sentence, the people gave vent to their joy in the wildest applause. They forthwith proceeded to the public buildings, pulled down the king's arms, and burned them in the streets. Bonfires at night lighted up the river. The rejoicings were continued until midnight, when a thunder-storm put an end to the festivities.

Similar demonstrations were witnessed at Boston, New York, and other places, at the first reading of the Declaration to the citizens. In the latter city the patriots in their enthusiasm pulled down the gilded leaden statue of George III., the English tyrant, on Bowling Green. It was afterwards cut into pieces, and run into bullets; for forty-two thousand of which it furnished material, thus providing a good supply of "melted majesty" to be poured into the redcoats and their allies. Of the Signers of the Declaration at least twelve, besides the Secretary, Charles Thomson, were Irish by birth or descent. These were—

JOHN HANCOCK, the President of Congress. It is stated by reliable authorities that the ancestors of President Hancock emigrated from near Downpatrick, Down county, Ireland, and settled in Boston* towards the close of the seventeenth century. The "Hancocks have been for centuries actively and largely engaged in the foreign and domestic trade of Newry,"† and it was doubtless in a commercial capacity that the first of the name came to Boston. The family to which President Hancock belonged is, it is said, now represented in Ireland by John Hancock, of Lurgan, Down county, and by Neilson Hancock, the founder of the Irish Statistical Society.

John Hancock was born at Braintree, Mass., in 1737, and when quite young was left in the care of his father's brother, a wealthy merchant of Boston, who sent him soon after to Harvard College, where he was graduated in 1754. He then became a clerk in his uncle's office, and, going to England on business in 1761, made the acquaintance of several of the leading public men there. His uncle died in 1763, and left him great wealth, the largest fortune in

---

* Tyrone (Ireland) Constitution, quoted in *Irish World* Centennial Number, 1876. The writer adds: "Those who are conversant with Reid's 'History of the Presbyterian Church in Ireland' are aware that multitudes of Protestants left Ulster for the plantations of North America, for causes sufficiently explained in that authority. John Hancock's ancestor was amongst that number."

† Article in Pittsburg *Leader*, quoted in *Irish World*. The name appears in the records of the Irish Parliament.

New England. He thenceforth took a prominent and leading part in public affairs, becoming a representative from Boston, in the Massachusetts General Assembly of 1766.

Incidents mentioned in his life show that he was not unmindful of his origin, nor oblivious of the claims of kindred. When a congregation of Irish Presbyterians, whose first place of worship in Boston was a barn, built a new church on the corner of Federal and Berry streets, Hancock presented them with a bell and vane. The first pastor of this church, Rev. John Moorhead, entered the ministry in Ireland, and was installed in Boston in 1730,* becoming a member of the Charitable Irish Society in 1739. It was to this church that the convention of which Hancock was president, adjourned from the Old State House, where it met to consider the adoption of the Federal Constitution in January, 1788.

He was from the first a sturdy opponent of the methods by which the London Parliament sought to injure and harass the colonists, and his example, efforts and influence contributed materially to the advancement of the National cause. One of the earliest "outrages," as the English called them, committed by the people upon the government officials, was caused by the seizure of Hancock's vessel, the *Liberty*, on a charge of containing concealed contraband goods. "The people turned out, beat the officers, burned the government boat, and drove the officials to the fort in the harbor for safety."† He delivered in 1774, the annual oration in commemoration of the "Massacre" of March 5, 1770, and was elected in the same year President of the Provincial Congress of Massachusetts, and also a

---

* Drake's Landmarks of Boston, p. 263.
† Lossing's Eminent Americans, p. 160.

delegate to the Continental Congress, which met in September, at Philadelphia. On June 12, 1775, he was declared an "outlaw" by a proclamation of General Gage. In this document "martial law" was proclaimed; those in arms, and their friends, were declared "rebels, parricides of the Constitution," and a free pardon was offered to all who would return to their allegiance, except John Hancock and Samuel Adams.

Hancock was again a delegate to the Continental Congress in 1775, and when Randolph, the first President, resigned through ill health fourteen days after it had met, the Massachusetts "outlaw" was chosen to fill his place. On July 4, 1776, Hancock, as President of Congress, and Charles Thomson, of Maghera, as Secretary, signed the Declaration of Independence, when it was adopted, and with only their names attached to it, "was sent forth to the world," the other signatures not being affixed to the document until August the second following.

The illustrious "First Signer," on account of weakened health, resigned his seat in Congress, in 1777. In the year following, however, when Sullivan was preparing to attack the British on Rhode Island, Hancock hastened to his aid at the head of the militia of Massachusetts, and took part in the stirring events, near Bristol Ferry, in August, 1778.* The year following he was elected Governor of Massachusetts, a position which he continued to hold for five consecutive years, when he declined a re-election. He was again chosen Governor in 1787, and re-elected annually until his death, which took place October 8, 1793.

WILLIAM WHIPPLE, of New Hampshire, was of Irish parentage. He was born in Kittery, Me., in 1730, and died at Portsmouth, N. H., November 28, 1785. Probably no

---

* Lossing's Eminent Americans.

man in New Hampshire took a more decisive part as a member of the Assembly, against the encroachments of English tyranny, than William Whipple. Bold, determined, and full of integrity and honor, he denounced oppression without fear, and secured the passage of resolutions declaring the acts of George III. grievous and tyrannical. In that momentous crisis, when everything depended on the union of the different States, and it was of the highest importance that New Hampshire should take sides with her sister provinces, Whipple's voice was loud, and his appeals resistless for the right. It was owing to his influence, and that of Langdon and Thornton, that New Hampshire wheeled into the ranks with Massachusetts and Virginia, and consolidated forever the glorious union. The British government, which had subsisted ninety-five years in the State, was in this manner brought to an end. Elected to the Third Continental Congress in 1776, he was present when the Declaration of Independence was adopted, and was one of the distinguished patriots who signed that charter of liberty, pledging his life, his fortune, and his sacred honor in its support. The next year, 1777, opened with sad presages to the nation, and not the least of them was the invasion by Burgoyne, with 10,000 men, by way of Lake Champlain. The people of New Hampshire were foremost in this pressing emergency. The Committee of Safety at Exeter called together the assembly, and in three days decisive measures were taken for the defence of the country. The militia of the State was formed into two brigades. William Whipple was given the command of the first; John Stark commanded the second. A portion of each was ordered to proceed to the western frontier under the command of the latter. The remainder, under Whipple, remained in quarters until their commander had received his commission, as brigadier-general, from Congress, when they, too, marched for the seat of war. Whipple served with his men under Gates, at the battles of Stillwater and Saratoga, doing good service in both, establishing his own reputation, and that of his troops for bravery and determination. After the British general, hemmed in, surrounded, harassed beyond measure, was forced to surrender, Whipple was stationed a short time at Ticonderoga. The following year he co-operated with General Sullivan in the siege of Newport. Brave to a fault, his soldiers followed wherever he led. Soon afterwards he received the appointment of financial reporter for the State of New Hampshire, which was bestowed on him by Congress. He filled this office from 1781 to 1784, when he resigned. The previous year he had been appointed a judge of the Supreme Court of his native State, and this position he held to the time of his death. His last illness was short but distressing, and he died before he had time to reap the fruits of that immortal struggle which he had helped to gain, and which made of the oppressed colonists a free people.

MATTHEW THORNTON, of New Hampshire, was born in Limerick county, Ireland, in 1714, and belonged to a family that had made itself formidable to oppression. "At an early age he emigrated to this country with his father, and settled in Connecticut. Here the young Irishman received a good education, and, selecting medicine for his profession, studied to make himself master of that branch of knowledge. Having acquired the requisite medical information, Thornton removed to New Hampshire in 1735, and established himself at Londonderry. In 1775, when the British Government was dissolved in New Hampshire, and a provincial convention formed for temporary purposes, Thornton was elected the president. The next year he was chosen a delegate to the Continental Congress. Though not present when the Declaration of Independence passed

that illustrious body, he placed his name to it on becoming
a member, and his signature stands among those of the
fifty-six patriots who have immortalized themselves by that
act.   In 1777 he was appointed a judge of the Superior
Court of New Hampshire, in which office he remained till
1782.   He had previously received the appointment of
Chief Justice of the Court of Common Pleas.   Judge
Thornton's last years were spent in retirement.   He preserved his intellectual vigor to the last, wrote political es-
says after eighty years of age, and died at the age of
eighty-nine,''* at Newburyport, Mass.

Robert Treat Paine, of Massachusetts.   According to
very reliable authorities, Paine was of Irish descent.
O'Hart tells us that "Henry O'Neill, of Dungannon, born
in 1665, sixth in descent from Shane the Proud, Prince
of Ulster, and cousin of Sir Neal O'Neill, who was killed
at the battle of the Boyne, changed his name to Paine,
which was that of a maternal ancestor, after the surrender of Limerick, in order to preserve a portion of his
estates.   He entered the British army, obtained grants of
land in Cork county and other parts of Ireland, and was
killed in 1698 at Foxford, in Mayo.   His youngest brother,
Robert, who also took the name of Paine, emigrated to
America a little before the occurrence alluded to.   He was
the grandfather of Robert Treat Paine,''† the signer
of the Declaration, who was born at Boston, March 11,
1731.   He graduated at Harvard, where he studied theol-
ogy in 1749, and acted as chaplain in 1755, of the Provincial
troops on the northern frontier.   A little later he visited
Europe, and on his return studied law, settling, in 1759,
at Taunton, Mass., where he remained for several years.

---

* Carleton's New Hampshire Worthies.
† Irish Pedigrees.

He was one of the delegates in 1768 to the convention called by prominent men in Boston, when Governor Bernard dissolved the General Court, for refusing to rescind the circular letter sent to the other colonies.

He conducted the prosecution of the English Captain, Preston, and eight of his soldiers, when they were tried for their murderous work in the "Boston Massacre," of March 5, 1770. In 1773 and the year following, he was elected to the General Assembly of Massachusetts, and was sent as a delegate to the Continental Congress, from 1774 to 1778, voting for, and signing, the Declaration of Independence. When, in 1780, the State Constitution of Massachusetts was adopted, he was made attorney-general, which office he held until 1790, when he became a judge of the Supreme Court. In 1804, he resigned his position, on account of deafness, and other infirmities of age, and died in 1814, at the age of eighty-three. O'Hart says that beside Henry and Robert O'Neill—Paine's ancestors—there were two other brothers, Brian and John, who went to France after Sarsfield's surrender, and finally settled in Portugal. Eight of their descendants, in 1807, when the French invaded the last-named country, went with the royal family of Braganza to Brazil, where many of their offspring are now to be found.*

JAMES SMITH, of Pennsylvania. James Smith was born in Ireland in the year 1713, and came from thence with his father to America while yet a young man. They settled on the Susquehanna river, nearly opposite Columbia. Young Smith was very fond of mathematics, and became an expert surveyor. He also studied and practised law in Lancaster. He was an educated, refined, and religious man. At the time of the Revolution he was a resident of

---

* Irish Pedigrees.

York, and extensively engaged in iron works. The first
step taken in Pennsylvania, relative to the existing oppressions, was the assembling of a convention of delegates from
each county in order to ascertain the feelings of the people
generally, regarding the course proposed by the people of
Massachusetts, where the Revolutionary storm had already
commenced. Of this convention Smith was a delegate,
and was one of the committee that prepared the instructions
to the members of the next General Assembly of the province, recommending, among other things, the appointing
of delegates to the General Congress convened at Philadelphia. So fully convinced was Smith of the issue, between
the colonies and England, that on his return home he at once
raised a company of volunteers, and was immediately elected
its captain by acclamation. *This was the first company raised
in the State of Pennsylvania to defend American liberty and
resist English oppression.* This company was organized nine
months before the first blood was shed at Lexington, and
showed the deep thought, penetration, and sagacious foresight of its projector. He introduced thorough discipline
in the corps, and imparted to its members the same holy
fire of patriotism that was illuminating his own soul.
Around this military nucleus, patriots gathered until it
formed a regiment. Smith was then elected colonel. He
was a member of the convention that met in Philadelphia
in 1775. He was one of the first to raise his voice for independence, to oppose force by force, and peril life for freedom. He was then called an ultra Whig, and considered
as treating the government with disrespect. His patriotism
had carried him six months in advance of the leading men,
and no one could outstrip him in the cause of justice and
freedom. He desired action, and his time soon arrived.
In the spring of 1775 he was appointed to organize a
camp for 4,500 troops to be raised in Pennsylvania. No

man was better calculated to render efficient aid in this important business. He prepared, and with the sanction of Congress published, an address to the volunteer and yeomen military of Pennsylvania, urging them to rally around the standard of liberty. Smith inspired the people with his own ardent patriotism, and the call, "to arms!" resounded over the land. As soon as he took his seat in the Continental Congress, he immediately enrolled his name with the apostles of liberty upon the chart of freedom. He declined a re-election to Congress, from ill-health, but his constituents insisted, and so he continued at his post with unabated zeal. So devoted was he in the service of his adopted country that, when Congress was compelled to fly to York, his place of residence, he closed his office against his clients and gave it up to the board of war. He sacrificed every private consideration for whatever would promote the public good. He was a great admirer of Washington. Franklin, Adams; and all the patriots of the Revolution loved and honored James Smith. He died on the 11th July, 1806. Not one of all the patriots hated English oppression or loved liberty more than that Irishman, who sleeps in the land he helped to free.*

GEORGE TAYLOR, of Pennsylvania, was born in Ireland in the year 1716. At an early age he was placed with a physician to study medicine, but, not liking the profession, he ran away from home without consulting his friends, and without a penny in his pocket. Finding a vessel ready to sail for Philadelphia, he entered on board as a "redemptioner." In colonial days it was not an infrequent thing for persons leaving Europe, and Ireland especially, to sell their services to those who would pay their passage to this country, hence they were called "redemptioners." Soon

---

* *Irish World.*

after he arrived in America, his passage was paid by Mr. Savage, of Durham, Bucks county, Pa., for which he bound himself as a common laborer for a term of years. This man was the owner of iron works where he lived, and assigned to his new servant the station of "filler," his business being to throw coals into the furnace when in blast. He soon found the work to differ widely from handling books and the pen. His hands became cruelly blistered, but being resolute and ambitious of gaining the approbation of all around him, he persevered without a complaint. The workmen, observing his condition, named the circumstance to Mr. Savage, whose humanity induced him to provide some less laborious employment for the young Irishman. On conversing with him he discovered his intelligence, education, and talents, and immediately promoted him to clerk in the counting-room of the establishment. He proved fully competent for his new position, and gained the friendship of all around him. Nor did he neglect the improvement of his mind. He applied to practical uses the theories he had learned at school. He became esteemed for his correct deportment, and admired for his clearness of perception and soundness of judgment. To add to his importance in society, the wife of Mr. Savage became a widow, and was subsequently married to Mr. Taylor, by which he became sole proprietor of a large property and the husband of a worthy and influential woman. He soon became favorably known, and, having the confidence of his fellow-citizens, he was by them elected, in 1764, to the Provincial Assembly at Philadelphia, and took a prominent part in its deliberations. He was a republican by nature, and a hater of oppression by instinct. He had watched with a freeman's eye the increasing advance of English tyranny. He was too patriotic and too bold to tamely submit to the yoke of bondage. In 1775 he was returned for the third time to the Assembly, and added fresh laurels to his fame. In addition to others, he was placed upon the Committee of Safety, then virtually the organ of the government. He was in favor of prudence in all things, but was not affected by the temporizing mania that at first paralyzed the arm of many who desired liberty, but dreaded its penalties. He continued to exercise a powerful and salutary influence in the Assembly of Pennsylvania until the summer of 1776, when he became a member of the Continental Congress, and sanctioned with his "rebel" signature to the Declaration of Independence, the principles of liberty he had so boldly advocated. In the spring of 1777 he retired from Congress and from public life, covered with the honors of a devoted and ardent patriot, an industrious and useful legislator, an enlightened and valuable citizen, a worthy and honest man. He died on the 23d of February, 1781.

GEORGE READ, of Delaware. He was the son of John Read, a wealthy planter who emigrated from Dublin, Ireland, and located in Cecil county, Maryland; and was born in 1734. At the age of seventeen he commenced the study of law, and his proficiency was so great that in two years he was admitted to the bar. Read was a republican to the core, and from the commencement to the close of the Revolution was a bold and unyielding advocate of equal rights and principles. In 1765 he was elected a member of the Assembly of the State of Delaware, and was instrumental in laying deep the foundation of liberty. He did not believe in petitions or remonstrances to the throne of Great Britain; he believed only in force. He boldly advocated war, and called on his countrymen to oppose with arms in their hands the oppressions and encroachments of England. He was a member of the Congress of 1774, and retained that elevated station during the Revolution. He

was also President of the Convention that formed the first
Constitution of Delaware in 1776, and a member of her
Assembly constantly for twelve successive years after his
first election.   A part of this time he was Vice-President
of his State, and in the autumn of 1777, when President
McKinly fell into the hands of the enemy, Read was called
from Congress to perform the duties of chief magistrate.
On his way home with his family he was compelled to pass
through Jersey, and in crossing the Delaware at Salem, his
boat was discovered by the British fleet then lying just below. An armed barge was sent in pursuit. Read's boat stuck
fast in the mud, and was soon come up to.   By effacing
the marks on his baggage during a few brief moments before he was boarded, and having with him his wife and
children, he convinced those from the fleet that he was a
countryman on his way to his farm, and solicited their assistance to put him ashore.   They promptly afforded their
aid, took his load out of the boat, and landed him and his
precious charge on the Delaware side of the river.   The
perfect and open calmness of himself and wife saved them
from the horrors of a prison-ship, and probably him from
an exhibition on the yard-arm of a man-of-war.   In the
midst of all the perils of the Revolution he stood firm, and
never doubted the final overthrow of English power in
the colonies. From the moment the first gun was fired
until he wrote his name on the Declaration, and from that
until his death, he was always the true patriot and soldier.
He was a talented, virtuous, and just man, and enjoyed the
esteem and gratitude of his countrymen.   This distinguished
Irish-American died in the year 1798.

THOMAS McKEAN, of Delaware.   William McKean, the
father of Thomas, emigrated from Ireland in the beginning
of the last century, and settled in Chester county, Pennsylvania, where the signer was born on the 19th of March,

1734. His father placed him at an early age under the tuition of the Rev. Francis Allison, then principal of one of the most celebrated seminaries in the province, and a man of profound science and erudition. He became a lawyer, and for many years followed that profession in his native place. In 1762 he was elected a member of the Delaware Assembly from Newcastle county, and continued in that station for eleven successive years. So much attached to him were the people of that county, that they continued to elect him for six succeeding years after his removal, although he necessarily declined the honor of serving. He was claimed by Delaware and Pennsylvania as a favorite son of each. In 1765 he was a member, for Delaware, of the Congress of New York. He was next appointed Judge of the Court of Common Pleas. He was a prominent member of the Continental Congress of 1776 that convened at Philadelphia. From that time to the peace of 1783 he was a member of Congress, and the only one that served the whole time. He was a strong advocate of the Declaration of Independence, and most willingly affixed his signature to that instrument. When it came up for final action, so anxious was he that it should pass *unanimously*, that he sent an express after Cæsar Rodney, one of his colleagues, the other showing an unwillingness to take the decisive step at that time. Mr. Rodney arrived on the 4th of July, just in time to give his vote in favor of the immortal measure, and thus secured its unanimous adoption. So devoted was McKean to the cause he had so nobly espoused, that he accepted a colonel's commission, and was appointed to the command of a regiment raised in Philadelphia, and marched to the support of Washington. On the 10th of July, 1781, McKean was elected President of Congress, and, on the surrender of Cornwallis, Washington dispatched a courier to carry the news to him. He was in bed when the messenger arrived, but at once arose, and presently the glad tidings were made known throughout the city; the watchmen proclaimed the hour, adding *"and Cornwallis is taken."* After the independence of our country was firmly established, and the last red-coat had left our shores, McKean retired from public life and took up his residence in Philadelphia, where he died on the 24th of June, 1817.

CHARLES CARROLL, of Carrollton. "Carroll," said Samuel Chase in 1772, "we have the better of our opponents, we have completely written them down." "And do you think that writing will settle the question between England and us?" asked Mr. Carroll. "To be sure," replied Chase, "what else can we resort to?" "The bayonet," replied Carroll, and his words were prophetic. Charles Carroll, of Carrollton, was born at Annapolis, Maryland, on the 20th of September, 1737. His grandfather, Charles Carroll, of King's county, Ireland, emigrated to America, about 1680. Belonging to a strict Catholic family, Charles, at an early age, was placed at the Jesuit College of Bohemia, a secluded spot on the eastern shore of Maryland. At the same time and place his cousin, John Carroll, afterward the first Archbishop of America, pursued his minor studies preparatory to entering the European colleges. From thence the two youths proceeded to France to finish their collegiate course in the college of St. Louis le Grand. At the age of twenty-seven the signer returned to his native land. In 1776 he, with his cousin John, then a Jesuit Father, Benjamin Franklin, and Samuel Chase, were deputed by Congress to go on a mission to Canada, the object being to win over the Canadians to the Colonial cause. The mission proved a partial success, and the patriots returned to Philadelphia just at the moment when Congress was wavering on the question of promulgating the immortal Declaration. Charles Carroll supported it strenuously, and on the memorable day when the roll was called, and the delegates walked up the aisle to affix their signatures to that imperishable document, Charles Carroll was asked by John Hancock would he sign. "Most willingly," said he, and went with the rest to stake by that act larger personal interests than any man present; for he was, not even excepting Boston's merchant prince, Hancock, the richest of all the delegates. As he took up the pen to sign, a bystander remarked, in words to which all at least mentally assented: "There go millions." But some one having suggested that there were so many Charles Carrolls, the British legislators would have some difficulty in securing the right one, Mr. Carroll immediately dashed off the expressive words which have ever since been appended to his name, whether written or spoken—words which ever distinguish him by the generous import they convey—"of Carrollton." He continued in Congress until 1778, when the alliance with France assured the success of the cause of Independence. Charles Carroll was one of the purest patriots that ever America produced. Years before the Revolution his genius and energies were employed in combating the tyrannical acts of the British government. In 1770 he wrote articles, under the signature of the "First Citizen," against the right of the government to regulate fees by proclamation. When a Mr. Stewart, a friend, imported tea into Annapolis, contrary to the known regulations of the conventon, he declined to interfere between Mr. Stewart and the excited people. "My advice is," said he, "that he set fire to the vessel and burn her with the tea that is in her, to the water's edge," an advice that was immediately complied with. Mr. Carroll held various offices under the government during and after the war. In 1788 he was elected United States Senator, from Maryland. He retired from public life in 1810, and devoted his time to the management of his estates.   He was a gentleman of polished manners, generous, proverbially hospitable, and philanthropic in all his views, a devout Catholic, and a true patriot. The demise of John Adams and Thomas Jefferson, on July 4, 1826, left Charles Carroll, of Carrollton, the last surviving signer, and chief mourner at the performance of their obsequies.   His devotion to his religious duties was exemplary and edifying.   Often might his venerable form be seen, kneeling in prayer, before the altar in the chapel of Doughoregan Manor, and even when past eighty years of age he was accustomed to serve Mass.   In 1829 the assembled Bishops of the First Council of Baltimore went to pay their respects to the survivor of the illustrious men who had declared the United States an independent Republic, to testify their affection for him, and their devotion to the institutions which he had so nobly aided in establishing. He lived to the patriarchal age of 96, dying November 14, 1832.   Almost his last words were: "I have lived to my ninety-sixth year; I have enjoyed continued health; I have been blessed with great wealth, prosperity and most of the good things this world can bestow—public approbation and applause; but what I now look back on with the greatest satisfaction to myself is, *that I have practiced the duties of my religion.*"

THOMAS NELSON, of Virginia.   The grandfather of the signer, came from Strabane, Tyrone county, Ireland, to America, about the beginning of the last century.   The name was originally O'Neill, but changed to its English synonym in the course of time.   The eminent Irish antiquarian, Eugene O'Curry, many years ago made out the pedigree of the Delegate to Congress from Virginia, tracing his descent from Donald O'Neill, Prince of Ulster, who addressed, in 1315, the famous "Remonstrance" to Pope

John XXII., in which he exposed and denounced the atrocities perpetrated by the English in Ireland, and justified the bringing over of Edward Bruce, brother of King Robert of Scotland, to aid in expelling the invaders. William Nelson, of Strabane, cousin of the signer, was an officer of the Irish volunteers in 1782, and in 1798 he subscribed liberally to provide the United Irishmen with arms. Colonel John Nixon, of the Friendly Sons of St. Patrick of Philadelphia, who first read to the people the Declaration of Independence, was also a relative of Thomas Nelson. The latter was born at Yorktown, in 1738. At the age of fourteen, he was sent to London to be educated, and in a short time was entered a member of Trinity College, Cambridge. In 1761, he returned to America, and three years later, was elected a member of the House of Burgesses, of Virginia, where he at once joined the patriots in supporting the resolutions, condemnatory of the "Boston Port Bill," which led to the dissolution of the Assembly by Lord Dunmore. Nelson was a member of the First General Convention of Virginia which met at Williamsburgh, in August, 1774, and sent delegates to the First Continental Congress. In the following year he was again elected to the convention, and there proposed that the militia of the State should be organized to defend the rights of the people. He was warmly supported by Patrick Henry, Richard Henry Lee, and other patriots; his project was indorsed by the body, and he was thereupon appointed to the command of one of the three regiments ordered to be raised, with the rank of colonel; Lee and Henry, receiving similar commissions, and being placed at the head of the other two. In August, 1774, he was sent as a delegate to the Continental Congress, and was unanimously re-elected, for 1776, when he signed the Declaration. Ill health compelled him to resign in 1777, and he returned home, but when Congress again

6

called for aid, he raised a volunteer corps, and went at their head to join Washington. He was again a delegate to Congress in 1779, but sickness once more compelled him to withdraw. When Jefferson's term as Governor of Virginia expired in 1781, Nelson was chosen his successor. As commander-in-chief of the forces of his State, he placed himself at their head, and joined Lafayette, who was then endeavoring to check Cornwallis. He continued in this capacity until the British surrendered at Yorktown, making constantly great personal sacrifices, guaranteeing, himself, the payment of a loan of two million dollars raised by Virginia, and insisting that his own house should be shelled and ruined, because the British occupied it. Soon after the surrender he resigned, and remained in private life until his death, which took place in 1789. During his last years he lived, alternately, at his house at Yorktown, and on his estate at Offly.

EDWARD RUTLEDGE, of South Carolina. Dr. John Rutledge, father of Edward, was a native of Ireland, and emigrated to America in 1735, bringing with him his eldest son John, afterwards a member, with his brother, of the first Continental Congress, and later Chief-Justice of the United States. Edward, whose name is attached to the Declaration, was born in Charleston, S. C., in 1749, and was the youngest of seven children. His father died soon after his birth, leaving him to his mother's care, and she, being a very intelligent woman and imbued with republican ideas, moulded and fostered them in the mind of her son. After receiving a good education, he commenced the study of law with his elder brother, who stood high at the Charleston bar, and who sent him to London to complete his legal studies. He returned in 1772, and soon acquired a merited eminence as a bold, discreet and able advocate, and was always ready to enter the arena when duty called him. It was evident that talents like his were well calculated to promote the cause of independence, and he was among the first elected members to the Continental Congress in 1774, and was re-elected in 1775 and 1776, signing the Declaration with his colleagues on August 2 of the latter year. This alone was sufficient to place him on the roll of imperishable fame. The Revolution found him on the side of liberty, and during the years it lasted, Rutledge, with voice, and pen, and sword, resisted the assaults of tyranny. After the disastrous battle of Long Island, in 1776, Lord Howe, thinking the Americans were awed by the power of England, and despairing of their cause, offered to treat with the " rebels," not doubting but they would submit to whatever terms he chose to propose. Edward Rutledge, Benjamin Franklin, and John Adams were the committee sent to wait upon him. During the whole of the doubtful and protracted struggle, Rutledge remained its powerful and zealous advocate, and gave his best exertions in its behalf. As a sound, judicious statesman he ranked high, as an orator he was regarded as the most eloquent in the Continental Congress, and as a soldier his courage was unquestionable. On account of ill health, as well as because of the disturbed condition of South Carolina, he withdrew from Congress in 1777, but was returned again in 1779. During the investment of Charleston, in 1780, he was given command of a battery of artillery, by his brother John, then Governor, and displayed great bravery in his efforts to succor Gen. Lincoln, who commanded in the city. He was, however, taken prisoner, and was sent to St. Augustine, Florida, where he was kept in durance for nearly a year before his exchange was effected. After the evacuation of Charleston by the British, in 1781, he found himself unable, on account of the debilitated state to which he had been reduced by his imprisonment, to continue his previous active career;

and resumed the practice of his profession.   Some years later, he was called on to enter the Legislature of his State, where he rendered good service, and displayed his aversion to the slave trade.   He was elected, in 1794, to the United States Senate, and four years later was made Governor of South Carolina, which position he filled at the time of his death, which took place in January, 1800.

THOMAS LYNCH, of South Carolina.   The grandfather of Lynch came from the province of Connaught—and according to the most popular belief, from the city of Galway— and settled on the banks of the North Santee river, in what was known later as Prince George's parish, about the beginning of the last century.   By unremitting industry he gradually acquired considerable wealth, and at his death left to his son, Thomas, a valuable estate.   The latter, known as Thomas Lynch, Sr., was a man of great influence, and so highly esteemed that he was elected a delegate to the first Continental Congress, which met at Philadelphia in 1774.   His son, Thomas Lynch, Jr., was born in 1749, and after having received a good academical education, at Georgetown, S. C., was sent to England to pursue his studies further.*   He took a degree at Cambridge, and afterwards entered on the study of the law, in one of the inns of the Temple, where he acquired a thorough knowledge of the profession.   Becoming acquainted with some

---

* It was usual at that period to send American youths, especially those intended for the legal profession, to Europe, to complete their education. Their sojourn in England did not, however, in most cases, have the effect of making them more favorably disposed towards the British government. It may be added that several of the most distinguished Irish Patriots were, when young, sent to pursue their studies at English Universities and schools, but instead of being rendered more loyal thereby, they became the most inveterate and determined opponents of British rule in Ireland.

of the leading British Whigs while there, he obtained a knowledge of the designs of the Ministry in regard to the Colonies, and returned home, in 1772, determined to thwart them as far as lay in his power, and to strike a blow, if possible, for liberty. His views and purposes were fostered and encouraged by his patriotic father, and responded to by the people of his parish. The first attempt of young Lynch at public speaking was at a meeting in Charleston in 1773. His father had just addressed the assembled multitude on the subject of English oppression, amid the cheers of his fellow-citizens. As he sat down his youthful son rose. A profound silence ensued. A thousand eyes were turned upon him. For a moment he paused, but speedily a burst of eloquence followed, that carried the flame of patriotism to the hearts of his astonished and delighted audience with irresistible force. Tears of joy ran down the furrowed cheeks of his father, and loud bursts of applause greeted the two patriots. When the first provincial regiment was raised in South Carolina, in 1775, young Lynch accepted a captain's commission in it, saying to his father, who desired to see him enter the service with higher rank, that the commission was quite as important as his experience would warrant him in receiving. Along with Captain —afterwards General—Pinckney, he made a tour through North Carolina, for the purpose of raising men for the regiment alluded to; but while performing this duty he suffered severely from the inclemency of the weather, and his constitution received a shock from which it never recovered. About this time, his father, through ill health, resigned his seat in Congress, but had the satisfaction of seeing his son elected to replace him. In October, 1775, Franklin, Lynch and Harrison (father of President Harrison), were sent as a committee from Congress to consult with Washington, then in camp at Cambridge, in relation to a new organization of the army, and also with respect to future operations, and they discharged the duty intrusted to them with credit to themselves and advantage to the national cause. Lynch signed the Declaration of Independence with his colleagues, August 2, 1776. The serious illness of his father, who had remained in Philadelphia, and his own increasing weakness, however, compelled him to resign soon after. Both set out on the return journey, but on the way back, the parent was stricken with paralysis, and died at Annapolis, Maryland. The son's health, after his return to South Carolina, failed slowly but steadily, and his physicians at length urged him, as a last resource, to spend some time in the south of Europe, the climate of which they hoped might benefit him. He accordingly sailed, accompanied by his devoted wife, in 1779, for the West Indies, hoping to find a neutral vessel there in which he might embark for Europe, and so escape the risk of being captured by the British. The ship, unfortunately, never reached her destination. She was supposed to have foundered at sea, for no tidings were ever heard from her after she had been a few days out of port. Thus died, at the early age of thirty, one of the truest and bravest of the founders of the Republic.

CHARLES THOMSON, "perpetual secretary" of Congress. Charles Thomson was born at Maghera, Derry county, Ireland, in 1730, and at the age of eleven, was brought to America, along with three other brothers, by his father. The latter died when within sight of the capes of the Delaware, and the boys were left to their own resources. An elder brother, however, who had arrived some years before, did what he could for them, and through his aid, Charles secured admission to the seminary of Dr. Francis Allison, an eminent Irish professor, who taught for a time at New London, Chester county, and afterwards at Philadelphia, and by whom several of the revolutionary leaders were educated. At Dr. Allison's establishment, young Thomson made so much progress in his studies that he was before many years deemed competent to undertake the management of a Friends' Academy, at Newcastle, Delaware, his methods of instruction giving great satisfaction. At a very early period in the controversy between Britain and the Colonies, Thomson became known as an ardent advocate of the people's rights. His opinions and the arguments with which he supported them, had great weight, for his integrity and good judgment were unquestioned. The Delaware Indians adopted him, and conferred on him the title of "The man of truth," a strict regard for which he maintained through life, so that, according to Rev. Dr. Green, it was a popular mode of vouching for the truth of anything to say, "It is as true as if Charles Thomson's name were to it."

He was intensely earnest in his efforts against British despotism, and on one occasion, it is said, that he fainted, while hotly engaged in discussing the proper course to be pursued, in order to aid the people of Boston—at a meeting at the Coffee-house in Philadelphia where Dickinson, Mifflin, Reed, and others also spoke. Nor did he confine his exertions to the city. On pretence of making a summer tour, he and another patriot traveled through the rural districts, seeking to stir up the feelings of the country people, and to test their disposition in the event of a revolution.* John Adams spoke of him as " The Sam Adams of Philadelphia—*The life of the cause of Liberty.*" When the first Continental Congress met, in September, 1774, he was unanimously chosen Secretary, and retained that position until his resignation in 1789. He would re-

---

* Watson's Annals of Philadelphia.

ceive no pay for his first year's services, and Congress presented his wife, the aunt of President Harrison, with a silver urn as a mark of its appreciation of his unselfish patriotism.   He made copious notes of the proceedings of Congress and the progress of the Revolution, and after retiring from public life prepared a history of his own times, but his natural kindliness of heart prevented him from publishing it.   A short time before his death, he destroyed the manuscript, assigning as a reason that he was unwilling to blast the reputation of families rising into repute by placing on record the want of patriotism of their progenitors during the war.   As a literary man his abilities were of the highest order, and his writings were spoken of in terms of warmest praise by eminent Europeans, as well as by Americans.   He died in August, 1824, in the ninety-fifth year of his age, at Lower Merion, Montgomery county, Pennsylvania.   In 1830, his nephew removed his remains to Laurel Hill Cemetery, where a beautiful monument was placed over them, bearing an appropriate inscription, which was written by J. F. Watson, author of the *Annals of Philadelphia.*   The Abbe Claude C. Robin, chaplain in the French army, thus describes his appearance when he came, with other patriots, to greet Count Rochambeau: "Among others Charles Thomson, Secretary of Congress, *the soul of that political body*, came to receive and present his compliments.   His meager figure (he was about six feet high) furrowed countenance, his hollow, sparkling eyes, his white straight hair, that did not hang quite so low as his ears, fixed our thorough attention, and filled us with surprise and admiration."   Only his signature, besides that of President Hancock was affixed to the Declaration, July the Fourth, 1776.

Captain John Dunlap, a native of Strabane, Tyrone county, a member of "the Friendly Sons of St. Patrick" of

Philadelphia, and of the famous "First Troop of Cavalry" of that city, who published the first daily paper issued in the United States, held the position of printer to Congress, and was the first who printed the Declaration. " An Irishman, Charles Thomson, first prepared this immortal document for publication, from the draft of Jefferson; the son of an Irishman, Colonel Nixon, had the honor of first publicly reading it to the people from the State House, and another Irishman, Captain Dunlap, first printed and published it to the world."*

It may be added here that Alderman John Binns, of Philadelphia, a native of Dublin and a United Irishman, in 1815 published the Declaration, with fac-similes of the signers' autographs, at his own expense, for the first time, and received the thanks of John Quincy Adams, Lafayette, and other eminent men for his patriotic and valuable work.

---

* Account of Friendly Sons of St. Patrick, Philadelphia.

CHAPTER XIII.

THE IRISH IN THE WAR OF INDEPENDENCE.

WHEN the British had been driven from Boston, they resolved to try their fortunes at New York and Charleston. An attack on the latter seemed to offer the best chances of success, and accordingly, the British fleet under Admiral Parker, having on board General Clinton, and nearly three thousand infantry, sailed southward, and anchored near Sullivan's Island, ten miles below the city, at the entrance to the harbor. But John Rutledge, brother of Edward, the signer, and born in Ireland,* who had been a short

---

* "John Rutledge," says Lossing, in his *Lives of Eminent Americans,* "was the soul of patriotic activity in South Carolina, during the darkest period of the Revolution, whether in civil authority or as general director of military movements. He was a native of Ireland, and came to America with his father, Doctor John Rutledge, in 1735. He was chosen one of the representatives of his adopted State, in the first Continental Congress, with his brother Edward as one of his colleagues. When, in the spring of 1776, the civil government of South Carolina was revised, and a temporary State Constitution was framed, Rutledge was appointed president of the State, and commander-in-chief of its military. Under his efficient administration, Charleston was prepared for the attack made in June, by Clinton and Parker, and the enemy was repulsed. In 1779, he was chosen governor under the new constitution, and was invested with temporary dictatorial powers by the legislature. He took the field at the head of the militia, and managed both civil and military affairs with great skill and energy, until after the fall of Charleston, in 1780. When Greene, aided by the southern partisan leaders, drove the British from the interior to the sea-board, in 1781, Rutledge convened a legislative assembly at Jacksonborough, and thoroughly re-

time before elected President, and commander-in-chief of
South Carolina, was ready to meet the invaders. He had
caused over a hundred pieces of artillery to be mounted in
the best positions, around the harbor, had summoned the
militia of the State to arms, and made whatever preparations were possible for the expected struggle. Gen. Charles
Lee was sent down by Washington, to aid in the defense
of the city, and under him were Armstrong, Gadsden,
Moultrie, and Thomson, the last named a nephew of the
Irish Secretary of Congress.* Thomson's troops were
chiefly riflemen, and to him was confided the command of
the advanced post on the east end of Sullivan's Island,

---

established civil government. After the war he was made judge of the
Court of Chancery. He was a member of the convention that framed
the constitution of the United States ; and in 1789, was elevated to the
bench of the Supreme Court of the Republic, as associate justice. He
was appointed Chief Justice of South Carolina in 1791 ; and in 1796 he
was called to the duties of Chief Justice of the United States. In every
official station he displayed equal energy and sterling integrity ; and
while yet bearing the robes of the highest judicial office in the Republic,
he was summoned from earth. His death occurred in July, 1800, when
he was about seventy years of age."

* General William Thomson was a brother of Charles Thomson,
the secretary of Congress, and born, three years before the latter, at
Maghera, Derry county, Ireland. Soon after arriving in America, at
which time he was only fourteen years old, some friends of the family
brought him to South Carolina. When the Revolution broke out he
was placed in command of the third regiment of South Carolina,
known as the "Rangers," and fought at its head at Charleston in 1776.
He also served with Howe in Georgia, and was engaged with his command on the attack of Savannah under D'Estaing and Lincoln. He
displayed great bravery, and suffered much during the war, retiring at
its close to his estate at Belleville " with shattered health and fortune."
There he remained engaged in the occupation of an indigo planter until
1796, when, seeking to benefit his declining health by a visit to mineral
springs in Virginia, he died during his stay there.

facing which Clinton planted his batteries. On June 2d, the English fleet moved up to attack Fort Sullivan (now Moultrie), while Clinton's guns opened on Thomson. The Englishman had two batteries and over twenty-six hundred men, the Irish-American only two guns and a few hundred riflemen, but these "were among the best marksmen in the State. He allowed the English flotilla to approach within musket shot, when he opened a destructive fire upon it from his guns and small arms. Several attempts to advance were made, and every time the sure marksmen of Carolina swept many from the boats, and Clinton was obliged to abandon his design."* The British general made another attack the next morning, but "Thomson confronted him with such hot volleys that he was obliged to again retreat behind his batteries." This was the first contest between the Americans and a British fleet, and the patriots were naturally full of exultation at their victory, while their baffled enemies turned their prows northward, and sailed for New York. During this engagement, an Irish sergeant, William Jasper, afterwards killed at Savannah, distinguished himself by an act of remarkable daring. Early in the action, the staff in "the western bastion," from which floated the Crescent flag of South Carolina, was cut away by a shot from a British frigate, and the color fell outside the walls. Jasper sprang over the parapet, "walked the length of the fort, picked up the flag, fastened it upon a sponge staff, and in the midst of the iron hail, fixed it upon the bastion. Three cheers greeted him as he ascended the parapet again, and leaped unhurt within the fort."† On the day after the battle, Governor Rutledge came to the fort, and presented his daring fellow-

---

* Lossing's Field Book of the Revolution, vol. ii., p. 549.
† Ibid., p. 550.

countryman with his own sword, offering him at the same time, a lieutenant's commission; but the young hero, as modest. as he was brave, declined the well-deserved promotion, saying, "I am but a sergeant."* The thanks of Congress were, on the twentieth of July, tendered to Lee, Moultrie, and Thomson, and the officers and men under their command, for their gallant and successful defence of Charleston.

Toward the end of June, Howe sailed from Halifax— whither he had gone when driven from Boston—for Staten Island. On the eighth of July, he landed there with over nine thousand men, and was soon reinforced by the arrival of several thousand more British regular and Hessians, and still later by Clinton and the vanquished and vengeful redcoats from Charleston. They were rendered still more vindictive by the news that the Declaration of Independeuce had been adopted and published, and that the statue of their king, George III., which stood in Bowling Green, had been pulled down and run into bullets, so that they

---

* Sergeant William Jasper was born in Ireland and came to America while young. At the commencement of the Revolution he joined the patriots, and attaching himself to the Second South Carolina Regiment, soon became distinguished for his intrepidity. At the attack on Charleston, his bravery as well as modesty attracted the admiration of all. Refusing the offer of a commission tendered him by his countryman Governor Rutledge, he was detached on special duty by General Moultrie, with permission to select such men as he chose from his regiment to accompany him. On one occasion while engaged in this service, he with a single comrade, surprised eight British soldiers who were conveying some Americans to Savannah to be executed; released the prisoners, and brought the redcoats to the American camp at Purysburg. During the attack on Savannah, Oct. 9, 1779, Jasper lost his life while planting the colors of his regiment on the British works. One of the principal squares in that city perpetuates Jasper's name, and a splendid monument was recently erected there in his honor.

were likely to have "melted majesty" poured into them
before long.

Washington had expected that the British would first
endeavor to make themselves masters of Long Island, and
the event proved the correctness of his judgment. Greene,
who was stationed there with several thousand men, had
carefully studied the ground, and caused fortifications to be
thrown up at various points. He was unfortunately taken
ill, and Sullivan, who was unacquainted with the locality,
was assigned to his position, Putnam having the chief
command. The Americans numbered about nine thousand, a large proportion being raw men.

On August 22d, a largely superior British force landed
near New Utrecht, Long Island, and prepared for an attack. They moved forward on the evening of the 26th,
and, guided and aided by American loyalists, they almost
succeeded in surrounding the patriot forces. Sullivan, perceiving the peril of his army, ordered a retreat to the fortifications at Brooklyn, but in endeavoring to effect this
purpose a desperate struggle ensued. "Hemmed in and en-
trapped between the British and Hessians, and driven from
one to the other, the Americans for a time struggled bravely,
or rather desperately. Sullivan and his ensnared men,
fought fiercely hand to hand with the enemy. In the struggle, the soldiers of Maryland and Pennsylvania, composed
in great part of Irish-Americans, behaved with determined
bravery, and one-half of their numbers was slaughtered.
Moylan, and Hand, and Butler, with their regiments,
were engaged from early morning until night; and from
the wooded hills, now Greenwood Cemetery, to the Flatbush
Pass, from Gowanus to Fort Greene, the bitter conflict
raged. Though surrounded by the English and Hessians, all chance of retreat cut off, and wearied and exhausted from continual fighting all day, many succeeded

in hewing their way through the ranks of the enemy, and escaped to Fort Greene. Hundreds were slain in the affair, or drowned in Gowanus Creek, while those who fell into the hands of the English were sent to the loathsome prison ships. Sullivan was captured and sent as a prisoner to Lord Howe, as was also Lord Stirling. The loss of the Americans in this affair was nearly two thousand, that of the British only five hundred. Washington, apprehensive that the English fleet might try to cut off his troops in Brooklyn from communication with New York, ordered, after consultation with his officers, the evacuation of Long Island. The movement took place on the night of August 29th, under his own supervision. The regiments of Shee and McGaw, of the Pennsylvania Line, with the remnants of Haslet's and Smallwood's Marylanders, acting as a covering party. It was executed with secrecy and dispatch, and the commander-in-chief remained until all the troops had embarked for New York, and then crossed the river in the last boat of all.

Soon after it was decided to abandon New York, and on the thirteenth of September, the main body of the American army quitted the city.*

---

* Shortly after the battle of Long Island, and while Howe's fleet lay in New York harbor, an attempt was made to destroy his flagship, the *Eagle*, by means of an "infernal machine" called a "marine turtle," the invention of a man named Bushnell, of Saybrook, Connecticut. This machine was capable of containing one man within it, and could be navigated by him under water. A small magazine of gunpowder—with fastenings to attach it to a ship's bottom—was carried along with the "turtle." "This magazine," says Lossing, "was furnished with clockwork, constructed so as to operate a spring and communicate a blow to detonating powder and ignite the gunpowder of the magazine. The motion of this clockwork was sufficiently slow to allow the submarine operator to escape a safe distance after securing the magazine to a ship's bottom." Washington approved of the machine, and requested Gen.

In all the skirmishes and battles that ensued from that date until the army passed into Jersey, the Irish-Americans bore a prominent part. At East Chester, Hand defeated and drove back a Hessian regiment by a bayonet charge. At Throck's and Pell's Neck, the same general and his riflemen, in the very teeth of Howe, destroyed the bridge and drove the British general from the Causeway. At Fort Washington, McGaw, of the Pennsylvania Line, defended the place till one thousand redcoats and Hessians lay dead before the ramparts. Soon after Washington commenced his famous retreat through Jersey. So quickly did the victorious army of Howe advance upon Fort Lee, that the Americans were compelled to make a hasty retreat, leaving their tents, artillery, and provisions behind. For three weeks they retreated before Cornwallis, across the level districts of New Jersey. So near were pursuers and pursued all this time that the music of the British could be distinctly heard by the Americans. The term of service of many of the militia regiments had expired, and the men, refusing to re-enlist, left the ranks and returned home. Desertions were frequent, and when on the second of December, Washington crossed the Delaware, his army had dwindled down to scarcely three thousand men. Lee had been left behind at White Plains, in command of a detachment of nearly three thousand men, and Washington wrote to him requesting him to move immediately into New Jersey, to

---

Parsons to secure a competent man to manage it and destroy the *Eagle*. A young man named Lee was selected for the undertaking. He performed his duty with skill and coolness, got under the British vessel and remained there for two hours, on September 6, but found it impossible to penetrate the thick copper on her bottom in order to attack the magazine. He returned in safety, and received the congratulations of Washington and his officers for his daring. The commander-in-chief often employed him subsequently.

re-inforce his melting army. Lee paid no attention to the request of his chief, and it was evident that at this time, and afterwards on the field of Monmouth, he harbored unworthy designs. Sternly commanded by Washington to advance to his assistance, the Englishman commenced his tardy and reluctant march. So slow were his movements that three weeks elapsed before he reached Morristown. Two days afterwards he was captured by the enemy. Sullivan who had been exchanged a short time before, then took command of Lee's troops and soon formed a junction with the main body of the army on the banks of the Delaware.

When on that memorable Christmas night, 1776, Washington, with his band of patriots, crossed the river, determined to make a dash on the Hessians at Trenton, and by one bold deed raise up the sinking spirits of his country, the Irish were by his side. Sullivan, Greene, Knox, Ewing, and Hand were there, and out from Philadelphia, at the same moment, came Colonel Griffin, on the march against Count Donop, to make a diversion in favor of Washington, and keep Donop from aiding the garrison at Trenton. As in the gray of the morning, Washington leaped upon the astonished Hessians at one point, the cheers of Sullivan's men were heard from the opposite end of the town, as they, with the bayonet, drove the stricken and bewildered enemy before them. Rall, who, with savage ferocity, had fought against McGaw at Fort Washington, was shot down at the head of his Hessians, and the terrified mercenaries ran in the direction of Princeton. But Hand was stationed on the Princeton road; his riflemen had not forgotten Brooklyn and the Flatbush Pass. A volley greeted the flying fugitives and checked their flight. They threw down their arms and begged for mercy. When Washington recrossed the Delaware, he took with him one

thousand prisoners, six pieces of artillery, a thousand stand
of arms, and four colors captured in Trenton. The descendants of some of the Irish soldiers who crossed the Delaware
with Washington are still living at Trenton.

The same men, a few days afterwards fought the battle of
Princeton. Captain Moore, with a few men of the Princeton
Militia, as brave as himself, made a dash, during the battle,
at Nassau Hall, then filled with British troops, and commanded them to surrender. They did so, and he marched
his prisoners, far out numbering his own men, to the American rear. Washington ordered Major Kelly, of the
Pennsylvania Militia, to destroy the bridge over Stony
Brook, near Princeton. With a handful of men he proceeded to the bridge, but no sooner had he begun to de-
molish it than the van of Cornwallis' army appeared before
him. The enemy, perceiving his designs, opened on him
with grape and round shot. In the face of this terrible
fire Kelly maintained his ground, throwing the planks into
the stream until the bridge was rendered impassable for
artillery. He, however, fell into the hands of the British.
While engaged in cutting away a log in which some of the
timbers rested, it gave way and he tumbled into the stream.
His men, supposing him to be drowned, started for Princeton, but he succeeded in getting out of the water, though
his frozen clothes so impeded his progress, tired as he was,
that the enemy came up with him and made him a prisoner.

In this engagement Washington was, for a time, in the
most imminent danger. Mercer's men, disheartened by the
fall of their leader, became confused. The commander-in-
chief, perceiving this, rode up and called on them to stand
fast. Custis then describes what followed. "The dis-
comfited Americans rally on the instant, and form in line.
The enemy halt and dress their line. The American chief

is between the adverse posts, as though he had been placed there, a target for both. The arms of both are leveled. Can escape from death be possible? John Fitzgerald (Washington's aid, who was just returning after having conveyed an order to another point), horror-struck at what seemed the impending death of his beloved commander, dropped the reins upon his horse's neck, and drew his hat over his face that he might not see him die. A roar of musketry succeeds, and then a shout. It was the shout of victory. The aid-de-camp ventures to raise his eyes. Oh, glorious sight; the enemy are broken, and flying, while dimly amid the glimpses of the smoke is seen the chief, alive, unharmed, and without a wound, waving his hat and cheering his comrade, to the pursuit. Colonel Fitzgerald, celebrated as one of the finest horsemen in the American army, now dashed his rowels into his charger's flanks, and heedless of the dead and dying in his way, flew to the side of his chief, exclaiming, "Thank God, your excellency is safe," and then the favorite aid, a gallant and warm-hearted son of Erin, a man of thews and sinews, and unused to the melting mood, gave loose to his feelings, and wept like a child for joy. Washington, ever calm, amid scenes of the greatest excitement, affectionately grasped the hand of his aid and friend, and then said, "Away, my dear colonel, and bring up the troops, the day is our own."*

During the spring of 1777, eighteen new Brigadier-Generals were appointed by Congress, six of them, at least,

---

* Custis' "Recollections of the Life and Character of Washington." "Colonel Fitzgerald," says Mr. Custis, "was an Irish officer in the old Blue and Buffs, the first volunteer company raised in the South in the dawn of the Revolution, and commanded by Washington. In the campaign of 1778, and retreat through the Jerseys, he was appointed aid to the commander-in-chief.

being Irish by birth or descent. These were Wayne,
("Mad Anthony"), Hand and Reed of Pennsylvania,
George Clinton of New York, Poor of New Hampshire,
and Conway, formerly of the Irish Brigade in the service
of France.* Moylan was given the command of a regi-

---

* Major-General Wayne.   " The elder Wayne came from Ireland to
America in 1722," writes Armstrong, the American biographer, in his
life of" Mad Anthony." Anthony was born on the 1st of January, 1745,
in Chester County Pa., "and a better New Year's gift," says Headley,
" fortune could not have presented to the nation." Sent to school at an
early age to his uncle, he passed from thence to the Philadelphia Academy,
where he remained till seventeen years old, devöting most of his time to
mathematical studies. Having completed his education, he returned to his
native place and opened a surveyor's office. He was sent to Nova Scotia
in 1765, to locate a grant of land from the crown to several gentlemen
in Philadelphia. They made Wayne superintendent of the settlement.
This post he held until 1767, when he returned home, married a young
lady in Philadelphia, and resumed his profession as surveyor. In 1773
he was appointed a representative to the Assembly of his State. He
quitted the council for the field in 1775, where he was appointed a colonel in the Continental army, and went to Canada with Gen. Thomas.
At the close of the campaign there in 1776, he was promoted to brigadier-general. He was with Washington at Germantown, Brandywine,
Monmouth, in all of which engagements he was distinguished for his
valor. The capture of Stony Point raised him to the highest mark in
the admiration of his countrymen. In 1781, he went with the Pennsylvania Line to the South, and in Virginia co-operated with Lafayette.
After the capture of Cornwallis, he was sent to conduct the war in
Georgia, and was very successful. As a reward for his services, the
legislature of Georgia made him a present of a valuable farm. He was
a member of the Pennsylvania Convention that ratified the Federal
Constitution. In 1792 he succeeded St. Clair in the command of the
army to be employed against the Western Indians, and gained a victory
over them in the battle of the Miamis, August, 1794. He concluded a
treaty with the Indians in August, 1795. While engaged in the public
service, and returning home from the West, he was seized with the gout,
and died in a hut at Presque Isle, in December, 1796, aged 51 years.
He was buried, at his own request, under the flag-staff of the fort on

ment of horse, at whose head he afterwards often rode to victory in some of the most desperately contested battles of the war.

---

the shore of Lake Erie, from whence his remains were conveyed, in 1809, by his son, Colonel Isaac Wayne, to Radnar churchyard, in Delaware county. The venerable church near which the body of the hero lies was erected in 1717. The Pennsylvania State Society of the Cincinnati caused a handsome monument to be erected over his remains. General Wayne became a member of the Friendly Sons of St. Patrick of Philadelphia in 1774, and took an active interest in the affairs of the society. Charles Clinton, father of Vice-President George Clinton, and of Major-General James Clinton, was born in Longford county, Ireland, in 1690. In 1729 he chartered a vessel to convey his family and a number of others to America. The captain formed the project of starving them to death, with a view, it is said, to becoming master of their property, but was induced by the offer of a large sum of money to land them at Cape Cod. A son and daughter of Clinton's, as well as a number of other passengers, died in consequence of the hardships of the voyage. In the spring of 1731 Charles Clinton founded a settlement in Orange county, New York. He was soon after made a county judge, and appointed a lieutenant-colonel in the militia, serving in 1758 at the siege of Fort Frontenac (now Kingston), Canada. He died in 1773, at the age of 83 years. Two of his sons, Alexander and Charles, adopted the profession of medicine. The two others, James and George, rendered good service to their country, and rose to positions of high honor and responsibility. James Clinton was the fourth son of Colonel Charles Clinton, and was born in 1736. He was appointed in 1756 an ensign in a militia regiment, from which rank he rose in 1758 to a lieutenancy, and in 1759 to a captaincy. In 1763 he was elevated to the post of commandant of the four regiments raised to defend the western frontiers of New York, and in 1774 he became lieutenant-colonel of the Second regiment of militia in his native country. In the French war he participated in the capture of Fort Frontenac, and won a reputation for gallantry, resolution and military skill. At the close of the war he married a Miss De Witt, and retired to private life. When the Revolutionary war broke out he at once joined the patriots. Congress gave him the commission of a colonel, and subsequently, in 1776, that of a brigadier. He afterwards attained the rank of major-general. Clinton served in the expedition against Canada under Montgomery ; but his chief military achievement was the

Burgoyne the commander of the British forces, in Canada, at the head of a large army, including a number of
Indians, compelled the Americans to evacuate Ticonder-

---

defence of Fort Clinton, on the Hudson, in October, 1777.   His brother,
Governor Clinton, as commander-in-chief, was at Fort Montgomery, its
neighbor.   The attack on these forts was part of a project devised by
Sir Henry Clinton, to create a diversion in favor of Burgoyne, and
open a passage to him.   At the head of four thousand men, the British
general advanced up the Hudson, and having surrounded Forts Clinton
and Montgomery, made a desperate assault upon them.   They were defended by only five hundred men, chiefly militia, who made a brave but
unavailing effort to prevent their capture.   In 1779, Clinton commanded
a detachment of sixteen hundred men, which was sent to assist Sullivan
in his expedition against the hostile Indians.   Clinton was for some time
in command of the northern department at Albany, was subsequently
attached to the main army, and was present at the capture of Cornwallis.   In later years he was one of the convention that formed the present
Federal Constitution.   His death took place in 1812, at Newburgh, N. Y.
Vice-President George Clinton was the youngest son of Charles Clinton, and was born in 1739.   When twenty years old he took part as a
captain of militia in the attack on Fort Frontenac (Kingston).   In 1768
he was elected to the Colonial Assembly, and in 1775 to the Continental
Congress, where he voted in favor of the Declaration of Independence.
He was made a brigadier-general in 1776, and in the year following was
elected both Governor and Lieutenant-Governor of New York.   He accepted the position of Governor, and by six successive elections was continued in that office for eighteen years.   It was in a great measure to his
efforts that the British in New York city were prevented from effecting
a communication with Burgoyne.   In 1788, Governor Clinton presided
over the convention which met at Poughkeepsie to consider the adoption
of the Federal Constitution.   He received fifty electoral votes as a candidate for Vice-President when Washington was elected for the second
term, and was, in 1801, again chosen Governor of New York.   In 1804
he was elected Vice-President of the United States, receiving the same
number of votes as was given Jefferson for the Presidency.   He was
again chosen Vice-President in 1808, Madison being elected President,
and died while discharging the duties of his office at Washington in 1812.
De Witt Clinton, Governor of New York, United States Senator, Mayor
of New York, and projector and inaugurator of the Erie canal, was the

oga, early in July, 1777, and pushing forward in spite of all opposition, reached the banks of the Hudson near Fort

son of General James Clinton. He was born in 1769. At the age of thirty-three, after having filled various positions in the State, he was elected United States Senator from New York. He introduced and strenuously supported in the New York Legislature a project for the construction of a canal from Lake Erie to the Hudson, and persisting in spite of all opposition saw with pride the completion of that great work in 1825. He was elected Governor of New York in 1816, and again in 1819. He died at Albany in 1828.

General Edward Hand was born at Clyduff, Kings county, Ireland, in 1744. After having served some time in the Irish Brigade he came to America and studied medicine at Lancaster, Pa. Promptly taking sides with the patriots, he received a commission as lieutenant-colonel in a regiment of riflemen, mostly composed of his own countrymen, and served at the siege of Boston. In March, 1776, he was promoted to a colonelcy, and led his regiment at the battles of Long Island and Trenton. Soon after he was made brigadier-general, and was placed in command at Albany, in October, 1778. He took part in Sullivan's expedition against the Indians of western New York, and other important movements of the war, and after its close was elected to Congress in 1784. His name is affixed to the Pennsylvania Constitution of 1790. In 1798, when Washington accepted the command of the army, which the prospect of a foreign war made it advisable to raise, he showed his appreciation of Hands' soldierly qualities by recommending him for the position of adjutant-general. This brave Irish-American officer died at Rockford, Lancaster county, Pa., in 1802.

General Enoch Poor was a native of New Hampshire, of Irish origin. He served as a colonel in the Continental army during the expedition to Canada in 1776, and afterwards at Crown Point. He was appointed brigadier-general in 1777, and took part in the battles which resulted in the surrender of Burgoyne. He soon after joined Washington in Pennsylvania; was with his command at Valley Forge, and participated in the pursuit of the British on their retreat from Philadelphia and in the battle of Monmouth which followed. He died in 1780, at Hackensack, N. J., his funeral being attended by Washington and Lafayette. General Poor was greatly esteemed by the latter, who, according to Lossing "was much affected when visiting his grave, when in this country, in 1825."

Edward, on the 30th of that month.   His progress excited
great apprehensions among the people of the North: the
whole frontier of Massachusetts and New Hampshire, was
uncovered and there was no force available, fit to withstand
the British.   But the patriots did not lose heart.   The New
Hampshire Assembly was convened on three days' notice,
and the Speaker, John Langdon—Sullivan's comrade in
the attack on Fort William and Mary—addressing the body
said, after offering almost all that he possessed for the
public service, and urging prompt action, "Our old friend
Stark, who so nobly sustained the honor of our State at
Bunker Hill, may be safely intrusted with the conduct of
the enterprise, and we will check Burgoyne."

The Assembly stirred to enthusiasm, at once proceeded
with the work of preparation.   The militia of the State was
formed into two brigades.   The first was placed under the
command of William Whipple, one of the Irish American
Signers of the Declaration, and the second under that of
Stark.   The latter was then a private citizen.   He had
commanded as Brigadier-General in the battles of Trenton
and Princeton, and when the army went in winter quarters
at Morristown, had returned to New Hampshire to raise recruits.   When he learned, however, that Congress had
passed him over in the appointment of general officers, he
felt indignant at the slight, and resigned his commission.
But now in the hour of trial and danger, he responded
promptly, when called upon.   He stipulated, however, that
he should be held accountable only to the Assembly of
New Hampshire, and that he should be allowed to act according to his own discretion, declining to place himself
under the orders of General Lincoln, who had been sent by
Schuyler, then in command of the Northern Department to
take charge of the newly raised force.

Meanwhile Burgoyne, learning that the Americans had

accumulated considerable stores at Bennington, about twenty-four miles east of the Hudson, sent Colonel Baum, at the head of a strong force, on August 13th, to capture the place. On the same day Stark arrived at Bennington, and made preparations for defence. Baum having reconnoitered the American position, sent back to Burgoyne for large reinforcements, which were promptly dispatched to his assistance. The British forces, composed of English, Germans, Indians, and Tories, then proceeded to entrench themselves, and place their artillery in position. But the Americans became impatient, and their sentiment was voiced by Rev. Mr. Allen, of Pittsfield, a clergyman who had come with the Berkshire county contingent. Addressing the commander before daylight, on the morning of the 16th of August, he said, "General, the people of Berkshire, have been frequently called upon to fight, but have never been led against the enemy. If you do not now give them a chance, they have resolved never to turn out again." "Do you wish," asked Stark, "to march now while it is dark and raining?" "No, not just now," replied the minister. "Then," said the stern old Irish-American veteran, "if the Lord should once more give us sunshine, and I do not give you fighting enough, I'll never ask you to come out again."

Stark had already determined to attack the British, without delay, and when the sun came out early in the day, he formed his troops, and pointing to the enemy's works said, "See men, there are the redcoats. We must beat them to-day, or Molly Stark will be a widow." A very large proportion of those whom he addressed—perhaps the majority —had sprung from the same stock as himself, and his grimly humorous, and determined utterance, was responded to with a yell which "greatly alarmed the loyalists in their works below," and gave promise that the men of New Hampshire would do their whole duty, and that, as far as it depended on their efforts, the estimable Mrs. Stark, would not be compelled to assume widow's weeds, for some time to come.

Two columns were then sent forward to assault the British works at different points, and as soon as the firing began, Stark threw himself in the saddle, and led the main body forward. The Americans rushed upon their enemies, drove them from the entrenchments, and pursued them across the Walloomscoick, where the struggle was renewed. The General in his report said, the battle "lasted two hours, and was the hottest I ever saw. It was like one continual clap of thunder." A British reinforcement which had been sent forward, arrived in time to meet the flying redcoats. They rallied, and again attempted to check the patriots' advance, but opportunely at this critical time a fresh American regiment came up and fell vigorously on them, again driving them back, and following them until dark, when Stark, ordered the pursuit to cease. "Another hour of daylight," said he, "and I would have captured the whole body." Over two hundred of the British were killed, including their commander Baum, many more wounded, and seven hundred made prisoners. Four pieces of artillery were captured, as well as several hundred stand of arms, and a quantity of military stores. The American loss was not over one hundred killed, and as many wounded. Stark's horse was killed under him, but he escaped unhurt himself. His victory startled and weakened Burgoyne, and gave fresh hope and confidence to the Nation's defenders.

"Nothing succeeds like success." When Congress was informed that Stark declined to obey the orders of Lincoln, it censured his conduct as "destructive of military subordination, and highly prejudicial to the common cause." After the victory of Bennington, however, it resolved "that the thanks of Congress be presented to General Stark of the New Hampshire militia, and the officers and troops under his coommand, for their brave and successful attack upon, and signal victory over the enemy, in their lines at Bennington ; and that Brigadier Stark, be appointed a Brigadier-General in the army of the United States.''*

---

* Journals of Congress, iii., 327.

Major-General John Stark was born in Londonderry, N. H., August 28, 1728. According to the New Hampshire Worthies, "he was of Irish descent; his parents emigrated from Ireland to America in 1719. In 1736 they removed to Derryfield, now Manchester, where John remained till he was twenty-four years old. In 1752 young Stark, lured on by his adventurous disposition, went on a hunting expedition among the wild regions of northern New Hampshire. Here he was captured by a party of the Abenaqui Indians and carried into Canada. For months he lay in captivity, when he was redeemed by a friend in Boston, for the sum of one hundred and three dollars. The next year he went on another excursion to the head waters of the Androscoggan. As guide, hunter, and trapper, two more years of his life went by. The old French war broke out, and longing for more toils and dangers, Stark threw himself into that struggle. When the news of the battle of Lexington reached him he was engaged at work in his saw-mill. Fired with indignation and a martial spirit he stopped for nothing, and in ten minutes was on his way to Boston. Receiving a colonel's commission, he availed himself of the enthusiasm of the day, and his own popularity, and in two hours enlisted over eight hundred men. His station was at Medford, but on that eventful day when the storm of battle hung over Bunker Hill he was in the fight with his troops, and during the whole of that dreadful conflict he evinced that intrepid zeal and consummate bravery which entitle him to honor and perpetual remembrance in the pages of history. The next year he went with his regiment to New York, where soon afterwards he joined our Northern army on its retreat from Canada. He took part in the disastrous attack on Three Rivers, and had command of the body of troops who were employed in fortifying the post of Mount Independence. We next find Stark at Trenton, where he shared largely in the glories of that ever memorable engagement. In the battle of Princeton he stood beside Washington and exhibited all that daring and intrepidity so peculiar to himself, and

On September 14th, Burgoyne crossed the Hudson, and encamped at Saratoga. The American army was at Bemis Heights, only a few miles away. Gates held the chief command—having been ordered by Congress to supersede Schuyler and under him, amongst others were Generals Stark, Whipple, Poor, and Nixon, as well as Morgan and his dreaded Irish-American riflemen. An attack made by the British on September 19th, was repulsed with heavy loss, and in a second battle on October 7th, they suffered a crushing defeat. During this conflict, the British General Fraser, with a body of picked men, pushed forward to turn the left flank of the Americans. His movement was noticed, and Morgan with his riflemen along with the brigade of Poor and a part of Learned's brigade were sent forward to meet him. Morgan drove Fraser back, and then wheeled and fell on the right flank of the British, "with

---

which never failed to inspire his men with confidence and courage. The following March he resigned his commission and retired to his farm. Insulted by Congress, triumphed over by younger and less able men, justice and self-respect impelled him to this course. But his patriotism still remained burning with undiminished vigor, and when Burgoyne came marching down from Canada, all was forgotten, and he took the most active measures in recruiting troops. Rallying around their favorite leader, the militia came pouring from all directions, and at the head of 1,400 men he marched upon the enemy and came up with them at Bennington. Here Stark reached the climax of his fame, by a glorious victory achieved over the British. The whole country hailed with joy, and the dark clouds were dispelled, which had rested like an incubus upon the land. He participated in the honors of Saratoga, and assisted in the council which arranged the surrender of Burgoyne. He also served in Rhode Island in 1778, and in New Jersey in 1780. In 1781 he was appointed Commander-in-Chief of the Northern department of the American army, and made Saratoga his headquarters. The two following years, though engaged in no battle, his duties were complicated and onerous, nor did he relinquish his valuable services till he could greet his native country as an independent nation."

such appalling force and impetuosity that their ranks were
at once thrown into confusion." He ordered his riflemen
to aim particularly at the English officers, in accordance
with the usual custom in the American army, and one of
them, Timothy Murphy, hit and mortally wounded Fraser.
Some people have seen fit to censure the American commanders for requiring their men to direct their fire upon
the British commissioned officers, rather than upon the
privates, and have censured Morgan for having given the
order referred to. But as Lossing says,* many "who
gloat over the horrid details of the slaying of thousands of
humble rank-and-filemen, as deeds worthy of a shout for
glory, and drop no tear for the slaughtered ones, affect to
shudder at such a cold-blooded murder of an officer, (the
killing of Fraser), upon the battle field. * * * * * * If
it is right to kill at all upon the field of battle, I can perceive no greater wrong in slaying a *general* than a *private*.
True he wears the badge of distinction, and the trumpet
of renown speaks his name to the world, but his life is no
dearer to himself and wife, and children, and friends, than
that of the humblest private who obeys his commands.
If Daniel Morgan was guilty of no sin, no dishonor, in ordering his men to fall upon, and slay those under the command of Fraser, he was also guiltless of sin and dishonor,
in ordering the sacrifice of their chief. Indeed it is probable that the sacrifice of his life saved that of hundreds, for
the slaughter was stayed."† The brutal conduct of the

---

* Lossing's Field Book of the Revolution, i., 62.

† Murphy was, like nearly all of Morgan's Irish-American riflemen, a
dead shot. He accompanied General Sullivan in his expedition against
the Indians in western New York, and nearly lost his life. In the
autumn of 1778 he was stationed in Schoharie county, where a girl of
sixteen fell in love with him and he resolved to marry her, though he
was twelve years her senior. The girl's parents did not approve of the

British General Prescott, toward Ethan Allen, when the latter was taken prisoner, and many similar instances of the vindictiveness of British officers, had filled the minds of the American soldiers with especial indignation, toward those who bore commissions in the British service, and who, so far from refusing to fight against the cause of liberty, as they could have done with propriety by resigning from the army, actually showed themselves the most malignant and inveterate of its enemies. The feeling against them naturally found vent in the most practical manner on the battle-field. After the battle, Burgoyne retreated to Saratoga, where he surrendered on October, 17. For many months previous to this event, Franklin, Deane, and Arthur Lee, as commissioners from Congress, had been in Paris urging the French Government to acknowledge the Independence of the United States. The French king and his ministers were favorably disposed: they sent substantial aid, though privately, to the Americans, and when the news of the surrender at Saratoga, reached Paris, hesitated no longer. A treaty of alliance was signed between the two nations, on Feb. 6, 1778, by which neither of the powers was to make war or peace without the consent of the other. This was the turning point of the contest.

Meanwhile Washington, who had remained in New Jersey, recruiting his army, learned that Howe, who had arrived in the Chesapeake, in July, was advancing toward Philadelphia. The commander-in-chief hastened forward to meet the British, and encountered them at Chads Ford, on the river Brandywine, about twenty-five miles south-west of

---

match, but she stole away barefooted one evening, went to the fort where her lover was stationed, and together they started for Schenectady, where they were married. In later days, Murphy became a man of considerable influence in political and other affairs. He died in 1818 of cancer in the throat.

Philadelphia, on September 11. The first encounter of
the day took place between a strong detachment of Knyphausen's division of Hessians, and the brigade of General
Maxwell.* The Irish American officer, drove the mercenaries back, but they were strongly reinforced, and he
was compelled to retreat across the river. He returned
again, and drove the enemy from the ground it occupied,
but heavy masses of British troops being sent against him
he was a second time forced to retire beyond the stream.

Sullivan who commanded the right wing of the American
army, misled by the reports of his scouts, was not fully
prepared for action, when the British burst upon him. His

---

* General William Maxwell was a native of Ireland. He joined the
army at the commencement of the war. In 1776, he was appointed
colonel and raised a battalion of infantry in New Jersey. He was with
General Schuyler on Lake Champlain, and in October, 1776, was appointed a brigadier-general in the Continental army. After the battle
of Trenton, he was engaged in harassing the enemy and during the
winter and spring of 1777, was stationed near the enemy's lines at Eliza-
bethtown. In the autumn of that year he was engaged in the battles of
Brandywine and Germantown, and during the succeeding winter he was
with the suffering army at Valley Forge. He was active in pursuit of
Clinton across New Jersey the following summer, and sustained an important part in the battle of Monmouth. After that engagement he was
left with Morgan to annoy the enemy's rear in their retreat towards
Sandy Hook. In June, 1780, he was engaged in the action at Springfield,
and in August of that year, he resigned. He was highly esteemed by
Washington who, on transmitting his resignation to Congress, said: "I
believe him to be an honest man, a warm friend to his country and
firmly attached to its interests." He died in November, 1798. Lossing's
Field Book of the Revolution, ii., 152.

There were two other Maxwells in the Revolutionary army who may
be alluded to here. Hugh, born in Ireland in 1733, who held a captain's commission at Bunker Hill, where he was wounded, was major in
Bailey's regiment at Saratoga, and lieutenant-colonel at the close of the
war; and his brother Thompson, born at Bedford, Mass., who was also
a brave soldier during the Revolutionary war.

men gave way, with the exception of Stirling's brigade—
in which was General Conway with eight hundred men,
who stood "firm as a rock," until the artillery of Cornwallis, who commanded the British advance, made fearful
havoc in their ranks.   Two of Sullivan's aids were killed,
Lafayette who fought beside him was wounded, and finally
the remnant of his division, finding itself unsupported, was
obliged to retreat.   Washington with Greene's division,
pushed forward to the support of Sullivan, and covered his
retreat; a Pennsylvania regiment, under Colonel—afterward
General—Walter Stewart, a native of Londonderry* dis-
playing great bravery on the occasion.   When Knyphausen
noticed the movement of Greene's division, which weakened the American line in his front, he advanced across the
river.   He was met, and held in check by Wayne, with a
much inferior force, until information was received of the
retreat of the main body of the Americans, when he too
fell back.   The approach of night ended the conflict, and
the national troops retreated to Chester, marching toward
Philadelphia next day, while the British remained on the
field.   The forces of the latter at the battle of the Brandywine, amounted to over seventeen thousand men, while the
Americans hardly numbered eleven thousand, and many of
their regiments were only raw militia.

---

* General Walter Stewart was born in Londonderry, Ireland.   He
came to America when quite young, and was so highly esteemed for his
soldierly qualities that he was made a colonel in the Continental army
when hardly twenty-one years of age, being known as "the boy colonel."
His conduct, however, justified the opinion of his friends, and he soon
was promoted to the rank of brigadier-general and took part in some of
the most important engagements of the war.   He became a member of
the Friendly Sons of St. Patrick of Philadelphia in 1779, and later assisted in founding the Hibernian Society of that city.   He married a
daughter of the patriotic Blair McClenachan.

The British, after an ineffectual effort on the part of Washington to prevent them, entered Philadelphia on September 26, Congress adjourning to Lancaster, and then to York, where it continued its sittings, until the enemy evacuated the city in the following summer. On first taking possession of Philadelphia, Howe stationed the main body of his army at Germantown. Washington determined, although his force was greatly inferior, to attack the enemy, and it was decided that the divisions of Sullivan and Wayne, flanked by Conway's brigade, should assail their front, while the Pennsylvania militia were to attack them in flank and rear. Washington accompanied the columns of Sullivan and Wayne. On the morning of October 4, Conway's brigade, being in advance, first drove the British back some distance, but some regiments of militia unable to withstand the superior numbers of the enemy by whom they were confronted, gave ground, and their retreat caused confusion in the American ranks. "Sullivan's division with a regiment of North Carolinians under the command of Colonel Armstrong, and assisted by a part of Conway's brigade, having driven the enemy to School-house Lane, in the center of Germantown, found themselves unsupported by other troops, and their ammunition exhausted. They could dimly perceive that the enemy were collecting in force on the right. At that moment, hearing the cry of a light horseman, that the enemy had surrounded them, and perceiving the fire at Chew's house, which was far in the rear, the Americans became panic stricken, and retreated with great precipitation. * * * The prize of victory was abandoned at the moment when another effort might have secured it."*

At the close of the year, 1777, Washington placed his

---

* Lossings's Field Book of the Revolution, ii., 112.

army in winter quarters at Valley Forge, about twenty miles north-west of Philadelphia. His troops at the time they commenced to build huts, December 19, numbered only eleven thousand, of whom nearly three thousand were unfit for duty, while the British army in Philadelphia, composed of "Britons, Germans, and provincials," was nearly twenty thousand strong. At this time, Conway was inspector-general of the army, a position conferred on him a little before by Congress, with the rank of major-general.* The winter of 1777–8 was extremely severe, and

---

* Major-General Thomas Conway was born in Ireland in 1733. He was educated in France, entered the army, attained the rank of colonel, and was made a Count. In 1777, on the recommendation of Silas Deane, he came to America to join the Continental army. He was almost immediately made a brigadier-general, and joined the army at Morristown. He fought bravely at Brandywine and Germantown, and proved that he had profited by his thirty years' experience in the art of war. He was soon appointed inspector-general of the army, with the rank of major-general, by Congress, notwithstanding the fact that Washington wrote a letter to a member of that body remonstrating against his promotion. Much has been said about his prominence in the "cabal" formed against the commander-in-chief, but the facts do not at all bear out the assertion that he was the instigator of the scheme. It is acknowledged that Generals Gates and Mifflin, and even the veteran patriot "Samuel Adams, with two or three others of the New England delegation in Congress, and one of the Virginia deputies," were among the "conspicuous actors" in this affair. Lossing admits this, and he says: "Whether the movement originated in personal ambition, or a sincere conviction of the necessity of making a change on account of the alleged 'Fabian slowness' of Washington in his military movements, is a question of difficult solution;" and, in another place he remarks: "How extensive was the dissaffection towards him (the commander-in-chief) among the officers of the army, it is difficult to determine, and it is equally difficult to fix a direct charge upon any individual of actual attempts to supersede Washington."—(*Field Book of the Revolution*, ii., 130–134.) "It appears clear," however, to the eminent writer just quoted, that Conway had been engaged "for a long time" with Mifflin and Gates "in endeavors to effect the removal of

the soldiers of the Revolutionary army at Valley Forge, suffered terribly. Thousands were barefooted, many had no blankets, the clothes of nearly all were ragged, and at times the whole force suffered for want of sufficient food. There was a scarcity of horses in the camp, and the men, naked and starving as they were, often yoked themselves to vehicles of their own construction in carrying wood or provisions when procured. Wayne, taking detachments of his brigade, made many excursions, in quest of provisions, and often foraged to within sight of the spires of Philadelphia. The brigades of Conway, Maxwell, McIntosh, Learned, and Poor, whose ranks were filled with Irish and Irish-Americans, bore their privations with heroic fortitude, as indeed, did all the sufferers at Valley Forge. "On the first of February, 1778, four thousand of the troops were incapable of any kind of service from want of cloth-

---

Washington from the chief command." But when it is remembered that Conway was hardly a year in the service altogether, common fairness will compel the conclusion that this view is manifestly exaggerated. General Sullivan, in his letter to Washington, says that Conway was "imprudently led into the cabal," and his statement is no doubt correct. Conway deserved blame, but others still more, and it must not be forgotten that after his duel with Cadwallader he wrote a frank and manly letter of regret and apology to the illustrious chief against whom he had offended, while others connected with the scheme sought to shelter themselves by evasions or denials of well proven facts, or by throwing all the blame on him after his return to France. In the letter referred to he expressed his "sincere grief for having done, written or said anything disagreeable" to Washington. "Justice and truth," he added, "prompt me to declare my last sentiments. You are, in my eyes, the great and good man. May you long enjoy the love, veneration and esteem of these States whose liberties you have asserted by your virtues." Conway, having resigned his commission in the spring of 1778, returned soon after to France, where he was made, in 1784, a marechal-de-camp, and appointed Governor of all the French possessions in India. He died in 1800.

ing.   The condition of the rest was very little better.   In
a word, out of the eleven or twelve thousand men that were
in camp, it would have been difficult to muster five thousand
fit for duty."*   In this crisis the hearts of the patriot
soldiers were gladdened by the arrival of relief from a distant quarter.   General Moylan, who had resigned his post
of commissary-general, in order to take command of a regiment of horse, had made known to his friends in Cork, his
native city, and to his brother the Catholic Bishop of the
diocese, the almost destitute condition of the American
army.   The sympathy of the men of the Irish city was
aroused.   They had a short time before assisted Ethan
Allen and his comrades, while being transferred as prisoners, to America, and now they privately and expeditiously
secured a ship and loaded her with large supplies of provisions, and clothing.   She was then sent to Boston, which
port she reached in safety, and her cargo was forwarded to
Valley Forge, for the patriot army."†

Sir Henry Clinton succeeded Howe as Commander-in-
Chief of the British, in the spring of 1778.   Fearing that
Washington might make a dash on, and capture New York,
he quietly evacuated Philadelphia, on June 18, and proceeded by land to the former city.   When the intelligence
reached Washington, he sent off Maxwell at once to check
Clinton's progress as much as possible, and then started in
pursuit at the head of his whole force.

The Americans following up the retreating invaders,
struck them near Monmouth court-house on June 2d, the
brigades of Maxwell and Morgan being the first to engage
the enemy.   Twenty thousand men were engaged in the
battle.   During the whole day the battle raged without

---

* Spencer's History of the United States, i., 520.
† Mooney's History of Ireland, p. 831.

advantage to either side. Twice the British attempted to turn the American flank, but they were repulsed. They then tried an assault on the right, but a battery under the immediate command of Knox, swept down their lines, and drove them back, bleeding and disheartened. Wayne was stationed with an advanced corps of his Pennsylvanians on a rising eminence, with a park of artillery. From this position he kept up a galling fire upon the English center, and repeatedly repulsed the royal grenadiers who had advanced to dislodge him with the bayonet. Moncton, their leader, perceiving that victory depended on driving Wayne from his position, harangued his men, and placing himself at their head, advanced in solid column upon the Pennsylvanians. The English advanced until within a few rods of the Americans, when their general, waving his sword, gave a shout and ordered his grenadiers to charge. At the same moment Wayne gave a signal; a terrible volley burst upon the assailants, and almost every British officer fell. Among them was their leader, Moncton. Over his dead body the Americans and English fought desperately, until at last the patriots secured it and carried it to the rear. At the same time a general assault was made along the whole line, and the enemy, beaten at every point, fell back. It was during the hottest part of the conflict that one of Knox's gunners, an Irishman, was shot down while in the act of firing his cannon. His wife (the same that had fired the last shot at Fort Clinton), saw him fall, and rushing to the spot, picked up the match, and fired the piece against the advancing columns of the enemy. She vowed she would fill her husband's place at the gun and avenge his death, and maintained her post at the gun, firing it with good effect until the battle was won. Lossing thus describes her: "It was during this part of the action that Molly, the wife of a cannonier, displayed great courage and presence of mind.

We have already noticed her bravery in firing the last gun at
Fort Clinton.   She was a sturdy young camp-follower, only
twenty-two years old, and in devotion to her husband she
illustrated the character of her countrywomen of the Emer-
ald Isle.   In the action in question, while her husband was
managing one of the field-pieces, she constantly brought him
water from a spring near by.   A shot from the enemy killed
him at his post; and the officer in command, having no
one competent to fill his place, ordered the piece to be
withdrawn.   Molly saw her husband fall as she came from
the spring, and also heard the order.   She dropped her
bucket, seized the rammer, and vowed she would fill the
place of her husband at the gun and avenge his death.
She performed the duty with a skill and courage which attracted the attention of all who saw her.   On the following
morning, covered with blood, General Greene presented her
to Washington, who, admiring her bravery, conferred upon
her the commission of sergeant.   By his recommendation
her name was placed on the list of half-pay officers for life.
After leaving the army she retired to Fort Montgomery,
among the Hudson highlands, where she died.   She usually
went by the name of *Captain Molly.*   The venerable widow
of General Hamilton, yet living (1852), told me that she
had often seen *Captain Molly.*   She described her as a
stout, fair-haired, young Irishwoman, with a handsome
piercing eye.   The French officers, charmed with the story
of her bravery, made her many presents.''*

The Americans slept on the field they had won, on the
night of the battle, but the British took advantage of the
darkness to steal away in the direction of Sandy Hook.
From this place they were conveyed by the British fleet,
under Lord Howe to New York, arriving there on the first

---

* Lossing, ii., 155.

of July. A few days later, the French fleet, twelve ships of the line, and six frigates with four thousand men, arrived at the entrance of Delaware Bay, having on board Silas Deane, one of the American commissioners, and M. Gerard, the first minister sent by France to the United States.

CHAPTER XIV.

THE IRISH IN THE WAR OF INDEPENDENCE (CONTINUED).

ON the arrival of the French fleet a plan was formed for driving the English from Rhode Island. Ten thousand men under Sullivan and Greene were assembled near Providence, and it was arranged that d'Estaing with his squadron should co-operate with the American land forces in an attack upon the British who had fortified themselves near Newport. Before Sullivan had made all his preparations, an English fleet under Howe appeared off the harbor of Newport, and the French Admiral sailed out to engage his enemy. They spent the principal part of that day (August 10, 1778) manœuvering for position, and on that following a violent storm arose which separated the combatants and severely damaged many of the ships. The action was consequently indecisive, and a few days after d'Estaing again appeared off Newport Harbor, but was prevented by his officers, who urged him to go to Boston and refit his fleet, from joining Sullivan in the projected attack. Upon the withdrawal of the French, for the purpose of repairing damages, the Americans were forced to abandon Rhode Island much to their disappointment and vexation.

The principal events which occurred during the latter part of 1778, were the massacre by the Tories and Indians of the people of Cherry Valley in November, and the capture of Savannah by the British on December 29.

On February 14, 1779, Gen. Pickens * with Colonel Dooly † (both Irish-Americans) and about three hundred and fifty men defeated a much superior force of Tories under Boyd at Kettle Creek, on the Broad River, in Oglethorpe county, Georgia. The fight lasted for two hours, when the Tories fled in confusion leaving over seventy dead on the field, and seventy-five of their number prisoners in the hands of the patriots, whose loss was only nine killed and twenty-three wounded. Lossing says that "This was one of the severest blows which Toryism in the South had yet received." It emboldened Lincoln, then in command

---

* Andrew Pickens was born in Paxton township, Pennsylvania, on the 19th of September, 1739. His parents were from Ireland. In 1752, he removed with his father to the Waxham settlement in South Carolina. He served as a volunteer in Grant's expedition against the Cherokees, in which he took his first lessons in the art of war. He became a warm republican when the Revolution broke out, and he was one of the most active of the military partisans of the South. From the close of the war until 1794, he was a member of the South Carolina legislature, when he was elected to a seat in Congress. He was commissioned a Major-General of the South Carolina militia in 1795; and was often a commissioner to treat with the Indians. President Washington offered him a brigade of light troops under General Wayne, to serve against the Indians in the Northwest, but he declined the honor. He died at his seat in Pendleton district, South Carolina, the scene of his earliest battles, on the 17th of August, 1817, at the age of 78 years. His remains lie by the side of his wife (who died two years before), in the grave-yard of the "old stone meeting-house" in Pendleton. In 1765, he married Rebecca Calhoun, aunt of the late John C. Calhoun, one of the most beautiful young ladies of the South.—*Lossing*, ii. 511.

† Col. John Dooly, born in South Carolina, of Irish parents, entered the Continental army in Georgia as captain, in 1776, and rising to the rank of colonel, was very active in the neighborhood of Savannah, until 1780, when a party of Tories, sent out from Augusta by Colonel Brown, entered his house in Wilkes county at midnight, and barbarously murdered him in the presence of his wife and children.—*McCall's History of Georgia*, ii. 306.

of the Southern army, to make an effort to drive the British back to Savannah.

Later in the spring of that year the mercenaries of King George, aided by the American Loyalists, burned Norfolk, Portsmouth, Suffolk, and Gosport in Virginia, as well as New Haven, Fairfield, Norwalk and other places in Connecticut.

On the first of June, 1779, Sir Henry Clinton captured the small forts at Stony Point and Verplancks, which commanded the passage of the Hudson and permitted free communication between the New England States and those to the South. Washington much regretted their loss, and determined to recapture them. After having made some changes in the position of the main army he directed Wayne to retake Stony Point. It was then the strongest fortress on the Hudson, and garrisoned by six hundred British regulars under the command of Lieutenant-Colonel Johnson. "The position of the fortress was such," says Lossing, "that it seemed almost impregnable. Situated upon a huge rocky bluff, an island at high water, and always inaccessible dry-shod, except across the narrow causeway in the rear, it was strongly defended by outworks and a double row of *abattis*. Upon three sides of the rock were the waters of the Hudson, and on the fourth was a morass deep and dangerous." But Wayne was not easily deterred by obstacles, and tradition avers that while conversing with Washington on the subject of this expedition he remarked with emphasis. "General I'll storm h—ll if *you* will only plan it." He resolved at all hazards to storm the fort, and waited for the ebbing of the tide and the first deep slumber of the garrison to move toward the works. His troops were divided into two columns. Lieutenant De Fleury led the van of the right, with one hundred and fifty volunteers. The van of the left was led by Major Stewart, an Irishman, and consisted of one hundred volunteers, each with unloaded muskets and fixed bayonets. An advance guard of twenty picked men for each company, under Lieutenants Gibbons and Knox, preceded them to remove the *abattis* and other obstructions. These composed the forlorn hope. Besides Gibbons and Knox, there were many other distinguished Irish officers with Wayne, who led the right division himself on that occasion. Colonel Moylan rushed side by side with him up the heights. Colonel Butler led the left division, having with him Major Murphy and two companies of the latter's command.

The Americans advanced to within pistol shot of the pickets before they were discovered, and driving before them the British outposts, forced their way onward at the bayonet's point. Wayne was struck on the head by a bullet, but though he believed for a moment that the wound was fatal he shouted to his aids as he fell, " Carry me into the fort for I will die at the head of my column." Fortunately he was not seriously hurt and in a few moments he was amongst his men, inside the works, and exulting in the surrender of the British. The latter lost seventy-three killed, while their commander and five hundred and forty-three officers and men were taken prisoners, the loss on the side of the victors only amounting to fifteen killed and eighty-three wounded. As soon as success was assured " Mad Anthony " sent the following brief dispatch to the Commander-in-chief.

STONY POINT, 16th July, 1779.
2 o'clock, A. M.
DEAR GEN'L :
   The fort and garrison, with Col. Johnston, are ours. Our officers and men behaved like men who are determined to be free.
Yours most sincerely,
GEN'L WASHINGTON.   ANT'Y WAYNE.

An attack ordered to be made upon the fort at Verplancks Point at the same time having failed, it was deemed advisable to dismantle and evacuate Stony Point. This work was completed on the eighteenth, and Wayne with his gallant band rejoined the main army. Everyone praised the dash and bravery of the intrepid Irish-American General, for what he had accomplished on this occasion. Even Gen. Chas. Lee, who was not on terms of the most cordial friendship with him, wrote saying, " I do most seriously declare, that your assault of Stony Point is not only the most brilliant, in my opinion, throughout the whole course of the war on either side, but it is the most brilliant I am acquainted with in history." Dr. Rush said in a letter, " Our streets rang for many days with nothing but the name of General Wayne. You are remembered constantly next to our great and good Washington. You have established the national character of our country, you have taught our enemies that bravery, humanity and magnanimity are the national virtues of the Americans." Congress voted Wayne its thanks " for his brave, prudent and soldierly conduct, " and resolved that a gold medal should be struck and presented to him. It also decided in accordance with the recommendation of Washington " That the value of the military stores taken at Stony Point be ascertained and divided among the gallant troops by whom it was reduced in such manner and proportions as the commander-in-chief shall prescribe." Gibbons, Stewart, Knox and De Fleury were also thanked and promoted by Congress.

In the month of July, Sullivan was sent at the head of a strong force to drive the Indians from Western New York, where they had committed great ravages, murdering, plundering and making prisoners of numbers of the people. Under him was placed Gen. James Clinton with fifteen hundred men. The two Irish-American Generals formed a junction at Tioga on August 22, their whole force amounting to five thousand men, with Hand, Maxwell, and Poor as brigade commanders, and Proctor's artillery, with a body of riflemen. They met the enemy near Elmira, the Indians being aided by a large force of Tories under the command of Brant and Sir John Johnson. After a hard struggle, lasting for over two hours, the savages and their more brutal allies were routed with heavy loss. Sullivan pursued his victory driving the enemy in all directions before him, until he reached the Genesee Valley. He then retraced his steps, the object of the expedition being accomplished, only taking care to send Col. Z. Butler of Wyoming to lay waste the Indian towns on the eastern shore of Cayuga Lake and leaving some small detachments behind for the protection of the people. This precaution proved to be of great advantage, for a short time after a large body of Tories and Indians, under Brant, Johnson and others, made another irruption into this district and attacked the Middle Fort (Middleburgh). The commander of this post, Woolsey, "concealed himself," according to Campbell's *Annals*, "at first with the women and children, and when driven out by the ridicule of his associates, crawled around the entrenchments on his hands and knees, amid the jeers and bravos of the militia who felt their courage revive as their laughter was excited by the cowardice of the major." The Irish rifleman, whom we have met before, Timothy Murphy, was, however, among the garrison, and his determination made amends for the commander's poltroonery. When Sir John Johnson sent a flag of truce to demand a surrender, he fired on the bearer, as a warning not to approach, and when ordered by Woolsey to desist he refused to obey and excused himself by saying that the enemy never had shown any regard for military courtesy. Another flag was sent later which Murphy again warned back by a bullet, and when Woolsey again ordered him to cease firing, the simple rifleman plainly expressed the opinion that his commander was a coward who meant to surrender the fort, and that he would not allow it. This proceeding was repeated; once the officers and regulars threatened Murphy with death for his disobedience of orders, but the militia who esteemed him highly took his part and set the others at defiance. His boldness was rewarded by success. Johnson, suspecting from the refusal to treat with his messenger that the garrison was much stronger than it really was, gave up the siege, and moved in another direction.

The siege of Savannah took place in September, 1779, and some regiments of the Irish Brigade in the French service took part in it. Here it may be as well to say that even before the Treaty of Paris several Irish officers in the French service came to America to aid the patriots. Amongst these were Col. Roche de Fermoy, Col. Hand and others of the supernumerary or reformed officers of the Irish brigade. "As this corps," says the announcement of the sailing of those gentlemen for America, "is known to contain some of the best disciplined officers in Europe, there is no doubt but that they will meet with all suitable encouragement." When hostilities between France and England broke out the Irish regiments in France, who considered themselves entitled to serve *before* all other corps against the English *—a claim more especially advanced on this occasion by the

---

* Lieutenant-General Count Arthur Dillon commences his narrative of the services rendered in this war, by his own and the other Irish regiments, in these words : "*On a vu que les regimens Irlandois ont ete constamment employes dans toutes les guerres precedentes ; ils ont toujours reclame le privilege de marcher les premiers contre les Anglais dans tous les climats ou la France leur feroit la guerre,*" *&c.* That is, "the Irish regiments, as we see, have been constantly employed in all the preceding wars. These regiments have always claimed the privilege in all the countries in which France waged war against England, of marching foremost against that nation. It was owing to this principle that the regiment of Dillon demanded and obtained the right of serving in America."

regiment of Dillon—were not long left unemployed. The Regiment just named embarked April 5th, 1779, at Brest, to the number of 1,000 men, subsequently increased to 1,400, in the squadron of M. de la Motte. The junction of this squadron from Brest, with that of the Count d'Estaing at Martinique, enabled the French to undertake the conquest of the island of Grenada in the West Indies. The object aimed at in attacking the British possessions in that quarter, was to create a diversion in favor of the Americans, and compel a withdrawal from the continent of at least a portion of the British forces. On July the 2d, 2,300, men, for the most part Irish, under the command of Dillon, landed in Grenada and attacked their ancient enemies, the Count d'Estaing himself leading the Irish Grenadiers. The assault was successful, and Lord Macartney, the Governor, surrendered at discretion. After having defeated the English Admiral, Byron, and driven him to take refuge at St. Christopher's, d'Estaing sailed with his troops for Savannah, and joined General Lincoln in an attack on that city, then held by the British. This took place on October 9. Owing to a heavy fog a part of the Franco-American forces lost their way in a swamp through which lay their march, and the assault was not successful. Colonel Browne, of Dillon's Regiment, planted the French colors twice on the fortifications and in a third attempt was killed. Here also fell the heroic Irish Sergeant Jasper and Count Pulaski of the American forces. D'Estaing too was wounded in the arm and thigh early in the action and carried to his camp. Colonel Browne was a warm friend of the French Commander, and on the latter's deciding to attack Savannah, contrary to the opinion of the other officers, the brave Colonel remarked to the Count that though he disapproved of his opinion, he should have no cause to complain of his conduct. Accordingly he marched

his regiment immediately to the attack, and fell during the
hottest of the conflict. The Count de Segur thus speaks
of another distinguished officer of the Brigade, who took
part in the attack on Savannah and was subsequently Colonel
of the regiment of Walsh. " I will narrate an anecdote of
my friend Lynch that will give an idea of his singular
bravery, and of the originality of his disposition. Lynch,
after being engaged in the campaigns of India, served,
before he was employed in the army of Rochambeau, under
the orders of the Count d'Estaing, and distinguished himself particularly at the too-memorable siege of Savannah.
M. d'Estaing, at the most critical moment of that sanguinary affair, being at the head of the right of one column,
directed Lynch to carry an urgent order to the third column,
which was on the left. These columns were within grape-
shot range of the enemy's entrenchments, and on both sides
a tremendous firing was kept up. Lynch, instead of passing through the centre, or in the rear of the column, proceeded coolly through the shower of balls and grape-shot
which the French and English were firing at each other. It
was in vain that M. d'Estaing, and those who surrounded
him, cried to Lynch to take another direction. He went on,
executed his order, and returned the same way; that is to
say, under a vault of flying shot, and where everyone expected to witness his instant destruction. ' Zounds !' said
the General on seeing him return unhurt: ' the devil must
be in you surely ! Why did you choose such a road as
that, in which you might have expected to perish a thousand
times over ? ' ' Because it was the *shortest*,' answered Lynch.
Having uttered these few words he went, with equal coolness, and joined the group that was most earnestly engaged
in storming the place. He was," adds Segur, " afterward
promoted to the rank of Lieutenant-General, and commanded our infantry in the first engagement we had with
the Prussians on the Heights of Valmy, in 1792."

In consequence of the lateness of the season, d'Estaing sailed a few days after for the West Indies, while Lincoln and his little army proceeded to Charleston.

On May 12, 1780, Sir Henry Clinton succeeded in becoming master of Charleston, notwithstanding all the efforts of Lincoln, and the disaster caused great depression throughout the South, which was intensified by the massacre of Buford's regiment by Tarleton at the Waxhaws—the home of the future victor of New Orleans—seventeen days after the surrender of Charleston. The English General had proposed terms to Buford which he knew were too humiliating to be accepted, and almost without waiting for the American's reply, Tarleton with his cavalry dashed on the patriots and hewed them down, unprepared and in many cases unarmed as they were. Lossing says that this affair " was nothing less than a cold-blooded massacre," and that " Tarleton's quarter became proverbial as a synonym for cruelty;" and even Stedman the British historian admits that " on this occasion the virtue of humanity was totally forgot." Horror seized on the people in the vicinity. Women and children fled as fast as possible from the monsters who had perpetrated the atrocity, and amongst them were the widowed mother of Andrew Jackson, with himself and his brother Robert. Both these boys were, however, made prisoners by the British, and both were severely wounded by a ruffianly officer whose boots they refused to clean; Robert dying soon after from the effects of the sabre cut which he had received, while Andrew bore the mark of the Englishman's sword to his grave. But he paid back the deep debt at New Orleans.

The tidings of these and other reverses suffered by the patriots in the Carolinas, soon reached the North, and excited deep apprehension, and dismay amongst many who wished well to the cause of freedom. But soon there ap-

peared a rift in the cloud. At this time, as Hood * says,
"when everything depended upon a vigorous prosecution
of the war, when the American army, morever was in imminent danger of being compelled to yield to famine, a far
more dangerous enemy than the British, when the urgent
expostulations of the commander-in-chief and the strenuous
recommendations of Congress had utterly failed to arouse
a just sense of the dangers of the crisis; the genuine love
of country and most noble self sacrifices of some individuals
in Philadelphia, supplied the place of the slumbering patriotism of the country and saved her cause from most dis-
graceful ruin.   In this great emergency was conceived and
promptly carried into operation ' the plan of the Bank of
Pennsylvania, established for supplying the army of the
United States with provisions for two months.' On the
17th of June, 1780, ninety-three Philadelphia merchants
signed the following paper:—

' Whereas, in the present situation of the public affairs in
the United States, the greatest and most vigorous exertions
are required for the management of the just and necessary
war in which they are engaged with Great Britain: We, the
subscribers, deeply impressed with the sentiments that
should, on such an occasion, govern us in the prosecution
of a war, on the event of which our own freedom and that
of our posterity, and the freedom and independence of the
United States, are all involved, hereby severally pledge our
property and credit for the several sums specified and mentioned after our names, in order to support the credit of a
bank to be established for furnishing a supply of provisions
for the armies of the United States.   And do hereby severally promise and engage to execute to the directors of the
said bank, bonds of the form hereunto annexed. Witness
our hand, this 17th day of June, in the year of our Lord,
1780.' "

Then follow the names of the subscribers with the sums

---

* " Account of the Friendly Sons of St. Patrick of Philadelphia."

respectively subscribed, amounting to £300,000 ($1,500,-
000), payable in gold or silver. Of this amount twenty-seven
members of the Friendly Sons of St. Patrick subscribed
£103,500—more than one-third.

Twenty of these who were of Irish birth or blood—the
others being honorary members—subscribed the following
amounts:—

Blair McClenachan	£10,000	John Patton	2,000
I. M. Nesbitt & Co	5,000	Benjamin Fuller	2,000
Richard Peters	5,000	George Meade & Co	2,000
Samuel Meredith	5,000	John Donaldson	2,000
James Mease	5,000	Henry Hill	5,000
Thomas Barclay	5,000	Kean & Nichols	4,000
Hugh Sheil	5,000	James Caldwell	2,000
John Dunlap	4,000	Samuel Caldwell	1,000
John Nixon	5,000	John Shee	1,000
George Campbell	2,000	Sharp Delany	1,000
John Mease	4,000	Tench Francis	5,500
Bunner, Murray & Co	6,000		

Total..................... £88,500 = $442,500.00

The Society of the Friendly Sons of St. Patrick was
founded in 1771, its first President being General Moylan,
brother of the Catholic Bishop of Cork. It included among
its members some of the purest and bravest of the citizens
and soldiers of the young Republic, and even the Father of
his country himself was enrolled in its ranks and attended
its gatherings.

Within a month after the fresh proof of Irish-American
patriotism, fidelity and generosity above alluded to had been
given, a French fleet under Admiral de Ternay, having on
board 6,000 men, at the head of whom was Count Rochambeau, arrived at Newport, R. I. The spirits of the patriots
rose again, and they prepared with confidence for the final
struggle against British despotism.

On August 7th, Sumter attacked the British and Tories

at Hanging Rock, N. C. His troops were chiefly Irish-Americans belonging to the district. Opposed to them were the Prince of Wales' American regiment, the infantry of Tarleton's legion, and several Loyalist corps. After a hard-fought engagement lasting four hours, the patriots forced their enemies to give ground; but just at that moment a reinforcement from Tarleton arrived and under those circumstances Sumter did not feel strong enough to follow up his advantage and contented himself with bringing off the prisoners and booty he had already captured. Amongst his killed and wounded on that day were some gallant Irish-Americans, including Captain John McClure * "one of the master spirits of South Carolina," Capt. Read of North Carolina, Capt. McCulloch, Ensign McClure, and many of the bold and determined patriots known as the "Chester Rocky Creek Irish." Among other officers, who under Sumter, about this time proved themselves worthy of honor and remembrance, were Cols. Irvine, Lacy and Neil, who was killed at Rocky Mount.

Gates' defeat at Camden on August 16, where Col.

---

* John McClure was a nephew of the venerable and patriotic Judge Gaston, whose nine sons fought beside him in the patriot ranks. General Davie said, speaking of McClure, "Of the many brave men with whom it was my fortune to become acquainted in the army, he was one of the bravest ; and when he fell, we looked on his loss as incalculable." The hero sank to the earth, pierced by two bullets, at the first fire of the Loyalists, and with him fell four of his cousins, sons of Judge Gaston. "When his friends came to his aid, he urged them to leave him and pursue the enemy. After the battle, he was taken with other wounded soldiers to Waxham church, where his mother went to nurse him. Thence he was removed to Charlotte, and on the eighteenth, the very day when his commander was surprised at Fishing Creek, he expired in Liberty Hall, where the celebrated Mecklenburg Resolutions had been drawn up. McClure was a native of Chester district, and his men were known as the Chester Rocky Creek Irish."—*Lossing*, ii. 457.

Rutherford * was taken prisoner, led to his being superseded by Greene who was more fortunate than his predecessors.

On Jan. 31, 1781, Morgan who commanded the Western division of the army of the South, met Tarleton at the Cowpens, S. C. The patriot general had under his command 400 continental infantry under Col. Howard † of the Maryland Line, a dashing Irish-American officer, besides a considerable force of militia and a body of dragoons under Col. Washington. His advance was composed of a body of militia, numbering about three hundred, headed by Gen.

---

* General Griffith Rutherford was an Irishman by birth. He resided in the Locke settlement, and in 1775, represented Rowan county in the convention at Newbern. In 1776, he led a large force into the Cherokee country, and assisted the people of North Carolina in destroying their towns and villages. He was appointed Brigadier-General by the Provincial Congress, in April, 1776. He commanded a brigade at Camden, and was taken prisoner by the British. He was soon exchanged, however, and was in command at Wilmington when that place was evacuated by the British at the close of the war. He was a State senator in 1784, and soon afterward removed to Tennessee, where he died. A county in North Carolina bears his name, as does also one in Tennessee.—*Lossing*, ii. 391. Drake says that he was "a brave and patriotic man." One of his descendants to-day is Senator Lucas, of West Virginia, the foremost of Southern orators, whose finest address was made on "Daniel O'Connell, the Liberator," before the West Virginia University ; and who, on the paternal side, is descended from the famous Irish patriotic Lucas family.

† John Eager Howard was born in Baltimore county, Maryland, in 1752. His mother was Johanna O'Carroll, one of the family of Ely O'Carroll. He fought at White Plains, Germantown, Monmouth, Cowpens and Guildford Court House. In 1788, he was chosen Governor of Maryland, which office he held for three years. Washington offered him a seat in the Cabinet as Secretary of War, but for private reasons he declined the honor. In 1796, he was elected to the Senate of the United States, where he served until 1803, when he retired from public life. He died in 1827.

Andrew Pickens, who had under him Captains Beatty * and Hammond of South Carolina, men of the same stock with himself. The battle began about nine in the morning. It was long and fiercely contested. Several of the American officers displayed dauntless bravery and great skill, and their exertions were rewarded by the defeat of the red-coats, who lost, besides their wounded and five hundred prisoners, over a hundred killed, and left in the hands of the victors, two pieces of artillery, eight hundred muskets, two standards, a hundred dragoon horses, besides military stores of all kinds. Congress voted a gold medal to Morgan, a silver one to Howard, a sword to Pickens, and special thanks to the other officers engaged.

The battle of Guildford Court House, fought on March 15, 1781, though resulting in a nominal victory for the British, proved of little advantage to them. The Americans would have won in all probability had it not been for the conduct of some newly raised North Carolina militia, who weakened at a critical moment. Two Maryland regiments under Cols. Ford and Gunby, Col. Lynch with a battalion of Virginia riflemen, Washington and Howard with their veteran troops, fought bravely, and proved themselves well able to meet the British regulars, on anything like an equal footing.

In June, 1781, Augusta surrendered to the Americans. In the siege of that post Captains O'Neill and Armstrong, at the head of some companies of cavalry, rendered good service and shared in the glory of compelling the British to lay down their arms.

At the battle of Eutaw Springs, which was fought September 8th, when Greene commanded, and the Americans

---

* Capt. William Beatty was born of Irish parents in Frederick county, Maryland, in 1758. He was killed at the battle of Guildford Court House, and to his fall is attributed the defeat of the Americans.

lost the fruits of victory by the same conduct which prevented the Irish insurgents of '98 from holding possession of New Ross after having taken it; Pickens commanded a South Carolina division and did much with Howard, Lee and other officers to retrieve the fortunes of the day, when they were endangered by the carelessness and over-confidence of the patriot soldiers.

A short time after the battle of Guildford Court-House Cornwallis moved northward leaving one of his subordinates in command in the South. Lafayette when at Elkton, Maryland, heard of the Englishman's arrival at Petersburg, Va., and advanced to meet him, but had not sufficient strength to cope with his foe. Washington was at this time contemplating an attack on New York, but various circumstances induced him to defer it, and instead to move against Cornwallis. The latter had fortified himself at Yorktown, Lafayette being within a few miles but too weak to strike, when the French fleet under the Count de Grasse arrived in the Chesapeake, and soon after Washington with Rochambeau reached Williamsburg. The allied armies completely invested Yorktown on the last of September 1781, and on the nineteenth of October the English general surrendered. He had been guilty of outrages in America almost as atrocious as those afterwards carried out under his orders in Ireland during '98, had acted more like a marauder than a general, and had caused a loss to the people of nearly fifteen millions of dollars, but now his day was over, and he was compelled to submit to those he had regarded and treated as rebels, and whom he had once hoped to have completely at his mercy. What that would have been we may judge from his conduct towards the Irish insurgents, seventeen years later.

By this surrender, there fell into the hands of the allies over seven thousand prisoners, exclusive of seamen, seventy-five brass and one hundred and seventy iron guns, nearly seven thousand five hundred muskets and twenty eight regimental standards, besides large quantities of military supplies. Two Generals and thirty-one field officers were among the prisoners.   Cornwallis feigned illness in order to avoid the humiliation of delivering up his sword, and sent one of his generals (O'Hara) to perform his part in the ceremony. Lincoln was then deputed by Washington to receive the sword of his conquered foe.

When the English marched to the field of humiliation to throw down their arms and deliver up their standards and battle-flags, Ensign Wilson, of Clinton's Brigade, an Irish-American aged eighteen years and the youngest commissioned officer in the army, received them from the hands of the conquered Britons.   Washington immediately dispatched one of his aids Col. Tilghman, to announce the glad tidings to Thomas McKean, President of the Continental Congress at Philadelphia.

McKean rose from his bed at midnight and spread the news over the city.   The watchmen too, when proclaiming the hour, adding "and Cornwallis is taken," and the old State House bell rang out its notes of gladness. Philadelphia was illuminated that night, and next day Charles Thomson read the dispatch to Congress, which thereupon passed appropriate resolutions, and thanked particularly Washington, Rochambeau and De Grasse.

Knox, for his splendid services as chief of artillery, received the commission of a major general on the occasion, a well-merited honor.

The Continental army after the surrender, was sent into winter quarters in Pennsylvania, New Jersey, and on the Hudson.   The French remained in Virginia ready to render service in the North or South until the summer of 1782, when they marched to the camp of the Continentals on the

Hudson, proceeding thence to New England in the autumn and sailing to the West Indies in December.

The English were still reluctant to acknowledge the independence of America, the king and Royal family being especially bitter against those whom they had so long hoped to punish as " rebels."

The Marquis of Rockingham died July 1, 1782, and was succeeded by Lord Shelburne. According to Franklin, King George III. said to the new minister on his acceptance of office, " I will be plain with you. The point *next my heart; and which I am determined, be the consequence what it may, never to relinquish but with my crown and life, is to prevent a total unequivocal recognition of the independence of America.* Promise to support me on this ground and I will leave you unmolested on every other, and with full power as the prime minister of the kingdom."

But the impotence of Britain to place its hated yoke again upon the neck of a free people was palpable to all, and on November 30, 1782, Provisional Articles of Peace were signed at Paris between the Commissioners of the United States and those of England. On January 20th of the following year, it was agreed that hostilities should cease between the belligerents, and the news reaching America on the 24th of March, Washington issued a proclamation of peace on the eighth anniversary of the battle of Lexington, April 19, 1783. A definite treaty was finally signed at Paris, on September 3d of the same year, by which Britain acknowledged the Independence of the United States, it being out of her power to prevent it any longer.

When peace was proclaimed a solemn *Te Deum* was chanted in St. Joseph's Church, Philadelphia, at the request of the Marquis de la Luzerne, Minister Plenipotentiary of the French Government. Washington was present with his principal generals, as were also the members of Congress and of the Assembly and State Council of Pennsylvania. The Abbe Bendale preached on the occasion.

"*Who but He,*" exclaimed the sacred orator, "*He in whose hands are the hearts of men, could inspire the alliea troops with the friendship, the confidence, the tenderness of brothers?* . . . . Let us beseech the God of mercy to shed on the councils of the king of France your ally, that spirit of wisdom, of justice, and of mercy, which has rendered his reign glorious. Let us likewise entreat the God of wisdom to maintain in each of the States that intelligence by which the United States are inspired. . . . Let us offer Him pure hearts, unsullied by private hatred or public dissension; and let us, with one will and one voice, pour forth to the Lord that hymn of praise by which Christians celebrate their gratitude and His glory—*Te Deum Laudamus.*"

When information of the signing of the definitive treaty reached the English headquarters here, Sir Guy Carleton gave notice that he should be ready for the final evacuation of New York on the 25th of November. George Clinton, by virtue of his office as Governor of New York, was to take charge of the city, and repaired to its vicinity to await events, accompanied by Washington. By request of Carleton, to prevent any disorder which might occur as the British retired, a detachment of American troops marched into the city on the morning appointed, down to near the junction of Third Ave. and the Bowery, to a point where they remained until the afternoon.* As the rear guard of the

---

* The prospect of peace and the acknowledgment by the British Government of the Independence of the United States, was far from affording pleasure to those here who had signalized themselves as loyalists. Their active and merciless zeal in the cause of Britain during the war had made them extremely obnoxious to their neighbors and to portions of their own families. They feared with reason the vengeance of those who escaped from the sugar house and provost, and North Dutch Church (then a prison house, where hundreds died of cold and starvation), and whose exasperation had been kindled to a flame. They therefore judged

British army began to embark, they moved slowly forward to the Battery and took possession of the fort. Major General Knox was appointed to the command of the United States troops on the occasion, with directions to make all suitable arrangements for the triumphal entry of the victors.

The American soldiers marched into the city in the following order:—

A Squadron of Dragoons.
Advanced Guard of Light Infantry.
A Battery of Artillery.
Battalion of Light Infantry.
Battalion of Massachusetts Troops.
Rear Guard, commanded by Major Burnett.

After the troops had taken possession Gen. Washington and Governor George Clinton made their public entry in the following manner:—

The General and the Governor, with their Suites, on horseback.
The Lieutenant-Governor and the Members of the Council for the temporary government of the Southern District of New York.
Major-General Knox and the Officers of the Army, eight abreast.
Citizens on horseback, eight abreast.
The Speaker of the Assembly and Citizens on foot, eight abreast.

Later in the day Gen. Clinton gave a dinner at Fraunce's tavern, at which the Commander-in-Chief and other general officers were present. Among the toasts were the following:—

The American Army.
The fleets and armies of France which have served in America.
The memories of those heroes who have fallen for our freedom.

---

it best to prevent the evil and hide themselves. Some of them found a home in " the mother country," where their descendants now live, and others in Canada and Nova Scotia. The first of these expatriated colonists set sail in a fleet of transports in October, 1782. Similar depopulations took place during the following twelve months. According to the manuscript report of Brook Watson, British Commissioner-General, dated New York, November 24, 1783, the total number of persons—men, women and children—who *left New York during the year was twentynine thousand two hundred and forty-four.*

May justice support what courage has gained.

The vindicators of the rights of mankind in *every quarter of the globe.*

May America be an asylum to the persecuted of the earth.

May a close union of the States guard the temple they have erected to liberty.

May the remembrance of this day be a lesson to princes and tyrants.

Gen. Washington lingered a few days after the British had left, fixing his headquarters at Fraunce's, where on Dec. 4th, his officers assembled to bid him farewell. The scene was an affecting one. The dangers and privations of years had knit officers and General together as comrades, and now that the object of all was attained the pang of separation was felt. As the moment came he turned to the company and with kindliest parting words said: " I now take leave of you, and most devoutly wish that your latter days may be as prosperous and happy as your former ones have been glorious and honorable. I cannot come to each, but would be obliged if each one would come and take me by the hand." They obeyed in silence—Knox first, whom he kissed, and then the others embraced him in turn while the tears ran down their cheeks. Then turning silently from the weeping group he passed from the room and walked to Whitehall, followed by his comrades where a barge was in waiting to convey him to Paulus Hook (now Jersey City). Having entered the boat, he bade them adieu with a silent gesture, and the officers returned to their place of rendezvous, mute and dejected at the loss of their leader. Washington proceeded to Annapolis, where Congress was then in session, and resigning his commission as commander-in-chief, hastened to Mount Vernon to resume the duties of a private citizen.

CHAPTER XV.

THE capture, already alluded to, of the English vessel
Margaretta, by Jeremiah O'Brien at Machias, Maine, on
May 11, 1775, led to the first steps taken by the Provincial
Congress of Massachusetts, towards employing a naval force.
O'Brien brought the prisoners he had taken to Watertown,
where the Provincial Congress was in session, and by order
of that body was placed in command of a cruiser, in which
he did good service. On June 7th, the Massachusetts Congress first acted on the subject of a navy. It is curious to
notice the caution with which it moved. It appointed a
committee to consider the expediency of establishing a
number of small armed vessels to cruise on our sea coasts,
for the protection of our trade and the annoyance of our
enemies: and that the members be enjoined, by order of
Congress, to observe secrecy in the matter. On the 8th,
this committee was ordered to sit forthwith. On the 10th,
an addition was made to it. On the 11th, in a proposed
address to the Continental Congress, it apprised that body
of the proposition under discussion to fit out armed vessels.
The committee reported on the 12th. On the 13th, the
report was considered and postponed till three o'clock,
when the committees of safety and supplies were notified.
A very long debate on the report then took place, and the
further consideration of it was postponed until the following
Friday. The battle of Bunker Hill prevented further proceeding. Nothing beyond building a few boats appears to

have been done until after this period,—among them, barges called fire-boats.*

On October 13, 1775, the Continental Congress ordered two small cruisers to be fitted out for the purpose of intercepting supplies intended for the British.   On the 29th of the same month a resolution was passed, by which merchant vessels were prohibited from flying pennants in presence of continental ships, and the day following two more cruisers, larger than those first authorized, were ordered to be equipped.   The wanton burning of Falmouth (Portland) by the English under Admiral Graves, prompted Congress to pass a general prize-law, by which the capture of British vessels was authorized, and on December 13th the construction of fourteen additional cruisers was authorized.

" By the close of the year 1775, Congress had authorized the equipment of seventeen men-of-war, varying in force from ten to thirty guns.   These ships, however, were much inferior to what vessels of the same rate would be now. Their armaments were light sixes, nines, or twelves, carronades not having yet been introduced.   A serious difficulty was found in procuring suitable officers.   Competent seamen there were enough, but officers accustomed to the discipline of a navy were rare: indeed, except a few who had left the royal service before the war, none were to be had.   A large number of Americans, it is true, were in the British navy, where they occupied all ranks, from that of a midshipman up to post-captain; but there is only a single authenticated instance of such a person having thrown up his commission.   Congress was accordingly compelled to select its officers principally from such masters and mates of merchant-vessels as were most conspicuous for seamanship, presumed courage, habits of enterprise, and the capacity for command." †

---

* Frothingham's *Siege of Boston*, iii.

† Peterson's *American Navy*.

One officer of the right sort was speedily found in the person of John Barry, a native of Wexford, Ireland, who, having followed the sea from his youth, was then in command of the *Black Prince* of Philadelphia. He was regarded by those best qualified to judge, as eminently fitted, by his skill and patriotism, for the position of a commander in the infant navy and was honored with one of the first naval commissions given by Congress. He promptly gave up " the finest ship and the first employ in America and entered into the service of his country " with alacrity. To him was committed the duty of superintending the fitting out of the first American fleet, a difficult one, but performed by him with rare ability. When this task was completed he was appointed to the command of the brig *Lexington*, of sixteen guns, in which vessel he left the capes of Delaware on his first cruise as a naval officer, in February, 1776. This was the " first armed continental ship that went to sea, an honor long claimed for the squadron under Commodore Hopkins, but in violation of the truth.'¹* On April 17th, he fell in with the British armed tender *Edwards*, which he captured after a hot action of over an hour. This was the first capture of any English vessel of war by a regular American cruiser commissioned by the Continental Congress. His reputation was so much enhanced by this action, that he was soon after given command of the *Effingham*, one of the three large frigates then building at Philadelphia, but as during the severe winter his ship, when finished, was kept ice-bound in the Delaware, he joined the army until navigation opened, acting as aid to Gen. Cadwalader and rendering efficient service in the operations in the vicinity of Trenton. When the British army under Lord Howe took possession of Philadelphia, it was thought necessary to

---

* *Ibid.*

send the American vessels of war up the Delaware and they were, accordingly, removed to Whitehall. About this time the English Commander, recognizing the great abilities of Barry, caused an offer to be made to him of fifteen thousand guineas ($76,000) and the command of a British ship of the line, if he would abandon the Revolutionary cause. But the faithful Irishman spurned the tempter's proposal, and indignantly replied " I have devoted myself to the cause of my country, and not the value or command of the whole British fleet can seduce me from it." Soon after this, he gave the English a proof that they had not under-estimated his talents by performing an act which has been justly regarded as unequalled during the war, for boldness of design and dexterity of execution. With only twenty-eight men in four boats he pulled down the river, intending to strike a blow at some of the enemy's vessels anchored near Philadelphia. He was noticed when passing the city, but dashing on, escaped without injury, and met off Port Penn a British schooner of ten guns, with four transports loaded with supplies for Howe's army. He boarded and captured the schooner and seized the transports, but just then, two more of the enemy's cruisers approached, on which he destroyed his prize and escaped back to his post without the loss of a man. " The courage that inspired this small and heroic band," says the *National Portrait Gallery*, " is not alone sufficient to account for his wonderful success, but it must be ascribed to a combination of daring bravery and consummate skill by which the diminutive power under his command was directed with unerring rapidity and irresistible force." *

---

* For this daring exploit, Barry received the following letter from the Commander-in-chief :

HEADQUARTERS, 12th March, 1778.

" To CAPTAIN JOHN BARRY—

" *Sir :* I have received your favor of the 9th inst., and congratulate

The British having succeeded in destroying the *Effingham* and the other ships at Whitehall, Barry was appointed to the command of the *Raleigh*, of thirty-two guns. He sailed from Boston in his new ship on September 25th, 1778. On the day following he encountered two English vessels, with which he had a long and desperate conflict, but was at last compelled to run his ship ashore in order to avoid capture. One of the enemy's vessels carried fifty guns and the other twenty-eight. Congress soon after appointed him to the command of a seventy-four, then building, but it was finally concluded to present her to the King of France, and he was transferred to the *Alliance* of thirty-six guns, the finest frigate in the United States service. In her he fought and captured the English ships *Atlanta* and *Trepassy*, after a hotly contested action. This was considered the most brilliant naval battle of the year. In 1782, when returning from Havana, he encountered a British squadron and attacked and disabled one of the frigates which belonged to it. This vessel's commander, Vaughan, afterwards Admiral, declared some years after that he had never seen a ship so ably fought as was the *Alliance* during that conflict. It was on that occasion that Barry, when hailed by a British commander with the question "What ship is that?" etc., replied "The United States ship *Alliance*, saucy Jack Barry,

---

you on the success which has crowned your gallantry and address in the late attack upon the enemy's ships. Although circumstances have prevented you from reaping the full benefits of your conquest, yet there is ample consolation in the degree of glory which you have acquired. You will be pleased to accept of my thanks for the good things which you were so polite as to send me, with my own wishes that a suitable recompense may always attend your bravery.

"I am sir, &c.,

GEO. WASHINGTON."

half-Irishman and half-Yankee—who — — are you?"*
After the Revolution Barry continued as senior officer at
the head of the navy until his death.†

Capt. Burke, who was appointed by Congress in February,
1776, commander of the *Warner*, one of the four vessels
then ready for service, showed himself an efficient and
active officer during the war.

Capt. Benjamin Dunn and Lieutenant John Fanning also
received commissions from Congress in 1776, and distinguished themselves in various engagements, as did several
other Irish-American naval officers.

Among the naval commanders supplied by Rhode Island
for the navy in the Revolution, were Captains Murphy,
Stacey, Read and Simmons, Irish-Americans, who showed
themselves to be brave and skillful in the performance of
their duties.

---

* " This is the ship *Alliance*
    From Philadelphia town,
And proudly bids defiance
    To England's king and crown.
As Captain on the deck I stand
    To guard her banner true,
Half Yankee and half Irishman ;
    What tyrant's slave are you ?"—*Collins.*

† John Barry, "the Father of the American Navy," was born at
Tacumshane, Wexford county, Ireland, in 1745. He early conceived a
fondness for a sea-faring life, and was placed at a youthful age on board of
a merchantman, sailing between Philadelphia and Cork. By attention
to his duties, as well as by study, he soon fitted himself for the command
of a ship, and was made in 1770, when only 25 years old, Captain of the
Black Prince, owned by Reese Meredith, of Philadelphia, father of Samuel Meredith, of the Friendly Sons of St. Patrick, of that city. General
Washington, on his visits to Philadelphia, always stayed at the house of
Mr. Meredith, and thus he became acquainted with young Barry and
his abilities. The Commodore died in 1803, and was interred in St.
Mary's Cemetery, where his monument may still be seen. He died

In 1778, Capt. James McGee, while commanding "in the service of the Commonwealth," was shipwrecked in Massachusetts Bay and seventy-two of his men lost. The survivors were very kindly treated by the inhabitants of Plymouth, who also "decently buried such bodies as were recovered." Capt. McGee was a member, and in 1810, President of the Charitable Irish Society of Boston.

---

childless, and left the greater part of his property to the Catholic Orphan Asylum of Philadelphia. Like the illustrious Charles Carroll, of Carrollton, he was remarkable through life for the strict performance of his religious duties.

The following, relating to the death of one of Barry's old officers, is taken from Nallette's *History and Reminiscences of the Philadelphia Navy Yard* (fourth paper); Potter's *Am. Monthly,* April, 1876.

"On Monday, September 11th, 1820, colors were placed at half-mast out of respect to the memory of Lieutenant James Traut, who had been attached to the Yard. It is related of this officer that from the time of the formation of the navy until the close of the War of 1812, he was a sailing-master in our service—an Irishman by birth, and is believed to have come to this country in the year 1781, with Captain Barry, in the Alliance. Few persons have given rise to more traditions in the service than Mr. Traut. His eccentricities were as conspicuous as his nautical peculiarities and his gallantry. His whole life was passed in and about ships, and his prejudices and habits were as thoroughly naval as those of 'Pipes' himself. For England and Englishmen he entertained to the last the most unmitigated hatred, with an Irishman's conceptions of wrongs done to Ireland. He was usually supposed to be a man of stern disposition, but he was not without some of the finest traits of human nature. He had been in numerous actions, and was always remarkable for decision and intrepidity. Owing to the latter quality, he was once captured while in charge of a vessel called the *Julia.* Towards the close of his eventful life, which extended to seventy years, he received the commission of a lieutenant, an honor that repaid him for all the hardships he had undergone, and all the dangers he had passed. Just before his death, which took place in this city on Sunday, November 10th, at nine o'clock in the evening, it is stated that he expressed a wish 'that his body be carried into blue water, and there consigned to the ocean's bed.' "

Matthew Mease, of Philadelphia, brother of James Mease, one of the founders of the famous First Troop of Cavalry of that city, and of John Mease, distinguished for gallant conduct at Trenton, entered the American navy and served under Paul Jones. He was severely wounded in the fight between the *Bon Homme Richard* and the *Serapis* off Flamborough Head.*

On the peace establishment, previous to 1801, are found the names of Captains Barry, McNeil, Barron, Mullowney, and James Barron; Lieutenants Ross, McElroy, McRea, O'Driscoll, Byrne, Somers, McCutchen, and McClelland; Midshipmen McDonough, Roach, Carroll, Magrath, Fleming, Hartigan, Hennessy, Dunn, O'Brien, Walsh, Blakely, T. McDonough, T. Moore, C. Moore, Rossitter, McConnell, Blake, Kearney, and Casey,—all Irish, by birth or parentage.†

---

* Matthew Mease was born in Strabane, County Tyrone, Ireland, and emigrated at an early age to America, settling in Philadelphia. Though educated for a merchant, he became purser of the *Bon Homme Richard*, under Paul Jones. In the desperate encounter between that vessel and the *Serapis*, not relishing the thought of being an idle spectator of the engagement, he obtained from Jones the command of the quarter-deck guns, which were served under him, until he was carried below to the cock-pit, dangerously wounded on the head by a splinter. He died in Philadelphia in 1787. His name is on the list of original members of the Friendly Sons of St. Patrick, of Philadelphia.

† McGee. Early Irish Letters in America.

CHAPTER XVI.

TESTIMONY of the most convincing kind, from unfriendly
as well as friendly sources, establishes the fact that at least
half the Revolutionary Army was composed of men of Irish
birth or descent. George Washington Parke Custis says,
" of the operations of the war—I mean the soldiers—up to
the coming of the French, Ireland had furnished in the ratio
of one hundred for one of any nation whatever. Then
honored be the old and good services of the sons of Erin
in the War of Independence. Let the Shamrock be en-
twined with the laurels of the Revolution: and *truth and
justice guiding the pen of history inscribe on the tablets of
America's remembrance, Eternal gratitude to Irishmen.*" *

Joseph Galloway, who, although he had been a delegate
to the first Continental Congress, afterwards abandoned the
national cause and became a bitter Loyalist, was examined
before a Committee of the London House of Commons,
June 16, 1779, on various matters connected with the Revolution. Amongst other questions he was asked. "What
were the troops in the service of the Congress chiefly composed of? Were they natives of America or were the
greatest part of them English, Scotch, or Irish?" Galloway replied: "I can answer the question with precision.

---

* Personal Recollections.

There were scarcely one fourth natives of America, about one half Irish, the other fourth English and Scotch." *

Major General Robertson was examined before the same committee on the 19th of August following, and was asked by Lord George Germaine, " How are the principal corps composed ? Are they mostly native Americans or emigrants from various nations of Europe ? " The officer replied, " Some of the corps consist mostly of natives, others, I believe the greater number, are enlisted from such people as can be got in the country and many of them may be emigrants. I remember Gen. Lee telling me that half the rebel army were from Ireland." †

Ramsay says, " that the Irish in America were almost to a man on the side of Independence. They had fled from oppression in their native country and could not brook the idea that it should follow them." Plowden asserts " that most of the early successes (of the patriots) in America, were immediately owing to the vigorous exertions and prowess of the Irish emigrants who bore arms in that cause." ‡

Even Froude, Ireland's most malignant traducer, declares that according to " all evidence " the foremost, the most irreconcileable, the most determined in pushing the quarrel to the last extremity, were those evicted tenants whom " the (Anglican) bishops and Lord Donegal and Company had been pleased to drive out of Ulster." § And he suggests the possibility—as indeed he might assume the certainty— that some exile from the vicinity of the Irish Bunker Hill, near Belfast, first gave that name to the historic height at Boston, where the " raw American rebels," until their ammunition gave out, proved themselves more than a match for

---

* Journals of House of Commons.
† Hist. Am. Revolution, 597.
‡ Plowden, Vol. ii. 198.
§ Froude " Hist. of Ireland," vol. i. 140.

the best troops of England. None dared to dispute the assertion of Lord Mountjoy in the House of Commons when he told the Ministers, "You have lost America through the Irish," yet this fact seemed only to embitter men of his class against those who sought to free his own country, for he went at the head of his regiment to put down the insurrection of '98, and lost his life at the battle of New Ross fighting against the cause of Irish Independence. In the Revolutionary struggle the evicted Irish tenants, newly arrived, displayed no less bravery or fidelity than did the men of their race who were descendants of those whom the persecutions and confiscations of Cromwell and William of Orange had driven from Ireland. At the battle of Long Island, for instance "the Delaware battalion, commanded by Col. Haslett, was composed principally of raw Irishmen who scarcely knew how to load a musket," * yet those men, undrilled and undisciplined, fought with cold steel and clubbed musket to the death.

Bearing in mind what has been stated in previous chapters, with regard to emigration from Ireland to America, and especially that in the years 1771, 1772, and 1773, nearly a hundred thousand Irish immigrants landed on these shores, driven from their homes by landlord cruelties and crimes, it will appear evident that Galloway's testimony does no more than justice to Irish-American patriotism. We may safely conclude then, that of the two hundred and thirty thousand men furnished for the Continental army by the various States during the war, one-half, or one hundred and fifteen thousand, were of the Irish race.

It may not be out of place here to refer to the erroneous opinion, still too prevalent, that the number of Tories or Loyalists in the colonies amounted only to an insignificant

---

* Memoirs Hist. Society of Long Island.

minority of the people. The truth of the matter is, that in some States the Tories out-numbered the " Rebels," as can easily be demonstrated. The *Historic Essay*, which Sabine prefixes to his work on the *Loyalists of the American Revolution*, contains such evidences as the following. With regard to Massachusetts, it seems to have been taken for granted, that because here the Revolution had its origin—that the people embraced the popular side almost in a mass. A more mistaken opinion than this has seldom prevailed. Upwards of eleven hundred loyalists retired in a body with the royal army at the evacuation of Boston, and other emigrations preceded and succeeded this. Maine had a considerable number of Tories—numbers of whom were proscribed and banished. In passing from Maine to New Hampshire we find the general state of things very similar.

" In Connecticut, the number of adherents of the crown was greater, in proportion to the population, than in Maine, Massachusetts, or New Hampshire.

" Rhode Island approached nearer the democratic standard than any of those already mentioned; though here, too, the King had supporters by no means insignificant. The political institutions in New York, which formed there a feudal aristocracy, were calculated to give the Tory party many adherents. Numbers entered the service of the Crown and fought in its defence. Whole battalions, and even regiments, were raised by the great landholders, and continued organized and in pay throughout the struggle. In fine, New York was undeniably the Loyalists' stronghold, and contained more of them than any other colony.

" Regarding the Tories, who opposed the Rebels in the field, our writers of history have been almost silent; and it is not impossible that some persons have read books devoted exclusively to an account of the Revolution, without so much as imagining that a part, and a considerable part of the force employed to suppress the 'rebellion,' was composed of our countrymen. From the best evidence I have been able to obtain, I conclude that there were at the lowest computation, 25,000 Americans who took up arms against their countrymen, and in aid of England. In fact, the addresses then presented by Loyalists to His Majesty, informed him that quite as many, if not more, Americans had joined the armies of King George as had entered those raised by the 'rebel' Congress!'' *

To this it may be added that of the thirty-seven newspapers published in America in 1775, twelve were in favor of English rule, twenty-three on the side of the patriots, and two were neutral.

It is gratifying to note the warm and kindly regard which Washington almost invariably entertained and manifested towards his Irish officers and soldiers, as well as towards his fellow citizens of the same race in civil life, and even their kindred in the Old Land. His choice of Reed, Moylan and Fitzgerald, as aids, his affection for Knox, and his esteem of Sullivan, Hand, Wayne and others, were often displayed and always in the most gratifying manner. Nor was his kindness to and regard for the feelings of his humbler comrades—the Irish of the rank and file—less marked. When at the camp, at Cambridge, they became excited and indignant over the projected burning of the effigy of the Pope, on what the English call Guy Fawkes' day, in 1775. The commander-in-chief speedily allayed their anger, and shamed those who sought to abuse their forbearance by issuing the following order.

''*November* 5th.—As the Commander-in-chief has been apprised of a design formed for the observance of that ridiculous and childish custom of burning the effigy of the Pope, he cannot help expressing his surprise that there

---

* Sabine's Loyalists of the American Revolution.

should be officers and soldiers in this army so void of common sense as not to see the impropriety of such a step.
* * * * It is so monstrous as not to be suffered, or
excused; indeed, instead of offering the most remote insult,
it is our duty to address public thanks to our (Catholic)
brethren; as to them we are indebted for every late success
over the common enemy in Canada." *

When the British were driven out of Boston, on the
17th of March, 1776, the commander-in-chief, gratified the
national feeling of his Irish soldiers, by giving " St. Patrick "
as the countersign, and naming Gen. Sullivan as " Brigadier of the day."

In his life-guard, formed in 1776, soon after the siege of
Boston, when the American Army was encamped on Manhattan Island, near the City of New York, Washington
had many Irish.   It consisted of a Major's command, one
hundred and eighty men.   These were selected with special
reference to their physical, moral, and intellectual character,
and it was considered a mark of peculiar distinction to be-
long to the *Commander-in-Chief's Guard*.   The corps varied
in numbers at different periods.   During the winter of
1779-80, when the American army under Washington, was
cantoned at Morristown, in close proximity to the enemy,
it was increased to two hundred and fifty.   In the spring it
was reduced to its original number, and in 1783, the last
year of service, it consisted of only sixty-four non-commissioned officers and privates.   Care was always taken to
have all the States, from which all the Continental army was
supplied with troops, represented in this corps.   The following names of Irish soldiers are taken from the muster
roll, 4th of June, 1783: E. Carrolton, T. Manning, J.
Crosby, David Brown, S. Daily, D. Manning, Peter Halt,
Jer. Brown, J. Moore, Samuel Baily, Wm. Martin, Robt.

---

* Washington's Writings.

Blair, John Fenton, Charles Dougherty, Wm. Karnahan, John Dowther, John Patton, Hugh Cull, James Hughes, John Finch, Denis Moriarty, John Montgomery, William Hennessy, Jeremiah Driscoll, Thomas Gillen.

On December 17, 1781, Washington was unanimously adopted a member of the Friendly Sons of St. Patrick of Philadelphia. Before giving an account of what took place on the occasion, something may be said of the origin and the members of this famous organization.

The Society of the Friendly Sons held its first meeting, September 17, 1771, when Stephen Moylan, afterwards General, brother to the Catholic Bishop of Cork, was elected President, as already stated.

"With the exception of its honorary members, the Society" says the *Account of the Friendly Sons of St. Patrick*, "was composed of Irishmen or of those whose parents (or one of them) were Irish. They were, for the most part, 'men of fortune,' and associated on terms of familiarity, friendship and equality, with the first men of the province, or rather included among them the very best men of the country. It is not, therefore, a matter of surprise to find many of them occupying the highest and most responsible stations in the army, navy, cabinet, and in Congress, and all of them 'distinguished for their firm adherence to the glorious cause of liberty in which they embarked' with a zeal, ardor and ability, unsurpassed in those days of intense patriotism.

"The objects of the society were social and convivial. Want and distress being, at the time of its formation, rare, did not require, so much as now, the union of individuals into associations for the purpose of charity. Yet it would be a great mistake to infer from this that the society was a useless one. As well might we condemn as useless the friendly intercourse which gives a zest to the dull routine of business and the stern requisitions of duty, as censure 'those happy meetings when' (to use the language of Curran in reference to similar scenes), 'the swelling heart conceived and communicated the pure and generous pur-

pose, the innocent enjoyment of social mirth expanded into
the nobler warmth of social virtue, and the horizon of the
board became enlarged into the horizon of man.' Certainly an association could not be deemed useless which
brought together, in familiar contact, such men as Dickinson, Barry, Morris, Wayne, Fitzsimmons, Peters, the Moylans, Hopkinson, and many others distinguished for their
genius, talents, wit and patriotism: which bound them together by the tie of friendship, and made them acquainted
with the character and qualifications of each other.

"The regular meetings of the society were held on the
17th days of March, June, September and December. Each
member was required to furnish himself with a gold medal,
of the value of three guineas, agreeably to the following
description: On the right, Hibernia; on the left, America;
in the center, Liberty joining the hands of Hibernia and
America, represented by the usual figures of a female supported by a harp, for Hibernia; an Indian with his quiver
on his back and his bow slung, for America; underneath,
Unite. On the reverse, St. Patrick trampling on a snake,
a cross in his hand, dressed in pontificalibus, the motto,
'Hiar.'

"These devices, designed some years before the Revolution, were certainly ominous, if not prophetic. The God-
dess of Liberty joining the hands of Hibernia and America,
with the superscription 'Unite,' was sufficiently signifi-
cant, considering that the effect of that union powerfully
promoted the subsequent dismemberment of the British
empire and the liberty and independence of America. The
motto *Hiar*, or, without the aspirate, *Iar*, in the Celtic
language signifies, 'West,' and from it, according to some
writers, came the name of the country, Eire, Erin, or Ireland, and Ierna, aspirated Hibernia.

"This medal the members were obliged to wear at the
meetings of the society under the penalty of 7s. 6d. for
neglect to do so on St. Patrick's day, and 5s. on the days
of the quarterly meetings.

"Ten honorary members were eligible. The qualifications for ordinary members were that the applicant should
be a descendant of Irish parents on either side in the first
degree, or a descendant of a member *ad infinitum* (honorary

members excepted). So that the applicant must either have been a native of Ireland himself or one of his parents must have been so, or he must have been a descendant of a member. Honorary members could not vote, and were not subject to fines.

"The meetings of the society continued to be regularly held till December, 1775. At this time the revolutionary feeling had become intense, and the side which the members of the Society of the Friendly Sons of St. Patrick had taken is very unequivocally indicated by the record of their proceedings at the meeting of December 17, 1775. A motion was made and seconded ' that Thos. Batt, a member of this Society, should be expelled for taking an active part against the liberties of America; the determination was postponed till the next meeting, in order for a more deliberate consideration.' At the next meeting, March, 1776, ' the question being put upon the motion made at the last stated meeting, whether Capt. Thomas Batt be expelled from the Society, it was unanimously carried in the affirmative.' At this meeting there were present twenty-one members, among them Generals Wayne, Shee, and Nixon, and several of the First Troop of Philadelphia Cavalry.

"The pent-up flames of the war at last burst forth, and most of the members of the Society of the Friendly Sons of St. Patrick became participants and actors in the stirring scenes that followed.

"The festivities of the society, the wit, the song and the joke, yielded to the stern requisitions of duty, and the excitement of the banquet was succeeded by that of danger, battle, and glory. The minutes of the society come down regularly to the meeting of June 17, 1776. Here there is a gap until September 17, 1778, with this only entry, namely: ' The State of Pennsylvania having been invaded, and the city of Philadelphia taken by the British army under the command of General Sir Wm. Howe, in September, 1777, the society had no meeting until September, 1778. The meetings from September, 1778, until the end of the war, were regularly held, and though those who were in the army and navy are generally noted as absent, yet we find many of them snatching occasional moments of enjoyment, amid the hardships of war, in a reunion at the festivals of the

society. *'Absent in camp,' ' absent at sea,'* are frequent
entries opposite the names of members, and at the meeting
of the 17th of June, 1779, it was 'agreed that such members of the society as are officers in the army, shall not be
subject to fines for absence while in service in the field.'
Gen. Wayne was present at this meeting, as were several
members of the First Troop—Colonel Walter Stewart, John
Patton, Com. Barry, and Mr. John Dunlap, afterward Capt.
of the First Troop.

"Intimately connected with the glory of the Society of
the Sons of St. Patrick, is the magnificent proof of the generosity and patriotism of its members, already referred to,
in subscribing nearly half a million of dollars, to provide
for supplying the Revolutionary army with provisions.

"At length the clouds which had hung heavily over the
liberties of America began to be dissipated by the glorious
sunburst of victory, and the surrender of Cornwallis extin-
guished the last hope of the British in America. Once
more the convivial reunions of the Friendly Sons of St.
Patrick revived, and in the winter of 1781–2, commenced a
series of brilliant entertainments, continued at intervals for
several years, which fairly entitle this epoch to the appellation of the Golden Age of the society.

"Gen. Washington had now become acquainted with the
talents, courage and patriotic devotion of most of the members of the society; not, to be sure, at the festive board,
but on many a hard-fought field, and by the substantial
evidence of pounds, shillings and pence. The steady courage of Moylan, Irvine and Nixon, the impetuous boldness
of Wayne, the fiery valor of Thompson, Stewart, and
Butler, the efficient services of the First Troop, were fully
appreciated by the calm observation of Washington. These
had all been among his dearest companions-in-arms—and a
fellowship in danger, hardship and victory already united
them to him by the strongest ties of affection. It was very
natural therefore, that, when these Sons of St. Patrick met,
during the short intervals of war, and at the close of each
campaign, they should desire that he who had been their
commander, their companion, and their friend amid other
scenes, should unite in their festive enjoyments, to smooth
the brow so long furrowed with care but now crowned with
laurels.

"Accordingly, at a meeting of the president of the society and his council, on the 7th December, 1781, Gen. Washington, being then in Philadelphia by the request of Congress, the secretary was directed to invite his Excellency and suite, in the name of the society, to dinner, on the 17th December, at the City Tavern. Gen. Washington was prevented by pressing public business from accepting this invitation. On the 17th, however, a numerous meeting of the society was held, and dined at Evans' Tavern. Generals Hand and Knox were proposed as members, and afterward duly elected. On the same evening, His Excellency Gen. Washington was unanimously adopted a member of the society. It was ordered that the president, vice-president and secretary wait on his Excellency with a suitable address on the occasion, and present him with a medal in the name of the society. Also, that they invite his Excellency and his suite to an entertainment to be prepared and given him at the City Tavern, on Tuesday, the first of January (1782), to which the secretary is requested to invite the President of the State, and of Congress, the Minister of France, M. Marbois, M. Otto, the Chief-Justice, the Speaker of the House of Assembly, Mr. Francis Rendon, M. Holker, Count de la Touche, and Count Dillon, with all the general officers that may be in the city."

In pursuance of this order the president and secretary waited on General Washington with the following address:

"May it please your Excellency:

" The Society of the Friendly Sons of St. Patrick, of this city, ambitious to testify, with all possible respect, the high sense they entertain of your Excellency's public and private virtues, have taken the liberty to adopt your Excellency a member.

"Although they have not the clothing of any civil establishment nor the splendor of temporal power to dignify their election, yet they flatter themselves, that as it is the genuine offspring of hearts filled with the warmest attachments, that this mark of their esteem and regard will not be wholly unacceptable to your Excellency.

" Impressed with these pleasing hopes, they have directed

me to present to your Excellency a gold medal, the ensign of this fraternal society, which, that you may be pleased to accept, and long live to wear, is the warmest wish of

" Your Excellency's most humble and respectful servant,
" By order and in behalf of the Society.
                    " GEO. CAMPBELL, President."

" To His Excellency Gen. Washington, Commander-in-Chief of the Allied Army."

To which His Excellency was pleased to give the following answer, namely:

" SIR:—I accept with singular pleasure the Ensign of so worthy a fraternity as that of the Sons of St. Patrick in this city—*a society distinguished for the firm adherence of its members to the glorious cause in which we are embarked.*

" Give me leave to assure you, sir, that I shall never cast my eyes upon the badge with which I am honored, but with a grateful remembrance of the polite and affectionate manner in which it was presented.

" I am, with respect and esteem,
    " Sir, your most obedient servant,
                " GEORGE WASIHNGTON."

" To George Campbell, Esq., President of the Society of the Friendly Sons of St. Patrick."

After which the president having requested the honor of His Excellency's company, together with the gentlemen of his suite, at dinner, at the City Tavern, on Tuesday, the 1st of January, he was pleased to accept the invitation, and, according to the order of last meeting, the secretary sent cards to all the persons therein specified, requesting the pleasure of their company at same place and time, namely, four o'clock.

At an extra meeting at George Evans', on Tuesday, the 1st of January, 1782, the following gentlemen were present:

His Excellency General Washington, Gen. Lincoln, Gen. Steuben, Gen. Howe, Gen. Moultrie, Gen. Knox, Gen.

Hand, Gen. M'Intosh, His Excellency M. Luzerne. M.
Rendon, His Excellency M. Hanson, His Excellency Wm.
Moore, Mr. Muhlenbergh, Col. French Tilghman, Col.
Smith, Major Washington, Count Dillon, Count De la
Touche, M. Marbois, M. Otto, M. Holker—21 guests.

Geo. Campbell, Esq., president; Mr. Thos. Fitzsimmons,
V. P.; Wm. West, Matthew Mease, John Mease, John
Mitchell, J. M. Nesbitt, John Nixon, Samuel Caldwell,
Andrew Caldwell, Mr. James Mease, Sharp Delany, Esq.,
Mr. D. H. Conyngham, Mr. George Henry, Mr. Blair
M'Clenachan, Mr. Alexander Nesbitt, Mr. John Donnald-
son, Mr. John Barclay, Mr. James Crawford, Mr. John
Patton, Mr. James Caldwell, Mr. John Dunlap, Mr. Hugh
Shiell, Mr. George Hughes, Mr. M. M. O'Brien, Jasper
Moylan, Esq., Col. Ephraim Blaine, Col. Charles Stewart,
Col. Walter Stewart, Col, Francis Johnson, Dr. John Coch-
ran, Mr. Wm. Constable, Henry Hill, Esq., Robert Morris,
Esq., Samuel Meredith, Esq.—35 members.

"This brilliant entertainment, it will be seen, was graced
by the presence of the bravest and most distinguished
generals of the allied army of America and France. The
French and Spanish ministers, with their secretaries, etc., were
also present. Several of the First Troop (members of the
Society), Colonels Charles and Walter Stewart; Colonels
Blaine and Johnston, with Robert Morris, Samuel Meredith, and Henry Hill, honorary members.

"The next regular meeting (the anniversary meeting of
the Society) was held at George Evans', on Monday, the
28th March, 1782—and was even more brilliant than the pre-
ceding one. Gen. Washington, was present with Generals
Lincoln, Dickinson, Moultrie and Baron Steuben; Messrs.
Muhlenberge, Moore and Hanson; Capt. Truxton, of the
Navy, etc. Of the honorary members, John Dickinson,
Robert Morris, Samuel Meredith, and Henry Hill, were

present. Com. Barry is mentioned as beyond sea, and Wayne, Butler, Irvine, and Cochran, at camp.

Amongst the prominent members of the Friendly Sons not hitherto mentioned were the following:

John Mease, brother of Matthew, already mentioned, was born in Strabane, Ireland; came to this country in the year 1754, and, for many years was an eminent shipping merchant of Philadelphia. He was an early and an ardent friend to the cause of independence, and one of the original members of the First Troop of City Cavalry. On the ever-memorable night of the 25th of December, 1776, he was one of twenty-four of that corps who crossed the Delaware with the troops under General Washington when the Hessians were captured.

Mr. Mease was one of five detailed to the service of keeping alive the fires along the line of the American encampment at Trenton to deceive the enemy, while the Americans marched by a private route to attack their rear-guard at Princeton. He served with the troop until the end of the war, and suffered great loss of property in his warehouses and dwelling. For the last thirty years of his life he was one of the admiralty surveyors of the port of Philadelphia, and died in 1826, at the advanced age of 86. He subscribed £4,000 to supply the army in 1780. Mr. John Mease was the only man who continued, in the latter days, to wear the old three-cornered hat of the revolution, and was familiarly called " *the last of the cocked hats.*"

Thos. Fitzsimmons was a native of Ireland and a Catholic. He was an extensive merchant of Philadelphia before and during the revolution, commanded a volunteer company and was engaged in active service during the war. After the war he was for many years a member of the State Legislature, and represented Philadelphia in Congress with distinction. He was for a long time a director in the Bank of North America, and president of the Insurance Company of North America, in which latter office he continued until his death. He was a man of high and honorable character, and his influence in the country, and especially among the merchants, was second to none. He married a sister of George Meade, and died without issue.

Mr. Fitzsimmons was one of the most efficient and able men who laid the foundations of the commercial and financial systems of the United States. He and Mr. Goodhue, of Salem, though they spoke but seldom and briefly, were always looked to in Congress for facts and the correction of errors in practical questions of commerce, exchange, etc., and the operation of legislative measures in relation thereto. To have been a counselor and adviser of Franklin, Hamilton, Jefferson, etc., the coadjutor of Robert Morris in what vitally concerned not only the present safety but the future prosperity of these United States, is fame that few men of those times could aspire to, and yet is nothing more than may with justice be claimed for Thomas Fitzsimmons. His house, namely, George Meade & Co., subscribed to supply the army, in 1780, £5,000. His name is attached to the Constitution of the United States and to the address of the Catholics to Washington

An interesting incident in the life of Fitzsimmons is his faithful friendship for Robert. Morris, who, although an Englishman, became an honorary member of the Friendly Sons. Of the latter, Bolter, in his *War of Independence* remarks, " The Americans certainly owed and still owe as much acknowledgment to the financial operations of Robert Morris as to the negotiations of Franklin or almost to the arms of Washington." But after all his service he was abandoned in his hour of need. Washington wished to make him Secretary of the Treasury, but he declined. He finally became embarrassed, and was thrown into prison for debt in 1798.

Says Sir Rom de Camden in his *Memorable Facts in the Lives of Eminent Americans:*

" During his incarceration few of his former *friends* evinced the least interest in him or his troubles; among the few the most attentive until he, too, became a prisoner, was his partner in the disastrous land speculations, John Nicholson; but another deserves special mention, because his friendship was of that purely unselfish type which is far too rare, and ever wins, as it merits, the respect of all, even of those incapable of emulating it—I allude to Thomas Fitzsimmons, an Irishman by birth, a Catholic in religion, a thorough American in devoted love to the Colonies and to their successors, the United States, and withal a noble-hearted man; a successful merchant, of the firm of George Meade & Co., of Philadelphia, he served with credit as a captain in the Revolutionary army; a man of enlightened views, he was a popular legislator, serving in the State Legislature, in the National Congress, and in the Convention for drafting the Constitution of the United States. He was at this time a merchant, not wealthy, but influential and successful; had his means been equal to his large heart, or had there been a number more like him, Mr. Morris would not have lain four years in prison. As it was, he was the great man's steadfast, constant, trusted friend, and as such frequently visited him in prison, comforted, advised and strengthened him."—*Potter's American Monthly*, Vol. vi., Feb. 26.

It makes an Irish-American as proud to read of this fidelity to a friend in adversity as of the heroism shown by the bravest on the battle-field.

John Maxwell Nesbitt. This eminent merchant and devoted patriot was a native of the North of Ireland, who emigrated to America before the revolution. In 1777 he joined the First Troop of Philadelphia Cavalry. He conducted one of the most extensive mercantile-houses in Philadelphia, under the firm of J. M. Nesbitt & Co., during the war, and afterward under the name of Conyngham & Nesbitt. He embarked his all in the cause of liberty, and with a devoted patriotism not exceeded in history, fearlessly staked his life, his fortune, and, what he valued more than both, his sacred honor, on the success of America. His benefactions to her cause had in them a simple greatness which should make his memory dear to America in every future age, as he was, while living, beloved and trusted by all his compatriots. Mention has been made of the formation of the Pennsylvania Bank for the supply of the army of the United States with provisions, to which J. M. Nesbitt & Co. subscribed £5,000. But before that event Mr. Nesbitt had already rendered most essential service to the army. This is related in Lingard's Reg. of Pa., vol. 6, p. 28: "So great was the distress of the American army in 1780 that General Washington was apprehensive that they would not be able to keep the field. The army, however, was saved by a combination of providential circumstances. General Washington having written to Richard Peters, Esq., giving him full information of the state of the army, that gentleman immediately called on J. M. Nesbitt, Esq., and explained to him the distress of the army and the wishes of the general." Mr. Nesbitt replied "that a Mr. Howe, of Trenton, had offered to put up pork for him if he could be paid in hard money. He contracted with Howe to put up all the pork and beef he could possibly obtain, for which *he should be paid in gold.*" Mr. Howe performed his engagement, and J. M. Nesbitt & Co. paid him accordingly. Mr. Nesbitt told Mr. Peters that he might have this beef and pork, and, in addition, a valuable prize just arrived to Bunner, Murray & Co., laden with provisions. "I need not tell you," continues Mr. Hazard's correspondent, "how pleased Mr. Peters was with the result of the application.

The provisions were sent in time and the army was saved.
Mr. Nesbitt was a faithful coadjutor of Robert Morris
during the war, in the supply of money and necessaries for
the army and in the support of public credit, when Mr.
Morris acted as financier."

Mr. Nesbitt was the second president of the Society of
the Friendly Sons of St. Patrick, succeeding General Moylan in 1773, and served at that time for one year.   He was
re-elected president of the society in June, 1782, and continued to be re-elected annually until his resignation in
March, 1796, having been president of the society, altogether, for nearly fifteen years.   He was one of the founders
of the Hibernian Society.

Gen. John Shee was a native of Ireland and a merchant in
Philadelphia, in partnership with Richard Bache (one of the
honorary members), the son-in-law of Dr. Benjamin Franklin.   He was taken prisoner at Fort Washington, York
Island, after the battle of Long Island.

Mr. Jefferson appointed him Collector of the Port of Philadelphia.   He was afterward a general in the militia, Colonel
of volunteers, and treasurer of the city.

Blair McClenachan was a native of Ireland.   He was in
business in Philadelphia before the Revolution, but on the
breaking out of the war engaged in privateering, in which
he was very successful.   He was most ardent and devoted
to the cause of liberty, and one of the founders of the first
troop of Philadelphia city cavalry, in which he served during the war.   He co-operated most liberally in all the patriotic exertions and schemes of Robert Morris and his compatriots in urging on, sustaining and establishing the cause
of American freedom.   He subscribed £10,000 in 1780 to
supply the starving army, and on various occasions aided
Congress by his money and his credit, and suffered much

thereby in a pecuniary way, though repaid by the approbation of the whole country and the triumph of the cause.

After the war he engaged largely in various mercantile operations, and was an extensive shipowner. His speculations, however, resulted in his embarrassment. Mr. McClenachan had a large family. One of his daughters married General Walter Stewart. Some of his descendants are living in Philadelphia. His granddaughter married Thos. Penn Gaskill, of Philadelphia, a member of the Hibernian Society.

George Meade, a native of Ireland, and a Catholic, was a highly respectable and wealthy shipowner and merchant in Philadelphia, and many years partner in trade with Thomas Fitzsimmons, one of the original members. Mr. Meade's high character and integrity may be inferred from the following anecdote: About the year 1790 he became embarrassed in his business and failed, owing to the insolvency of a house in France. His largest creditor was John Barclay, an extensive and liberal merchant of London. Immediately upon his failure Mr. M. wrote to Mr. B. informing him of the condition of his affairs, but expressing a hope that he might yet be able to retrieve his losses. Mr. B. in reply, requested Mr. M. not to trouble his mind on account of the debt he already owed, and directed him to draw at sight for £10,000 sterling more. With this generous assistance Mr. Meade was enabled to retrieve his fortunes, and had the satisfaction not only to repay Mr. B., but to discharge all his former obligations in full. He was one of the founders of the Hibernian Society, and subscribed £5,000 to supply the army with provisions in 1780.

Col. Ephraim Blaine, a native of Ireland, settled in Carlisle, Pa. " Became a colonel in the American army early in the war and was well known in Pennsylvania for his patriotic exertions in the cause of the Revolution."—*Account of*

Friendly Sons. Was the ancestor of Hon. James G. Blaine, of Maine.

But to pursue the history of the society in further detail would be unnecessary; suffice it to say that the usual conviviality, the elegant hospitality, and the harmony and friendship which had ever characterized the Society, continued until 1796, when the greater number of its members, with several others, formed themselves into a charitable association under the name of "The Hibernian Society for the Relief of Emigrants from Ireland," with the laudable view and intent (to use the words of the charter) to aid and assist poor and oppressed persons emigrating from Ireland into Pennsylvania. The object met the cordial approbation of the authorities, and a charter of incorporation was granted to the society on the 27th April, 1792, signed by Gov. Mifflin, who had frequently experienced the hospitality of the Society of the Friendly Sons of St. Patrick. The preamble recites that "it is highly proper to promote the designs of the said society, inasmuch as they may greatly contribute to the strength and prosperity of this State and of the United States by encouraging emigration from Ireland."

Hon. Thomas McKean, Chief-Justice and afterward Governor of Pennsylvania, was chosen first President of the new society.

In November, 1783, a number of Irishmen, the majority of whom were members of the Irish Volunteers, arrived in New York, and soon after landing "begged leave to extend congratulations to Gov. Clinton on the happy conclusion of the late cruel, oppressive, and unnatural war, and his Excellency's safe return to New York." Continuing they said: "We, armed in a similar cause and with the assistance of this country, contributed to procure the emancipation of our own from the slavery she was long obliged to acquiesce under."

This was signed on behalf of, and at the request of the meeting at New York, the 2d of December, 1783, by "Joseph Holmes, Secretary," and to it George Clinton, the Governor, responded appropriately.

The same volunteers also addressed congratulations to Gen. Washington, who replied as follows:—

"*To the Members of the Volunteer Association and other inhabitants of the Kingdom of Ireland who have lately arrived in the city of New York:*

"GENTLEMEN: The testimony of your satisfaction at the glorious termination of the late contest, and your indulgent opinion of my agency in it, afford me singular pleasure and merit my warmest acknowledgment. If the example of the Americans, successfully contended in the cause of freedom, can be of any use to other nations, we shall have an additional motive for rejoicing at so prosperous an event.

"It was not an uninteresting consideration to learn that the Kingdom of Ireland, by a bold and manly conduct, had obtained the redress of many of its grievances; and it is much to be wished that the blessings of equal liberty and unrestrained commerce, may yet prevail more extensively. In the meantime you may be assured, gentlemen, that the hospitality and beneficence of your countrymen to our brethren, who have been prisoners of war, are neither unknown nor unregarded.

"'The bosom of America is open to receive, not only the opulent and respectable stranger, but the oppressed and persecuted of all nations and religions, whom, we shall welcome to a participation in all our rights and privileges, if by decency and propriety of conduct they appear to merit the enjoyment.

GEORGE WASHINGTON."*

About the same time Washington received the heartiest congratulations from various quarters, and societies in Ire-

---

* *New York Gazette*, Dec. 4, 1783, quoted in *New York World*, Jan. 16, 1887.

land itself, to which he made fitting replies, one of which, that to the "Yankee Club" of Stewartstown, Tyrone, will serve to show how highly he appreciated the good will of American friends in Ireland.

MOUNT VERNON, 20 January, 1784.
To the Yankee Club of Stewartstown, in the County of Tyrone, Ireland.

GENTLEMEN:—It is with unfeigned satisfaction that I accept your congratulation on the late happy and glorious revolution.

The generous indignation against the foes to the rights of human nature, with which you are animated, and the exalted sentiments of liberty which you entertain, are too consonant to the feelings and principles of the people of the United States of America, not to attract their veneration and esteem, did not the affectionate and anxious concern with which you regarded their struggle for Freedom and Independence, entitle you to their more particular acknowledgements.

If in the course of our successful contest, good consequences have resulted to the oppressed Kingdom of Ireland, it will afford a new source of felicitation to all who respect the interests of humanity.

I am now, gentlemen, to offer you my best thanks for the indulgent sentiments you are pleased to express of my conduct, and for your benevolent wishes concerning my personal welfare, as well as with regard to a more interesting object, the prosperity of my country.

I have the honor to be,
Very sincerely yours,
GEORGE WASHINGTON."

Among the delegates who met at Philadelphia for the purpose of revising the Articles of Confederation and framing a Constitution, there were Thomas Fitzsimmons of Pennsylvania, Daniel Carroll of Maryland, George Read of Delaware, John Rutledge, and Pierce Butler of South Carolina, and other Irish Americans. In compliance with the request of the delegates. Conventions were called in the various States, to decide upon the adoption of the new Federal Constitution and soon eleven States, gave their endorsement. North Carolina did not accept it until 1789, nor Rhode Island until 1790.

Under the provisions of the new Constitution, Gen. Washington was unanimously chosen President. He was inaugurated at New York, where Congress was then in session, on April 30, 1789. Soon after he was presented with the following address on behalf of the Catholics of the United States, then almost exclusively of Irish birth or origin.

Address of the Catholics to George Washington, President of the United States.

" Sir: We have been long impatient to testify our joy and unbounded confidence on your being called, by an unanimous vote, to the first station of a country in which that unanimity could not have been obtained without the previous merit of unexampled services, of eminent wisdom, and unblemished virtue. Our congratulations have not reached you sooner, because our scattered situation prevented the communication and the collecting of those sentiments which warmed every breast. But the delay has furnished us with the opportunity not merely of presaging the happiness to be expected under your administration, but of bearing testimony to that which we experience already. It is your peculiar talent, in war and in peace, to afford security to those who commit their protection into your hands. In war you shield them from the ravages of armed hostility; in peace you establish public tranquility by the justice and moderation, not less than by the vigor, of your government. By example, as well as by vigilance, you extend the influence of laws on the manners of our fellow-citizens. You encourage respect for religion, and inculcate by words and actions that principle on which the welfare of nations so much depends—that a superintending Providence governs the events of the world and watches over the conduct of men. Your exalted maxims and unwearied attention to the moral and physical improvement of our country have produced already the happiest effects.

Under your administration America is animated with zeal for the attainment and encouragement of useful literature; she improves her agriculture, extends her commerce, and acquires with foreign nations a dignity unknown to her before. From these happy events, in which none can feel a warmer interest than ourselves, we derive additional pleasure by recollecting that you, sir, have been the principal instrument to effect so rapid a change in our political situation. This prospect of national prosperity is peculiarly pleasing to us on another account: because, whilst our country preserves her freedom and independence, we shall have a well-founded title to claim from her justice the equal rights of citizenship, as the price of our blood spilt under your eyes, and of our common exertions for her defence under your auspicious conduct; rights rendered more dear to us by the remembrance of former hardships. When we pray for the preservation of them where they have been' granted, and expect the full extension of them from the justice of those States which still restrict them; when we solicit the protection of Heaven over our common country we neither admit, nor can omit, recommending your preservation to the singular care of Divine Providence; because we conceive that no human means are so available to promote the welfare of the United States as the prolongation of your health and life, in which are included the energy of your example, the wisdom of your counsels, and the persuasive eloquence of your virtues.

" In behalf of the Catholic clergy,   ' J. CARROLL.
" In behalf of the Catholic laity,
                    " CHARLES CARROLL, of Carrollton.
                    " DANIEL CARROLL.
                    " THOMAS FITZSIMMONS.
                    " DOMINICK LYNCH."

To this President Washington made the following reply.

Washington's Answer to the Catholics in the United States of America.

" GENTLEMEN: While I now receive with much satisfaction your congratulations on my being called, by an unanimous vote, to the first station of my country, I cannot but duly notice your politeness in offering an apology for the unavoidable delay. As that delay has given you an opportunity of realizing, instead of anticipating, the benefits of the general government, you will do me the justice to believe that your testimony of the increase of the public prosperity enhances the pleasure which I would otherwise have experienced from your affectionate address.

"I feel that my conduct, in war and in peace, has met with more general approbation than could reasonably have been expected; and I find myself disposed to consider that fortunate circumstance, in a great degree, resulting from the able support and extraordinary candor of my fellow-citizens of all denominations.

"The prospect of national prosperity now before us is truly animating, and ought to excite the exertions of all good men to establish and secure the happiness of their country, in the permanent duration of its freedom and independence. America, under the smiles of a Divine Providence, the protection of a good government, and the cultivation of manners, morals, and piety, cannot fail of attaining an uncommon degree of eminence, in literature, commerce, agriculture, improvements at home, and respectability abroad.

"As mankind become more liberal, they will be more apt to allow that all those who conduct themselves as worthy members of the community, are equally entitled to the protection of civil government. I hope ever to see America among the foremost nations in examples of justice and liberty. And I presume that your fellow-citizens will not forget the patriotic part which you took in the accomplishment of their revolution, and the establishment of their government; or, the important assistance which they received from a nation in which the Catholic faith is professed.

"I thank you, gentlemen, for your kind concern for me. While my life and my health shall continue, in whatever situation I may be, it shall be my constant endeavor to justify the favorable sentiments which you are pleased to express of my conduct. And may the members of your society in America, animated alone by the pure spirit of Christianity, and still conducting themselves as the faithful subjects of our free government, enjoy every temporal and spiritual felicity.

"G. WASHINGTON."

CHAPTER XVII.

THE SEE OF BALTIMORE ESTABLISHED.—ALIEN AND SEDITION
LAWS.—IRISH PATRIOT EXILES.

AFTER the termination of the war of Independence, it was
deemed advisable by the Holy See, as well as by the Catholic
clergy of the United States, that the Church here should
no longer remain, as had been the case up to that time,
subject to the jurisdiction of the vicar-Apostolic of the London district. The Papal Nuncio at Paris, Monsignor Doria,
Archbishop of Seleucia, made Franklin, then Minister to
France, aware of the change contemplated, and the latter
having expressed a desire that Father John Carroll, who
had accompanied him on the embassy to Canada, a few
years before, and kindly nursed him when ill, should be
placed at the head of the Church in America, his wishes
were at once complied with, as the following extract from
his diary will show.

"1784, July 1st.—The Pope's Nuncio called and acquainted me that the Pope had, on my recommendation, appointed Mr. John Carroll, Superior of the Catholic clergy
in America with many of the powers of a bishop, and that
probably he would be made a bishop *in partibus* before the
end of the year. He asked which would be most convenient
for him, to come to France or to go to St. Domingo for ordination by another bishop, which was necessary. . I mentioned Quebec as more convenient than either. He asked
whether, as that was an English province, our government
might not take offence at his going thither. I thought not,

unless the ordination by that bishop should give him some
authority over our bishop. He said not in the least; that
when our bishop was once ordained, he would be independent of the other. * * * He added they had written
from America that there are twenty priests, but that they
are not sufficient, as the new settlements near the Mississippi have need of some." * Father Carroll continued to ad-
minister the affairs of the Church for nearly five years as
Superior or Prefect Apostolic, when, in compliance with a
decree of Pope Pius VI., "the priests exercising the ministry in the United States" assembled to elect a bishop and
determine in what city his See should be fixed. Their
choice fell of course upon Father Carroll, and his election
was ratified at Rome on November 6th, 1789. In consequence of the outbreak of the Revolution in France, the
first American prelate did not deem it advisable to go there
to be consecrated, and Ireland was still suffering under the
infamous Penal "Laws." Bishop Carroll therefore went
to England, where at Lulworth Castle, the residence of
Thomas Weld, his consecration took place on the Feast of
the Assumption, 1790. This was nearly forty years before
Catholic Emancipation was conceded. The new prelate
had many difficulties to contend with, but he set to work
vigorously to overcome them. In many respects the condition of the American Catholics was much improved by
the overthrow of British rule. Bishop England, referring
to this period, says: † " Many causes now combined to diminish the long-existing prejudices; not only had Catholics
fought and fallen in the Revolutionary struggle, but Catholic France had aided with her army and her navy; her
Catholic chaplains had celebrated our offices in the camps

---

* Sparks' Life and Writings of Franklin.
† Works of Rt. Rev. Dr. England, Vol. III. 238.

and in the cities.   *   *   *   The best and most gallant and
hardy portion of their own (American) troops, the Pennsylvania line was chiefly composed of Irish Catholics.   The
commander-in-chief, the noble and generous Washington, had
testified to their bravery and devotion.   A Catholic was the
man who had probably staked his largest property in their
cause, among that patriot band who had pledged life and
fortune and sacred honor to sustain the Declaration of Independence.   He had gone with Franklin and Chase, accompanied by a Catholic priest, (afterwards Archbishop Carroll), through pathless woods and unexplored mountains, a
long and perilous journey, to try whether they could wipe
away from the mind of the Catholic colony of Canada the unfavorable impressions which the ignorance, the folly and
the bigotry of those hostile to his creed had made to the
detriment of his country.   The feelings of hostility to Catholics, and the prejudices against our religion, thus began at
the period of the Revolution gradually to decline, liberty
of worship was soon restored in some of the States, penalties
were blotted from the statute-book, yet was the public mind
quite uninformed respecting our tenets and principles; the
ancient notions concerning Catholic doctrines and practises
continued to subsist though feelings of kindness began to
be entertained.''

This illustrious prelate continues, '' When the observer
contemplates the situation of the Catholic church under
those circumstances, he sees indeed a bishopric erected; the
see is filled by a man worthy of his age, of his station and
of his religion as well as of his country, but he is found to
be comparatively powerless because equally destitute of a
proper clergy and of the means for its creation.   The scattered Catholics were destitute of pastors, their children were
lost to the Church; the greater number of the few who exercised the minstry were unable to remove the erroneous

impressions of such a people as were found over the States. There were few opportunities; no books could be procured to defend Catholic doctrines; the principal portions of English literature, which necessarily became that of the United States, were filled with passages tending to destroy our religion by sophistry, by ridicule and by wit; and through the whole country there was not found a press nor a bookseller to counteract this evil. The people sought for information upon the subject, and every source from which they could draw it was poisoned, every fountain at which they drank was tainted. Need we wonder at the continuance of prejudice, the dislike of our religion, the obloquy to which our principles and practises were exposed, or at the false shame which drew the pusillanimous from the profession of their creed ? "

In this connection may be interesting to read Dr. England's opinion with regard to the loss sustained by religion through the causes above alluded to. " Fifty years ago," he said, writing in 1836, " the population of the United States was three millions; to-day it is fifteen millions. I shall suppose the natural increase of the original three to give us seven millions of our present number; this will leave us eight millions of emigrants and their descendants, together with those obtained by the acquisition of Louisiana and Florida.

" Of the population acquired by immigration and by cession, we may estimate at least one-half to have been Catholics, and supposing the children to have adhered to the religion of their parents, if there were no loss, we should have at least four millions of Catholics from these sources, without regarding the portion which was Catholic fifty years ago, and its natural increase, and the many converts and their descendants. Yet there are many who this day are well informed upon the subject of our churches, who doubt

if we have one million of Catholics.   Upon my first arrival
in the United States in 1820, I saw in a public document
coming from a respectable source, the estimate to be one
hundred thousand, and this from one by no means unfriendly.   I have since then made closer inquiries, taken
more special notice of details, and received better information, and I think the estimate may be safely fixed at
1,200,000.   *   *   If, I say, upon the foregoing data, that
we ought, if there were no loss, to have five millions of
Catholics, and that we have less than one million and a
quarter, there must have been a loss of three millions and
three quarters at least."

In the great majority of cases, when men forgot or for-
sook their Faith in this country, they also lost sight or became ashamed of their origin.   It has been often said that
the Irish are a "missionary race," and that the sufferings
and the persecutions which forced them to abandon their
native soil were "providential," because through their in-
strumentality the cause of religion has been advanced in
many lands.   But does it not seem more reasonable to conclude that had Ireland been a free nation, her sons, emigrating to America or elsewhere, well taught and trained,
and skilled, would be better fitted than they have been to
command respect for their principles and their nationality;
better able to serve the cause of religion, and to make their
children preserve with pride and fidelity the traditions of
their Motherland, and their attachment to her.

Within the limits of this little work, it will not be possible
to give a detailed account of the progress of the Church
up to our day, but the subject has been so ably and almost
exhaustively treated by several eminent authors, that the
task is rendered unnecessary.

The permanent seat of the Federal Government was fixed
on the Potomac by an Act of Congress on July 16, 1790,

and the choice of a site being left to George Washington, he selected a farm owned by Daniel Carroll—brother of Archbishop Carroll, and one of the authors of the Constitution of the United States—which was freely tendered for the purpose. Upon that land the Capitol was laid out, and the original proprietor lived to see ten Presidents inhabiting the " White House," where once his solitary cottage overlooked the now world-famed river.

In the latter part of Washington's administration the people began to divide into two parties. They were the Republicans and the Federalists. The Republicans had French sympathies; the Federalists English. At the head of the former appeared Thomas Jefferson. John Adams led the Federalists. He was elected President upon Washington's positive refusal to remain in office for a third term, with Alexander Hamilton as Vice-President.

Adams' administration commenced in 1797. Six years before that time the Society of the United Irishmen was instituted in Ireland. In '97 a branch of the association was started in America. The headquarters were at Philadelphia, where that great and good Irishman, Matthew Carey, father of Henry C. Carey, and himself a social scientist of very considerable abilities, gave it aid and comfort. Before the formation of the branch association of the United Irishmen in the United States, the publications of the parent society were reprinted on this side of the water; and, as far back as 1794, funds were collected, and arms were promised. The relations which then existed between Irish Revolutionists and the Republic of France tended, of course, to identify the two nations; so that the Federalists became not only anti-French but anti-Irish also.

In 1798—the year of the Irish rebellion—President Adams, under pretence of danger from this society of the United

Irishmen, proposed in a message to Congress and obtained from that body the passage of the famous "Alien Law." Never was autocratic ruler clothed with more absolute power. By this law the President could order any alien he chose to deem "dangerous" to quit the country. Other foreigners were to be licensed to stay at the President's pleasure, and the neglect to take out such license was an offence punishable by three years' imprisonment and perpetual disqualification for citizenship. Fourteen years' residence was the time fixed as necessary to citizenship. This "Alien Law" was, as might be expected, severely criticised by the press; and forthwith Mr. Adams called upon Congress to pass another law—the "Sedition Law"—which made it a seditious libel to reflect on the conduct of the President or question the motives of Congress. The law was passed.*

---

* Matthew Lyon, an Irishman by birth, and a Member of Congress from the State of Vermont, became the special victim of this infamous law. Born in the County Wicklow, in 1746, he emigrated to New York in 1755; and, being too poor to pay for his passage, was assigned by the captain of the ship, for a pecuniary consideration, to a farmer in Connecticut, in whose service he remained a number of years. Subsequently he removed to Vermont. At the breaking out of the Revolution he joined the patriot army, and in July, 1776, was commissioned as lieutenant in one of the companies of "Green Mountain Boys." Afterwards he served as Commissary-General, and eventually rose to the rank of Colonel. After the war he became one of the most enterprising manufacturers of New England. He engaged in paper making, iron casting, and a variety of other occupations, and published a newspaper, thoroughly democratic in its ring, called, "*The Scourge of Aristocracy and Repository of Important Political Truth*," of which the types and paper were manufactured by himself. He married a daughter of Governor Chittenden, and, becoming an active political leader of the Jeffersonian school, was, in 1797, elected to Congress by the anti-Federal party. He was, of course, strong in his opposition to the policy of the then existing administration. In 1798 Lyon was convicted of a libel on President Adams, and sentenced to four months imprisonment and a fine of $1,000 The libel consisted in the remark

The Irish Rebellion failed. At that time (1798) Rufus King, who had been appointed by President Adams, represented this Republic at the Court of St. James. He acted with more malevolence towards the unsuccessful Irish patriots than did even England herself. In the latter part of 1798 the British Government agreed to liberate Thomas Addis Emmet, Dr. McNevin, and others of the leaders of the United Irishmen, who had been confined in Fort George, Scotland, on condition that they would leave the British dominions never to return. Thomas Addis Emmet acted for the prisoners in the matter, and on their behalf applied for passports to the United States, which the Minister, in accordance with the wishes and sympathies of President Adams, declined to grant! When Mr. Marsden, English Under-Secretary, informed Mr. Emmet and his companions that Mr. King had remonstrated against their being permitted to emigrate to America, the Englishman remarked, "*Perhaps Mr. King does not desire to have Republicans in America.*" Had Mr. Emmet been granted passports at that time he would have been accompanied to this country by his brother Robert, who would thus have been saved from the clutches of the English executioner.

Eight years afterwards, Thomas Addis Emmet, who arrived here in 1804, and was then one of the leaders of the New York Bar, denounced in a vigorous and feeling letter King's conduct in the case, and with so much effect that the unworthy ex-minister, who was a candidate for the governorship of New York, was driven from public life. In the course of his letter Emmet said:

---

that " the pomp of the White House better became the court of a king than the residence of the president of a republic !" In 1799, while still a prisoner in jail, he was re-elected to Congress from Vermont. In 1801, at the expiration of his term, he removed to Kentucky: and at the very first election that was held in that State, after his arrival, he was chosen to represent Kentucky in Congress, and held his seat till 1811.

"Your interference was then, (in '98), Sir, made the pretext of detaining us for four years in custody, by which very extensive and useful plans of settlement within these States were broken up.   The misfortunes which you brought upon the objects of your persecutions were incalculable.   Almost all of us wasted four of the best years of our lives in prison. As to me, I should have brought along with me my father and his family, including a brother whose name [ROBERT EMMET] perhaps you even will not read without emotions of sympathy and respect.   Others nearly connected with me would have come partners in my emigration.   But all of them have been torn from me.   I have been prevented from saving a brother, from receiving the dying blessings of a father, mother, and sister, and from soothing their last agonies by my cares; and this, Sir, by your unwarrantable and unfeeling interference."

Thomas Addis Emmet was about forty years old when he came to this country.   Advised and encouraged by George Clinton, the Irish American governor of New York State, and by his nephew De Witt Clinton, then Mayor of New York City, the illustrious patriot devoted himself to the profession of the law, and being at once, notwithstanding some opposition, admitted to the bar, speedily acquired fame and aroused admiration among all who witnessed his efforts.   Yet his path at first was not strewn with roses. Haines says: *

---

* The feeling entertained towards Emmet, among the most eminent of his contemporaries, is well illustrated by the manner in which Charles Glidden Haines speaks of him in a biographical sketch.   "Helvetius remarks," he says, "that the sun of glory only shines upon the tomb of greatness.   His observation is too often true, but facts and living proofs sometimes contradict it.   Mr. Emmet walks on in life, amid the eulogiums, the admiration, and the enthusiastic regard of a great and enlightened community.   Without the glare and influence of public office, without titles and dignities, who fills a wider space, who commands more respect, than Thomas Addis Emmet?   Like a noble and simple column, he stands among us proudly preeminent,—destitute of

" Mr. Emmet's strong and decided attachment to Democratic principles was known even before he reached the American shores. Coming to a country where he could breathe and speak freely, he did not find it necessary to repress those bold and ardent sentiments which had animated his bosom while toiling for the emancipation of Ireland. He mingled in the ranks of the Republican party. Transatlantic politics, it is well known, had extended their agitations and influence to this country. The Federal party hated France, hated Ireland in her revolutionary character, and hated Charles James Fox and his Whig party in England. Mr. Emmet was viewed by the opponents of Mr. Jefferson's administration as a fugitive Jacobin. Hence he was doomed to some little persecution even in this country. The great men of the New York bar were Federalists. They therefore turned their faces against Mr. Emmet. They formed a combination, and agreed to decline all professional union and consultation with him. Mr. Emmet has told me the names of this shameful league, but as they are now his warmest friends and admirers, and as I respect and esteem them, their names shall not go from me. * * * When Mr. Emmet ascertained the existence of the league he did not hesitate what to do. His native boldness and decision of character governed his conduct. He determined to carry the war into the enemy's country. He did not wait

---

pretentions, destitute of vanity, and destitute of envy. In a letter which I recently received from a friend who resides in a western part of the Union, a lawyer of eminence, he speaks of the New York Bar. " Thomas Addis Emmet," says he, " is the great luminary, whose light even crosses the western mountains. His name rings down the valley of the Mississippi, and we hail his efforts with a kind of local pride."— Haines' sketch in Madden's United Irishmen, Third Series, Second ed. 146. Emmet never sought or held any public appointment after having resigned the position of Attorney-General of New York.

for an attack. He proved the assailant. Whenever he met any of the league at the bar he assumed the attitude of professional war, and he lost nothing by contact. If Mr. Emmet has any one extraordinary power, it is the ready talent of successful and over-awing reply. His spirit is always dauntless. Fear he never knew. Hence he generally came off victorious in the wars against the combination.

" The league was soon dissolved. Business flowed in and Emmet assumed a standing, and was able to maintain it, that put all opposition at defiance."

Mr. Emmet was seized with an apoplectic fit while attending the session of the U. S. Circuit Court, on September 14, 1827, and died soon after, being carried to his home. The different courts were adjourned, and his funeral was attended by the members of the Bar, students at law, the city council, and large numbers of citizens of every walk in life. The splendid monument erected to his memory in St. Paul's churchyard, Broadway, New York, in December, 1832, is a proof of the estimation in which he was held by his countrymen. It is a marble monolith of nearly thirty feet in height, bearing inscriptions in three languages, Irish, English and Latin. The first written by Bishop England, the second by Hon. S. Verplanck, and the last by Judge Duer.*

Among others who came with T. A. Emmet to America

---

* T. A. Emmet was born at Cork City, April 24, 1764. He joined the Society of United Irishmen soon after its formation, and while acting as counsel in 1795, for persons charged with administering the oath of the organization, took it himself in open court. He was taken and put in prison March 12, 1798, and kept in Kilmainham and Fort George for more than three years, being released in July, 1802. He came to New York in 1804, and resided there almost constantly until his death in 1827. The translation of the inscription in Irish upon his monument, written by Bishop England, is as follows: "He contemplated invaluable benefits for the land of his birth, he gave eclat to the land of his death, and received in return her love and admiration."

was William J. McNevin,* once a physician of extensive practice in Dublin, and an enthusiastic United Irishman. He was initiated into the organization by Miss Moore, afterwards Mrs. Macready, the friend of Lord Edward Fitzgerald, and famous for her beauty as well as her patriotism, one of the noble band of brave young Irish girls who gave all the aid in their power to those who sought to make Ireland a Nation. McNevin was imprisoned first at Kilmainham, and afterwards at Fort George, Scotland, along with Emmet. When released, he joined the Irish Brigade as a captain, hoping that Napoleon would soon invade Ireland, but being disappointed in this respect, he sailed for America, landing in New York, July 4, 1805. He soon achieved a distinguished reputation as a physician, wrote several valuable works, and continued till his death to take a warm interest in everything relating to his Motherland and her people. To his memory also a splendid monument has been erected in St. Paul's churchyard, Broadway.

Alexander Porter, afterwards U. S. Senator from Louisiana, and Judge of the Supreme Court of the State, came here a short time before the arrival of Emmet and McNevin. He was a son of the Rev. James Porter, the Presbyterian minister of Grey Abbey near Belfast, who had been one of the leading United Irishmen, and who, having taken the field in 1798, was captured, "tried" by court-martial, and hanged before his own door. Young Porter was admitted

---

* William James McNevin was born in 1763 at Ballyhowna, Galway County. At the age of eleven he was sent to Vienna—where his uncle Baron McNevin was physician to the Empress Maria Theresa—in order to be educated, the English Penal "Laws" prohibiting those of the old Faith from receiving an education at home. He returned to Dublin in 1783, obtained as a physician an extensive practice, became a member of the United Irish organization, was imprisoned in 1798 with Emmet, and released in 1802, came to New York in 1805, where he married five years later and died in 1841, aged 78.

to the Bar at Nashville in 1807, and settled in Louisiana three years later. In 1821 he was raised to the bench of the Supreme Court, and was United States Senator from 1834 to 1837. To his exertions is due in a large measure the adoption of the system of jurisprudence which now obtains in Louisiana.

The brothers John and Benjamin Binns came to the United States in 1801. John had been tried at Maidstone, England, in 1798, along with Arthur O'Connor and Father Coigley, for "treason." The two first named escaped at that time, but the priest was condemned and executed. A little later Binns was again arrested and placed in Gloucester jail, where he was kept for nearly three years, being, however, allowed to come to this country in 1801. Soon after his arrival he commenced with his brother the publication of the *Republican Argus*, at Northumberland, Pa., and from 1807 to 1829, he conducted the *Democratic Press* of Philadelphia. He was for many years an alderman of the City of Brotherly Love, where he died in June, 1860.

William Sampson, another prominent United Irishman, was the son of a Presbyterian clergyman of Londonderry. Born in 1764, he received a commission in a corps of the Irish Volunteers, when only eighteen years old, and in 1793, became a member of the National organization. Having studied law, he acted frequently as counsel for his comrades and thus attracted the suspicion of the English government. His name was included in the list of those marked out for arrest on March 12, 1798, and though he escaped to England, he was seized there and sent back to Dublin. Being at length set free, he came to the United States in 1806, and was soon called to the Bar, where he attained great eminence. He wrote several very interesting works, and died in New York, December, 1836. His daughter married young Theobald Wolfe Tone, and survived him some years.

Many patriots besides those named, including Nicholas Gray who was adjutant-general to Beauchamp, Bagenal, Harvey, during the Wexford campaign, Traynor, who made a remarkable escape from the provost-guard in Dublin, Henry Jackson, John Cormick and others, found a refuge in America from British power, and remained through life staunch advocates of the cause of Irish Independence.

CHAPTER XVIII.

In the Presidential election of 1800, Jefferson defeated Adams, and immediately after his inauguration March 4th of the following year, ordered the release of the prisoners who had been condemned under the Sedition Act, which he held to be " unconstitutional, null and void." Jefferson then succeeded in having all the obnoxious measures passed under the administration of his predecessor repealed, including the act which had extended the period of residence required before naturalization to fourteen years. This was now reduced to five, in compliance with his suggestion.

On Jefferson's re-election in 1804, George Clinton of New York, son of Charles Clinton of Longford, was chosen Vice-President, receiving one hundred and sixty-two electoral votes, to fourteen cast for his opponent, Rufus King.

In order to cripple France, with which it was at war, the British government in 1806, issued its " orders in council " declaring the several European ports under the control of the French in a state of blockade, a measure which afforded a pretext for the seizure of American vessels bound to these ports. Napoleon thereupon issued his "Berlin decree," which forbade the introduction of English goods even in neutral vessels, into any port of Europe. He followed this up by his " Milan decree, " which authorized the confiscation of such vessels as would submit to be searched by the English. The latter, however, insisted on their alleged " right of search," and carried their presumption so far that an English man-of-war, the *Leopard,* actually fired upon the United States frigate *Chesapeake,* in June, 1807, killing three and wounding eighteen of her crew, because her commander had refused to allow his vessel to be searched on the pretext that he had on board some seamen who were claimed as British subjects.

The *Chesapeake* was not prepared for action, and had to submit to the Englishman, who thereupon boarded and took from her the men whose presence was made the pretence for the outrage, and bore them off in triumph. The British government indeed, on being remonstrated with, admitted that its " right of search " did not extend to ships of war, but still continued to claim and enforce this " right " in the case of merchant vessels.

In December, 1807, Congress passed the " Embargo Act " by way of retaliation against England. By this measure United States trading vessels were prohibited from leaving their ports, and though this operated to the disadvantage of the English, it also seriously injured our own shipping interests and caused much dissatisfaction in certain quarters.

In 1808, Madison was chosen as successor to Jefferson, George Clinton again defeating Rufus King as a candidate for Vice-President. Soon after the accession to power of the new President, the British Minister at Washington, gave assurances that the English " orders in council " would be annulled, and Madison thereupon issued a proclamation suspending the " Non-intercourse Act," which had been substituted for the embargo, when the latter was found to be injurious to American commerce. The British government, however, refused to carry out the promise made on its behalf by its representative, and the latter was recalled, his place being filled by a Mr. Jackson. This official seemed to think that he could dictate to Madison and his administration as his predecessor Liston had done when Adams was in power, but he discovered his mistake when the President demanded of the British government that it should withdraw its offensive agent.

The Berlin and Milan decrees were revoked in November, 1810, but the English still refused to annul their "orders in council," and stationed their ships of war before the principal ports of the United States to show that they were determined to insist on their alleged "right of search." They even proceeded to still more unjustifiable lengths. During the first session of the Twelfth Congress, which was called together on November 4, 1811, the President sent a special message to that body, showing that a party named Henry had been employed by the British government as a secret agent, in an attempt to create disaffection in the New England States, and to induce them to secede from the Union, and again subject themselves to British rule.

The committee of the House, to whom the matter was referred, reported that " The transaction disclosed by the President's message presented to the mind of the committee conclusive evidence that the British government, at a period of peace, and during the most friendly professions, had been deliberately and perfidiously pursuing measures to divide the States and to involve our citizens in all the guilt of treason and the horrors of civil war." The rulers and agents of the alleged "mother" country were not successful, however, at that time. The detection of their infamous plot before it was ripe caused its abandonment.

On May 30, 1812, Foster the new British Minister at Washington presented the ultimatum of his government. The President promptly sent it to Congress, by whom the matter was referred to the Foreign Affairs Committee, of which John C. Calhoun, of South Carolina, son of Patrick Calhoun of Donegal, was chairman. The committee naturally reported in favor of declaring war, the House endorsed by a large majority the report, and passed an act in conformity with its decision, the Senate ratified the action of the House, and finally the President approved of the Declaration of War on June 18th.

An invasion of Canada was soon determined on. Among those who volunteered to take part in it, were a considerable number of Irish-born citizens, who fought in the battle of Queenstown Heights on October 13th under General, then Colonel, Scott. The contest ended with the surrender of the latter and his small body of troops to the greatly superior British force under General Sheaffe. The prisoners were sent to Quebec, and there a number of the Irish Americans were separated from their comrades and sent in irons to England, "in order to be tried and executed for the crime of high treason."

While the British officers were engaged in picking out the men, Scott, who was in the cabin of the transport, heard the bustle upon deck, and going up, found that twenty-three Irish soldiers had been already selected as victims, there being nearly three times as many still remaining among the other prisoners, the whole number of those captured amounting to two hundred and ninety men. As soon as Scott ascertained the purpose of the English officers, he shouted to his men to answer no more questions, but remain strictly silent, in order that no clue as to nationality should be given to the felon setters by the sound of an Irish accent. The men obeyed strictly in spite of threats freely made, and not another was added to the batch selected for slaughter. Scott was repeatedly ordered below, but he refused, and told those who were apparently doomed, that the United States would not fail to avenge their gallant and faithful soldiers, pledging himself moreover, in the most solemn manner, that retaliation and if necessary a refusal to give quarter in battle should follow the execution of even one of the party.* When, some time after, Scott was landed in Boston and exchanged, he proceeded to Washington, informed the President of what he had witnessed, and was instructed to make a full report of the whole transaction in writing, which he did at once.† His report was immediately sent to both Houses of Congress, and led to the passage of the " Act

---

* The names of the prisoners are given on page 632, vol. 3, of American State Papers. They are as follows, viz:—Henry Kelley, Henry Blaney, George M'Common, John Dalton, Michael Condon, John Clarke, Peter Burr, Andrew Doyle, John McGowan, James Gill, John Fulsom, Patrick McBraharty, Matthew Mooney, Patrick Karns, John Fitzgerald, John Wiley, John Donnelly, John Curry, Nathan Shaley, Edward M'Garrigan, John Dinnue, John Williams, George Johnson.

† Following is Scott's letter to the Secretary of War, written January 13, 1813.

SIR : I think it my duty to lay before the Department, that on the arrival at Quebec of the American prisoners of war surrendered at Queenstown, they were mustered and examined by British officers appointed to that duty, and every native-born of the United Kingdoms of Britain and Ireland sequestered, and sent on board a ship of war then in the harbor. The vessel in a few days thereafter sailed for England, with these persons on board. Over twenty persons were thus taken from us, natives of Ireland, several of whom were known by their platoon officers to be naturalized citizens of the United States, and others to have been long residents within the same. One in particular, whose name has escaped me, besides having complied with all the conditions of our naturalization laws, has left a wife and five children, all of them born within the state of New York.

I distinctly understood, as well from the officers who came on board the prison-ship for the above purpose, as from others with whom I remonstrated on this subject, that it was the determination of the British government, to punish every man whom it might subject to its power, found in arms against the British king contrary to his native allegiance.

I have the honor to be, sir, etc.,

WINFIELD SCOTT.

American State Papers, vol. 3, p. 634.

vesting the President of the United States with the power of retaliation," on March 3, 1813.

" Two months later, at the battle and capture of Fort George, Scott made a great number of prisoners. True to his pledge, he immediately selected twenty-three of the number to be confined in the interior of the United States, there to abide the fate of the twenty-three imprisoned and sent to England by the British officers. In making the selection, he was careful not to include a single Irishman, in order that Irishmen might not be sacrificed for Irishmen. This step led, on both sides, to the confinement as hostages, of many other men and officers, all of whom were, of course, dependent for their lives on the fate of the original twenty-three." *

When Lord Bathurst, the British Secretary, heard what had been done with regard to those English prisoners, he wrote a furious letter to Sir George Prevost in Canada, ordering him to " put in close confinement *forty-six* American officers and non-commissioned officers to be held as hostages for the *twenty-three* British soldiers stated to have been put in close confinement by order of the American government." Prevost was further instructed to notify Major-General Dearborn, the American commander on the Canadian frontier, of what had been done to his officers, and the letter continued, " You will at the same time apprise him that if any of the said British soldiers shall suffer death, by reason that the (American) soldiers now under confinement here, have been found guilty, and that the known law of Great Britain has been in consequence executed, you have been instructed to select out of the American officers and non-commissioned officers whom you shall have put into close confinement as many as may *double the number* of British

---

* Mansfield's " Life of Scott."

soldiers who shall so unwarrantably have been put to death, and *cause such officers and non-commissioned officers to suffer death immediately.*

"And you are further instructed to notify to Major-General Dearborn, that the commanders of His Majesty's fleets and armies on the coasts of America, have received instructions to prosecute the war with unmitigated severity against all cities, towns, and villages belonging to the United States, and against the inhabitants thereof, if, after this communication shall have been duly made to Major-General Dearborn, and a reasonable time given for its being transmitted to the American government, that government shall unhappily not be deterred from putting to death any of the soldiers who now are, or who may hereafter, be kept as hostages, for the purposes stated in the letter.

BATHURST."

Notwithstanding these threats, however, the British government did not dare to execute the Irish-American prisoners; though it did indeed "prosecute the war with unmitigated severity against all cities, towns, and villages belonging to the United States," as far as it was able. Madison at once directed that forty-six British officers should be set apart as hostages for the safety of the forty-six American officers and non-commissioned officers, designated by the English official.

"The new hostages were partly selected from Scott's captures, and partly from the prisoners taken by General Harrison at the battle of the Thames. Some other imprisonments were made on both sides, in the following winter. In the campaign of 1814, however, the American arms were crowned with such brilliant success, that Britain had little of either power or inclination to pursue the war of retaliation on American prisoners. In fact, it ceased. The prisoners

were not executed, and one day in July, 1815, when peace
had been some months concluded, and Scott (then a Major-
General) was passing along on the East River side of the
city of New York, he was attracted by loud cheers and bustle on one of the piers. He approached the scene, and great
was his delight to find that it was the cheers of his old Irish
friends, in whose behalf he had interfered at Quebec, and
who had, that moment, landed in triumph, after a confinement of more than two years in English prisons ! Twenty-
one were present, two having died natural deaths.*

Among the officers who distinguished themselves particularly on the Canadian frontier at the battles of Fort George,
Chippewa and Fort Erie, were General Brady and Colonels
Mullany, and McRee, Captain James McKeon (father of the
late Hon. John McKeon of New York),who was congratulated
publicly upon his bravery by the Tammany Society; Lieutenant Roach, adjutant of Scott's regiment, and afterwards
mayor of Philadelphia, with many other Irish Americans.
At the battle of the Thames, fought 1813 by the Americans
under Harrison against the British and Indians, according to the popular account, Tecumseh, the famous chief, received his death wound from Mason, an old Revolutionary
rifleman, and a native of Wexford, then nearly eighty years
old.†

In May, 1813,a marauding British force numbering several
hundreds attacked and burned Havre de Grace, Maryland,
which was abandoned on the advance of the enemy by the
few militia in the vicinity, but defended by Captain John
O'Neil and two others with great gallantry for some time,
when O'Neil was taken prisoner, and brought on board the
Maidstone frigate, where he would have been at once executed but for the strenuous efforts of General Miller, who

---

* Mansfield's " Life of Scott."
† McGie's " Early Irish Settlers."

threatened to put two British prisoners to death if the li..
of the brave Irish-American were taken.

The gallant defense of Fort Stephenson, Sandusky County,
Ohio, by Major George Croghan, a young Irish-American
officer, in August, 1813, was one of the most creditable
events of the war. General Harrison, having inspected the
fort, became convinced that it could not be held against an
enemy provided with artillery, and sent word to the commandant to destroy the public stores there, and retreat when
the British advanced in considerable force. But Croghan
determined to defend it to the last, and although he had
only one hundred and sixty men and one six pounder, he
repulsed the British general Proctor, who had under him
four hundred English regulars and a large body of Indians,
with several pieces of artillery

Intelligence of this gallant defense caused the liveliest
sentiments of admiration throughout the country, and congratulations were sent to Major Croghan from every quarter.
His general, in his official report, spoke of him in words of
highest praise. The ladies of Chillicothe, Ohio, purchased
and presented to him an elegant sword. Congress voted
him the thanks of the nation, and afterward gave him a gold
medal in commemoration of his signal service on that day.*

---

* George Croghan was a son of Major William Croghan of the Revolutionary Army. His father was a native of Ireland ; his mother was a
sister of General George Rogers Clarke, the Father of the Northwest.
He was born at Locust Grove, near the Falls of the Ohio, (now Louis-
ville), in Kentucky, on November 15, 1791. He joined the army under
Harrison at Vincennes, and was volunteer aid to Col. Boyd at the battle
of Tippecanoe. In March, 1813, he was promoted to major, and
became aid-de-camp to Gen. Harrison. In that capacity he distinguished
himself in the defense of Fort Meigs, and the sortie on the 5th of May
under the gallant Col. Miller. For his gallantry at Fort Stephenson he
was breveted a lieutenant-colonel, and was appointed colonel of a rifle
corps in February, 1814. At the close of the war he was retained in

A monument was erected on the spot by the people of Sandusky County in July, 1885, to perpetuate the memory of
the defenders of Fort Stephenson as well as that of those
who fell in maintaining the Union.

Though frequently beaten at sea, the British, having a
large naval force, were able to inflict serious injury upon the
American towns along the coast. An Order in Council,
issued early in the war, declared the ports and harbors in
the Chesapeake and Delaware Bays to be in a state of blockade, and Admiral Cockburn, who had command in that
quarter, signalized himself by committing the most horrible
atrocities upon the people within his reach. A repulse at
Craney Island, by the forces under Major Faulkner, an
Irish officer, only embittered the redcoats and they took a
brutal revenge at Hampton soon after.

The government at Washington felt confident that the
British would not venture to that point, and failed to take
adequate precautions for its defence. About the middle
of August, 1814, the British squadron in the Chesapeake
was re-inforced by a fleet of 21 vessels, under the command
of Admiral Cochrane, and later by a number of frigates,
under Commodore Malcolm. These ships carried land
forces amounting to several thousand men. Washington
and Baltimore were the chosen points of attack, and a portion of the fleet was sent up the Potomac at once. With
about 2,500 men, many of whom had only been under arms
three or four days, General Winder, the American commander, encountered the English at Bladensburg, but, as
might be expected, the raw troops which formed the greater

---

service, but married in 1817, and resigned. In 1824 he was appointed
postmaster at New Orleans, and returned to the service in 1825 as
inspector-general with the rank of colonel. In 1835 Congress awarded
him a gold medal for his gallantry at Fort Stephenson. He died at
New Orleans on January 8, 1849.

portion of his force, though they fought for the most part pluckily, could not resist the attack of seasoned veterans, and he was at length compelled to retreat. The British then moved across the Eastern Branch, and, finding that the Americans had retired beyond Georgetown, advanced on the capital on August 24th.

The main body of the invaders halted upon the level ground between the Capitol and the site of the Congressional Cemetery, while Cockburn, with General Ross and a few hundred men, went into the city. Near the Capitol a single shot was fired from behind the house of Robert Sewall, which killed Ross's horse. The house was at once destroyed. Then the incendiaries applied their torches to the Capitol itself, in which were the library of Congress and the national archives, and pushing on to the Executive Mansion, that, too, was given to the flames. The Treasury building was next set on fire, as was the *National Intelligencer* office and other buildings, public and private, including hotels, stores, and dwellings, until the light of the conflagration could be plainly seen in Baltimore, forty miles distant. Of the public buildings only the Patent Office escaped.

A more cowardly, unprovoked, or infamous transaction never disgraced the annals of war between civilized nations. There was no military or other necessity to justify the outrage; it could only gratify the vindictive hatred of the Republic by which those wretches were inflamed. Cockburn himself assisted in the work of destruction with the fury of a fiend. This burning was an act the memory of which should ever bring the blush of shame to the brows of Englishmen, yet there was none felt. The guns at the Tower of London were fired in honor of the British "victory," the perpetrators of the crime were voted the enthusiastic thanks of the members assembled in the Houses of Parliament, and a splendid monument was erected in Westminster

Abbey in honor of Ross, who was killed soon after at Baltimore.

The next day the British re-embarked and returned down the river. They compelled the people of Alexandria to give up to them all the merchandise and shipping which they possessed. They then sailed down the Potomac, and reached Baltimore on September 11th. Here, though the Americans were forced to retire before superior numbers, the redcoats failed in their attempt on Fort McHenry, and on the evening of the 13th retired baffled and disappointed to their ships.

But there was still a worse defeat in store for them. Andrew Jackson had been appointed Major-General in the United States army on May 31, 1814. After the repulse of a British attack on Fort Bowyer at Mobile Point, he marched upon Pensacola, which the British had made their base of operations in the South, and seized it on November 6th. He then sent the main body of his troops to New Orleans, and arrived there himself on December 2, 1814. On the 14th of that month the British captured five American gunboats and a schooner, which gave them command of the route to New Orleans. Jackson had previously called out the State militia. He had to oppose the enemy with a small force of regulars and militia from Louisiana, Mississippi, Tennessee and Kentucky, the privateersmen of Barataria and a colored battalion. General Keane landed with the British advance on December 16th and marched to within nine miles of the city on the 23d. Jackson then assembled his most available troops, amounting to a little over two thousand, and attacked the enemy. He was successful, but was prevented from following up his success by the arrival of large British reinforcements, and fell back to a canal four miles from the city, where he entrenched his forces. Sir Edward Pakenham arrived on the 25th, and the same even-

ing his batteries destroyed the American gunboat *Carolina.*
He made an attack on Jackson on the 28th and again on
New Year's Day, 1815, and was repulsed on both occasions.
The British forces numbered, at this time, about fourteen
thousand, including seamen and marines.   Two regiments
and six hundred seamen and marines were detached to attack the Americans on the western bank of the river on January 7th, and the main body advanced upon Jackson's works
on the morning following.   The Irish-American General's
line of defence was about a mile long.   Behind it were
posted about three thousand two hundred men, while eight
hundred more were placed in various positions close at hand.

With a view of strengthening the breast works bales of cotton were placed upon them, but the British artillery scattered these about and set fire to some, in consequence of
which they were all removed.   The British had fallen into
a similar error with regard to hogsheads of sugar which
they employed as a shelter until the first American cannon-
ball pierced their bulwarks and confounded their confidence
in the invulnerability of their defences.

Before dawn on the morning of January 8th the men of
both armies were in readiness.   The leading English column, numbering three thousand, under the command of
Gibbs, advanced, and, about six o'clock, drove in the
American outposts.

As they came within range the American artillery opened
fire, "cutting great lanes in the column from front to rear."
Carroll, who was posted at the point of attack, held in his
men until the British came within two hundred yards of his
works.   Then he gave the order to commence firing, and
the rifles of his Tennesseans riddled the hostile ranks.   Still
the British advanced a little further, but before they came
within a hundred yards of the American works they halted,
staggered, broke, and fled in disorder, having lost half their

number.   An attempt to rally the flying forces and retrieve
the fortunes of the day by pushing forward the Highlanders,
who advanced later, only led to a similar result.   They,
too, broke and sought refuge behind trees and in ditches.
Hardly twenty-five minutes elapsed between the first fire of
the Americans and the complete rout of the British, who lost
in the attack over two thousand men, including Pakenham,
the chief in command.   Jackson had seven killed and six
wounded.   Well, indeed, had he avenged the death of his
brothers and repaid English tyranny for having driven his
parents from their native soil, and America for having
sheltered them in their hour of need.

On the western bank of the river matters had not proceeded so favorably.   There the Americans abandoned
their position and fell back before the British.   Jackson
promptly sent a strong force across the river, under the
command of General Humbert—who had in '98 chased
the English before him at Castlebar—with orders to retake
the position which the enemy had gained.   Before Humbert
could make his arrangements, however, General Lambert,
the English commander, sent a flag of truce to Jackson,
asking for leave to bury his dead, and subsequently withdrew his troops from the western bank altogether.

It has been doubted whether the British used as a watch-
word on that day the expression "Beauty and Booty," but
there can be no question whatever that, had they taken the
city, the women would not have been safe from outrage nor
their homes from pillage.   Even wounded British officers,
who, as prisoners, were treated with every kindness, acknowledged that they would be unable to protect even their
benefactresses from the worst fate which woman can suffer.
A considerable number of the defenders of New Orleans were
of the same origin as the hero of the fight.   One of these,
Nicholas Sinnot, a '98 "rebel," who had fought at Oulart

and Vinegar Hill, was sent in command of a detachment to which was entrusted the charge of Fort St. John. When the sound of battle reached their ears there was great difficulty in preventing Sinnott from leading his men to the scene of action. "There," said he, "are the bloody villains murdering my countrymen, and myself stuck down in this infernal mud-hole."

The British finally retreated on the 18th and took refuge on board their ships.

General Jackson, upon their departure, requested the Right Rev. Dr. Dubourg, Catholic Bishop of New Orleans, to offer up to Heaven thanks for the victory. "Permit me," he wrote, "to entreat that you will cause the service of public thanksgiving to be performed in the Cathedral in token of the great assistance we have received from the Ruler of all events and of our humble sense of it."

The Bishop, in compliance with the General's request, appointed the 23d for the celebration. On that day Jackson, surrounded by his staff, marched to the Cathedral through streets lined with troops, and past windows and balconies filled with spectators. Passing under a triumphal arch, he received crowns of laurel from two young girls, another congratulating him on behalf of Louisiana, while there were ranged on each side ladies dressed in white, representing the several States of the Union. At the entrance to the sacred edifice he was met by Bishop Dubourg, who welcomed him most cordially and eloquently. The General, in the course of his reply, said, " I thank you, Reverend Sir, most sincerely for the prayers which you offer up for my happiness. May those your patriotism dictates for our beloved country be first heard, and may mine for your individual prosperity, as well as that of the congregation committed to your care, be favorably received.'

He was then conducted by the Bishop to a seat prepa\

for him near the high altar, and the *Te Deum* was sung with impressive solemnity.

It should be remembered that a treaty of peace had been agreed on between the United States and Britain fifteen days before the battle of New Orleans, but the news did not reach New York until February 11, 1815.

In the conflicts by sea which took place during this war, many Irish-Americans took a leading and creditable part.

Captain Boyle in the *Comet*, a privateer schooner, attacked and captured three British vessels, one of fourteen, and two of ten guns each, convoyed by a Portuguese brig of thirty-two guns, near the harbor of Pernambuco in January, 1813. He captured later the *Adelphi* of Aberdeen, carrying eight guns, the *Alexis* of Greenock, of ten guns, the armed vessel *Dominica* of Liverpool, and several others, and entered the harbor of Baltimore in triumph on St. Patrick's Day, 1814, having passed through the midst of the British blockading squadron in safety.

On another cruise during the same year in the *Chasseur*, which carried sixteen long twelve pounders, Captain Boyle captured eighteen British vessels including the *St. Lawrence*, a ship of fifteen guns, which was conveying reinforcements to New Orleans. He cruised around the British Channel during several months of the year 1814, inflicting great damage upon the British shipping, and having many remarkable adventures. As a burlesque on the " paper blockade" which the British sought to establish around the American coast, Boyle, while in the English Channel, issued a " proclamation" declaring " all the ports of Britain to be in a state of strict and rigorous blockade," which he sent to London with a request to have it posted up at Lloyd's Coffee House.

Captain Stafford, another Irish-American officer, in the *Dolphin*, fought and captured two British vessels in January

1813, off Cape St. Vincent, bringing them to Baltimore through the British blockading squadron. Captain Murphy, in the *Grampus*, after a successful career of many months, was at length decoyed by a British war-vessel disguised as a merchantman, of greatly superior force, but succeeded in making his escape after a desperate conflict, in which he received a fatal wound.

Captain Blakely, a native of Seaford, county Down, was when the war broke out a Lieutenant on the *Enterprise*, but was soon placed in command of the *Wasp*, and sent to cruise around the English coast. On June 14th he fought and captured the British man-of-war *Reindeer*, and a little later the *Avon* of eighteen guns, and the *Atlanta* of eight. From that time nothing authentic was heard of him, and his ship is believed to have been lost in a storm. The Legislature of North Carolina generously undertook to support his widow and only child.

Captain John Shaw, a native of Mountmellick, Queens County, who in the *Enterprise* achieved some remarkable victories during the trouble with France at the close of the last century, was at the time of Burr's conspiracy placed in command of the flotilla fitted out for the defence of the Mississippi, and in 1813 commanded the naval force which coöperated with General Wilkinson in the capture of Mobile. In 1815 he was placed in command of the Mediterranean squadron, and on his return was put at the head of the Boston navy-yard. Fenimore Cooper says of Shaw, that he was "second to none on the list of gallant seamen with which the navy of the United States commenced its brilliant career."

Commodore Charles Stewart, born of Irish parents at Philadelphia in 1778, became a Lieutenant in the United States navy at the age of twenty, and served under Commodore Barry on his first cruise along with Decatur, whose mother, it may be remarked, was Irish. In 1813, Stewart was put in command of the *Constitution*, and in that year he captured the British war-vessel *Picton* with the *Catherine* and *Phœnix*, and fought the frigates *Junon* and *La Nymphe* together. In the following year he captured the *Lord Nelson* and the *Susan*, and in February, 1815, fought the *Cyane* of thirty-four guns, and the *Levant* of twenty-one, together, the conflict continuing into the night, and ending in the surrender of both English ships. For this glorious triumph, the common council of New York tendered him the freedom of the city. The Legislature of Philadelphia presented him with a gold-hilted sword, and Congress voted him a gold medal. Commodore Stewart was the father of Mrs. D. T. Stewart Parnell, mother of Charles Stewart Parnell.

Commodore Thomas McDonough was born in Newcastle, Delaware, in 1783, and distinguished himself under Decatur in the war with Tripoli in 1805. In the following year, while first lieutenant of the *Siren*, he rescued in the harbor of Gibraltar from a boat belonging to a British frigate, an American seamen who had just been taken from on board a United States merchant brig. In 1812 he was sent to take command in Lake Champlain, and busied himself in superintending the construction of a small fleet. On September 11, 1814, Prevost the English commander at the head of twelve thousand men prepared to attack the Americans under General Macombe, who numbered scarcely fifteen hundred, at Plattsburgh. The British squadron at the same time attacked the American fleet, but the conflict resulted in a glorious victory for McDonough and the flag he fought under. He sunk or captured all the British vessels, and sent a dispatch to the Secretary of the Navy saying, " The Almighty has been pleased to grant us a signal victory on Lake Champlain." His efforts frustrated the

British plan of invasion, and the whole country felt proud of his victory. The Legislatures of New York and Vermont gave him tracts of land, and Congress voted him a gold medal and the thanks of the nation.

CHAPTER XIX.

AMERICAN SYMPATHY WITH IRELAND—JACKSON—·POLK—
THE MEXICAN WAR.

ALTHOUGH the war was ended by the treaty of Ghent, the feeling of hostility between the two nations still existed. The English had not abandoned their pretensions, and the Americans were more disposed than ever to resent them. The British press indulged in the coarsest abuse of the institutions and public men of this Republic, while the people here evinced in the most unmistakable manner their sympathy with the struggles of the Irish against British misrule. Their sentiments in this regard were of course strengthened by the large and constantly increasing emigration from Ireland to this country. This soon assumed extraordinary proportions, while that from England, owing to the fact that the people there were less oppressed by harsh laws, and that moreover, and especially since the Revolution, they had always felt jealous of and prejudiced against the Americans, remained as it had been inconsiderable. The efforts of the Irish to be allowed to educate themselves, and to abolish religious inequalities, naturally called for and received the approbation and support of the free people of this Republic. Associations were formed in many cities of " The Friends of Ireland," and the utterances heard at their meetings gave confidence to the Irish people, and created apprehension among their enemies.

Mr. Wyse, in his *History of the Catholic Association*, says, referring to what was transpiring at that period:

" The American papers were filled with the subject. Ireland often formed their leading article. The debates of their associations were given with the same punctuality, and read with an earnestness sca· :ely inferior to that which generally attended the proceedings of the Catholic Association of Ireland. The entire people became kindled by the subject, and every day the conclusions to which it tended were more and more perceptible. The last document from that country (it arrived in Ireland but a short time after the dissolution of the association) states, that in every hamlet in the land similar bodies were ere long to be established, and that delegates of the Friends of Ireland (it was thus the Philellenes preluded to the liberation of Greece) were to assemble in general congress from all parts of the Union at Washington, there to consider and devise the best means of assisting the efforts making in this country for emancipation. The exertions of individuals were favored by the government: the local authorities often presided; and it has been stated on the best information, that the President himself, General Jackson, had expressed his intention, of subscribing the first thousand dollars to the patriotic fund.

" Little doubt can exist, that if this sort of collateral or accompanying organization in America had been suffered to proceed, and thus to spread itself over every part of the States, the most alarming, and perhaps the most fatal, consequences might have ultimately resulted to this country. The suppression of the association in Ireland, (even if practicable), in such a state of things, would literally have effected nothing. No English statute could have travelled to the other side of the Atlantic; the exasperation produced by so arbitrary an act, on the temper of the Irish Catholics, would in an instant have communicated itself to their brethren in America. Indignation, legitimate indignation, would have added new fuel to their zeal: the associations would

of course have increased; their funds would have augmented; and a spirit very different from the spirit which
now exists would very probably have directed their future
application. * * * Nor would this have been the whole
of the evil. It must be remembered that America is a very
different power from what she was at the period of the last
rebellion. Her connection and sympathy with Ireland are
infinitely closer. The survivors of that eventful period occupy some of the highest stations in her government. They
cannot be supposed to have lost much of their old anti-
pathies. They have long watched with anxiety every chance
of retaliation. They have the will, and would not have
been long under such circumstances without the means to
effect it. They would have found in Ireland a most powerful
coöperation. The delay of emancipation on the one side,
and the habit of discussion on every topic connected with
government (generated by the debates on the Catholic
question) on the other, had produced views incompatible
with *the connection* (with Britain) in the minds of a large body
of the population. Many began to adopt a tone of thinking
quite in harmony with the first addresses from America.
They began to consider even Catholic emancipation but a
very partial remedy for the political and moral evils of Ireland. They looked to a regeneration far more sweeping
and decisive: they believed that Ireland had outgrown the
connection, and could now set up for herself. *Reasoning
on past experience, they were disposed to treat with distrust and
contempt all overtures from England. They had in history
proof that she had never made concessions to Ireland, except
upon compulsion. They looked only to such a crisis as might,
by its appalling force, loose the iron grasp altogether, and liberate the country forever from its dependence.* They laughed
at any thing less than self-government in its amplest sense;
separation and republicanism were the two chief articles of

their political creed. Such a party has, within these last years, been rapidly increasing in Ireland—far more formidable than the French party which haunted the imagination of Mr. Grattan, and which he so often denounced in parliament. It based its projects *on the practical model which it saw in America,* expanding to a greater maturity and vigor every day before them. They compared the resources, the advantages, the population, the energies, the intelligence, of the two countries. They opposed the oppression and wretchedness of one to the freedom and prosperity of the other. *They calculated that there was no other emancipation for Ireland than the absolute assertion of her independence;* and that the attempt if conducted with ordinary prudence and perseverance, quietly husbanding and augmenting their forces, and awaiting with patience the propitious and certain hour for the experiment, could not fail of the most entire success."

In the Presidential election of 1824,* General Jackson re-

---

* Jackson's parents emigrated from Carrickfergus, Antrim County, Ireland, where they had followed the occupation of linen-weavers in 1765, and landing at Charleston went with a number of relatives and friends to settle down in "the Waxhaws." The father was named Andrew Jackson, the mother, before her marriage, Eliza Hutchinson, and they brought with them across the Atlantic two sons, Hugh and Robert. Within two years the father died and the widow and her orphans sought shelter under the friendly roof of a brother-in-law, George McKemey, where a few nights after, March, 15, 1767, she gave birth to a boy whom she named after his dead father, Andrew Jackson—a name which he was destined to make one of the proudest in American history. Jackson was 9 years old when the Declaration of Independence was signed. Hugh, Andrew's eldest brother, fought at the battle of Stono, and died of exhaustion shortly after. A little later Andrew and Robert were present at Sumpter's attack on the British at Hanging Rock, where, when the battle was nearly won, the Americans, like the Irish at New Ross in '98, through indulgence in the liquor they had captured from the British, suffered defeat. It is recorded that whenever Andrew

ceived 99 electoral votes, 84 being cast for John Quincy Adams, 41 for W. H. Crawford, the Congressional Caucus nominee, and 37 for Henry Clay.   No candidate having received a majority, the election devolved on the House of Representatives, and Adams was chosen.   John C. Calhoun was elected Vice-President for the same term.*

---

was sent with farm tools to be mended to the blacksmith's shop he always brought home some new weapon to be used against the English. Sometimes, slashing at the weeds on the farm with a scythe, he would cry out : " Oh, if I were a man how I would sweep down the British with my grass blade !"   Jackson began in his 18th year the study of law, and was admitted to practice before he reached the age of 20.   In 1788 he was appointed public prosecutor of the western district of North Carolina, which included the present State of Tennessee, locating at Nashville.   He married in 1791 Mrs. Rachel Robards, was made District-Attorney of Tennessee when it became a federal territory, and when it was admitted as a State, in 1796, he was elected its representative in Congress.   He was chosen U. S. Senator in 1797, taking his seat on November 22, of that year, but returning to Tennessee on leave, in April, 1799, he resigned.   He was then elected a Justice of the Supreme Court of Tennessee.   When war was declared against England in 1812 he offered his services and those of the militia division of which he was Major-General to the Government, but was not then called on.   On May 31, 1814, he was appointed Major-General in the United States Army. He captured Pensacola, Florida, from the British in November of that year and reached New Orleans on December 2.   On January 8, 1815, he won the battle of New Orleans.   The Seminole outbreak was suppressed by Jackson in 1817-18.   He was appointed Governor of Florida when Spain ceded that State to the Republic.   In 1823 the Tennessee Legislature elected him U. S. Senator.   He received 99 electoral votes in the Presidential election of 1824, 84 being cast for John Quincy Adams, 41 for W. H. Crawford, and 37 for Henry Clay. No candidate having received a majority, the election devolved on the House of Representatives, and Adams was chosen.   In 1828 the hero of New Orleans was however again elected President, receiving 178 electoral votes, while only 83 were cast for Adams.   He was re-elected in 1832, securing 219 votes out of a total of 228. His death took place in 1845.

* John Caldwell Calhoun was born in Calhoun Settlement, District of

Jackson's star, however, had not sunk forever, and when four years more had elapsed his popularity was found to have increased, not waned. The campaign of 1828, when he was again a candidate against Adams, was exceedingly bitter. An instance may be given. Mrs. Jackson, during the excitement, once found her husband in tears. Asking the reason, Jackson pointed to a paragraph reflecting on his dead mother, and said: "Myself I can defend; you I can defend; but now they have assailed even the memory of my mother." Mrs. Jackson was fiercely attacked in the Washington *National Journal*, said to be the organ of the President. In consequence, Jackson, on his arrival in Washington for the session, refused to call upon Mr. Adams.

In the election of 1828 the hero of New Orleans received 178 votes, while only 83 were cast for Adams, and Calhoun was re-elected to the Vice Presidency. In the midst of his triumph, and while preparing to attend a banquet given in his honor, in Nashville, Jackson suffered the loss of his devoted and faithful wife, an event which cast a deep gloom over his remaining years

He was re elected to the Presidency in 1832, receiving 219 votes out of a total of 288. The Nullification crisis occurred between his second election and his inauguration.

Abbeville, S. C., March 18, 1782. His grandfather, James Calhoun, emigrated from Donegal, Ireland, to Pennsylvania in 1763, bringing his son Patrick then only 6 years old, who became father of the distinguished statesman. In 1770 Patrick Calhoun married Martha Caldwell, the daughter of an Irish emigrant. John was the third son of this couple. Calhoun was at an early age chosen a member of the State Legislature, and was sent to Congress in 1811, taking his seat in that body for the first time on November 4 of that year, Congress having been called together by the President's proclamation a month before the usual time. He was appointed Secretary of War in the Cabinet of President Monroe in 1817, was elected Vice-President of the United States in 1825, and re-elected four years later. He died at Washington in 1850.

The extreme Nullifiers asserted the right of any State of the Union to secede whenever it pleased. The difficulty was, however, averted for the time by a compromise measure introduced by Clay, which enabled the South Carolinians to abandon their resistance to the Government without having to yield to force.

In June, 1833, the President visited several cities in the North. At Boston, the Charitable Irish Society in a body, headed by its banner, paid its respects to him at the Tremont House. After all the members of the society had been introduced, President Boyd on behalf of his brother-members, addressing the chief magistrate said, after mentioning that the body was composed exclusively of Irish and their descendants, " We fill the place now that was once occupied by men who have done the State some service in times of peril and danger, men who did not withdraw themselves from the ranks of those who were fighting the battles of liberty, nor could withhold the most zealous support to the Constitution and Laws and Magistrates of this our adopted country. We hope, Sir, the present generation has not fallen off from the standing maintained by their fathers, and that if occasion required the motto on our Banner * would be a promise which would be willingly performed at any time." And then he expressed the pride which himself and his brothers felt at seeing the highest office in the Republic held by the son of an Irishman, and concluded by wishing that the remainder of the illustrious visitor's life " might be as long and happy as its past had been brilliant and successful."

The President, evidently very deeply affected by the Irish welcome tendered him, replied:

---

* The banner of the Charitable Irish Society of Boston has upon it an eagle, with the motto underneath, " *Fostered under thy wings, we will die in thy defense.*"

" I feel much gratified, Sir, at this testimony of respect shown me by the Charitable Irish Society of this City. It is with great pleasure that I see so many of the Countrymen of my Father assembled on this occasion. *I have always been proud of my ancestry* and of being descended from that noble race, and rejoice that I am so nearly allied to a country which has so much to recommend it to the good wishes of the world; would to God, Sir, that Irishmen on the other side of the great water, enjoyed the comforts, happiness, contentment and *liberty*, that they enjoy here. I am well aware. Sir, that Irishmen have never been backward in giving their support to the cause of liberty. They have fought, Sir, for this Country valiantly, and I have no doubt would fight again were it necessary, but I hope it will be long before the institutions of our Country need support of that kind; accept my best wishes for the happiness of you all."

Having concluded his reply, the members of the Society were about to withdraw, when the President again took Mr. Boyd by the hand, and in the most affectionate manner held it while he added:

" I am somewhat fatigued, Sir, as you may notice, but I cannot allow you to part with me till I again shake hands with you, which I do for yourself and the whole Society. I assure you, Sir, there are few circumstances that have given me more heartfelt satisfaction than this visit. I shall remember it with pleasure, and I hope you, Sir, and all your Society will long enjoy health and happiness." *

James K. Polk of Tennessee, a descendant of Robert Pollock, of Donegal, Ireland, † having received one hundred

---

* Extracts from records of Charitable Irish Society.

† About 1660 Robert and Magdalen Pollock, together with their six sons and two daughters, set sail from the County Donegal, Ireland, for America, and settled in the then colony of Lord Baltimore and now Somerset County, Maryland, at a place now known as Dane's Quarter. All the

and seventy electoral votes, to one hundred and seven cast for Henry Clay, took the oath of office as President of the United States on March 4, 1845. Soon after his inauguration war with Mexico, which had been anticipated for sometime broke out.

When the Independence of Mexico was established in 1821, Texas was a Mexican province, and remained so, until 1836, when the people of the Lone Star State formed for themselves a separate and independent government. They then desired to obtain admission into the Union, and on March 3, 1845, Congress ratified the treaty of annexation made by John C. Calhoun at Washington, on behalf of the United States with the Texan commissioners.

Mexico had not recognized the separate sovereignty of Texas, and the Mexican Minister withdrew from the National Capital as soon as the fact of the annexation became known. Nearly a year, however, was spent in negotiations before war actually broke out. In March, 1846, General Taylor, then at Corpus Christi, advanced to the banks of the Rio Grande, and erected Fort Brown opposite Matamoras. Soon after he fought the battles of Palo Alto and Resaca de la Palma. A little later Matamoras surrendered and Monterey was also compelled to submit. Among the officers who most distinguished themselves in those engagements, was the Irish

---

sons married and became the progenitors of numerous families. From one of the sons were descended the late *President James K. Polk,* General Thomas Polk, of Mecklenburg fame, Bishop and Lieutenant-General Leonidas Polk, and others. From another son, Governor Charles Polk, of Delaware, deceased ; and from another, Governor Trusten Polk, of Missouri.—*Potter's American Monthly, May,* 1876.

Lossing says, (*Eminent Americans, p.* 388,) that President Polk was born in Mecklenbnrg County, N. C.,—chiefly settled by the Irish and their descendants—which was known as the " Hornet's Nest," because of the zeal and activity of its people in the cause of liberty during the Revolution.

American, General W. O. Butler of Kentucky, the grandson
of an Irish emigrant, who having served under Taylor was
afterwards chosen to succeed Scott in the command-in-
chief, and in that capacity led the American forces home
when peace was restored.   Colonel Croghan, Captain Down-
ing, Lieutenants Moore, Calhoun and Blake, with many
others of the same origin, also covered themselves with
glory in the conflicts under Taylor.   At the battle of Buena
Vista (fought on Washington's Birthday, 1847, when twenty
thousand Mexicans contended for the mastery, with five
thousand Americans, Colonel McKee of Kentucky, who
was killed, Major Gorman of Indiana, who headed a rifle
battalion, and Captain O'Brien, who commanded a regular
battery, received the highest praise from all who witnessed
their daring.   The latter was brevetted Major for his conduct on the field.   Captain Connor, at the head of a company of Texas Volunteers, also fought bravely during the
day, sometimes against extraordinary odds, himself being
wounded and two of his officers killed.   Night put a stop to
this stubborn battle; both armies remained in the same
positions they had occupied in the morning, the Americans
slept on their arms; but when dawn appeared it was found
that the Mexicans had retreated during the night, leaving
many of their wounded behind.   They had lost in killed
and wounded more than fifteen hundred, the loss on our
side being nearly half that number.

Meanwhile General Scott had proceeded against Vera
Cruz, which soon surrendered.   He then after a brief rest
pushed on towards the city of Mexico, defeating the enemy
at Cerro Gordo, where General Shields was wounded, mortally it was at first believed, again at Puebla, and later at
Contreras, where Riley's brigade did such good service ; and
at Cherubusco, where Phil Kearney lost his arm, Colonel
Butler of South Carolina was wounded and Captain Burke

of the 1st artillery killed. The day following this last conflict, the Mexicans sent out a flag of truce from the Capital,
and an armistice was arranged. This battle was fought on
August 20, 1847.

Again the struggle was renewed when terms of peace
could not be agreed on, and on the 8th of September Chapultepec was won by our troops, Shields, who was badly
wounded, refusing to retire while the contest raged. Finally
on September 14th, the Stars and Stripes floated over the
Mexican capital, and the war was practically ended. Major
General Robert Patterson was one of the Irish officers who
greatly distinguished himself in this campaign, and he was
no less esteemed for his bravery than beloved by the men
who fought under him. General Patterson was born near
Strabane, Tyrone county, Ireland, in 1792. His father, who
had been a " rebel" in '98, left Ireland on the failure of that
struggle, bringing his little boy with him, and settled in Delaware county, Pa. General James Shields* was present at

* General James Shields was born in 1810, on the Hill of Altmore, about
four miles from Dungannon, Tyrone county, Ireland. At the age of
sixteen he came to America, and after some years established himself in
Kaskaskia, Ills. engaging in the practice of the law. While employed
in this manner he was involved in a difficulty with Abraham Lincoln,
which fortunately ended without serious results, and both became warm
friends in later years. In 1839 Shields was elected State Auditor of Illinois, and was chosen Judge of the Supreme Court of the State in 1843,
a position which he held until 1845, when President Polk appointed him
Commissioner of the United States Land Office. In the year following
the Mexican war broke out, and Shields was offered by the President the
Commission of Brigadier General, and he at once set out for Mexico. He
greatly distinguished himself at the siege of Vera Cruz, was shot through the
lungs at Cerro Gordo, and believed to be mortally wounded, yet in a few
weeks he was again in the saddle. At Contreras and Cherubusco he
rendered most essential service, and at Chapultepec he was again wounded
while leading on his men. For his valor in these actions he received the brevet of Major General. In 1849 he was elected U. S. Sen-

the siege of Vera Cruz, received a bullet through the lungs
at Cerro Gordo, and was in the advance all the way to the city
of Mexico in command of one of the best brigades in the
service.   Colonel   Riley was a native of Maryland, of Irish
descent.   He led the attacking party on both days of the
fight at Contreras, and finally carried the works at the bayonet's point.   " The charge of his brigade, " says Colonel
Smith, "down the slope in full view of friend and foe, un-
checked for even a moment until he planted his colors on the
enemy's works, was a spectacle that animated the army to
the boldest deeds.   He acted with equal bravery at the
gates of Mexico." Colonel Pierce Butler of South Carolina
highly distinguished himself in every engagement, until he
fell pierced with three wounds before Cherubusco.   Shields,
under whom he served, said in his report, " Colonel Butler
had risen from his sick bed to share the dangers of the com-
bat with his devoted regiment.   He survived the conflict of
the morning to lead his command where victory again
awaited it.   Although wounded twice, and having lost his
horse, which was shot under him, he still continued to press
on near the colors of his regiment until the last fatal ball
terminated his life."

---

ator from Illinois.   In 1855 he went to Minnesota to settle on lands
awarded him for his services in the army, and was elected U. S. Senator
from that State also on its admission into the Union in 1858.   When the
Civil war broke out he promptly tendered his services, and was appointed Brigadier General in August, 1861.   In March of the following year
he met and defeated Stonewall Jackson, at the Battle of Winchester, one
of the most fiercely contested actions of the war, where he was again
wounded. President Lincoln soon after nominated him as Major General,
but the Senate—of which he had been a member twice—through unworthy influences, refused to confirm his nomination, and the insulted
veteran resigned.   He then settled in Missouri, from which State he was
again elected to the U. S. Senate in 1879, and died June 1 of that year
at Ottumwa, Iowa, his body being brought to his home at Carrollton,
Missouri, for burial.

General S. W. Kearney * had fought on the Canadian border in the war of 1812, was engaged in New Mexico and California in 1846, and served with honor in several severe conflicts of this war. At the bombardment of Vera Cruz, Commodore David Connor, descended from an Irish family which settled in Pennsylvania about the middle of the last century, displayed the highest skill and intrepidity. The war was finally brought to an end by the treaty of peace signed by the envoys of the two contending powers at Guadaloupe Hidalgo, on February 2, 1848.

---

* Major General Stephen W. Kearney was the grandson, of Philip Kearney, whose father came from Ireland and settled in Monmouth county, New Jersey, in 1716. Stephen W. Kearney was born at Newark in 1794. While only in his eighteenth year he received, on the breaking out of the war of 1812, a First Lieutenant's commission in the 13th U. S. Infantry, and took part in the engagements on the Canadian frontier. At the battle of Queenstown Heights he particularly distinguished himself by heading a successful charge on an English battery, for which Lieut. Col. Christie, his commander, presented the young officer with his own sword upon the field. He was afterwards taken prisoner, sent to Quebec, and long detained in captivity. On the organization of the 1st. U. S. Dragoons in 1833, Kearney was appointed Lieut. Col. of the Regiment, and was made Colonel three years later. In 1846 he was commissioned Brigadier General, was placed in command of the Army of the West, and at its head, conquered New Mexico. He received the brevet of Major-General for his services in the district first named and in California. He was twice wounded in the battle of San Pasena, and commanded in the conflicts of San Gabriel and the Plains of Mesa. He was made Governor of California in 1847, and died at Vera Cruz, Oct. 3, 1848, through illness caused by his exertions in the Mexican war.

CHAPTER XX.

OF the causes which led to the last great influx of Irish people to these shores—"Famine," coercion and the unsuccessful attempt at revolution in '48—it is only necessary to speak briefly. For the appalling loss of life during the " famine " the British government is as directly responsible as if it had caused the death of its victims by bullet and bayonet. During the latter years of the repeal agitation grave apprehensions had been felt and expressed in England that the Irish people when convinced of the uselessness of peaceful efforts, to obtain even a small measure of justice, would not hesitate to have recourse to arms, as the Americans had done. When Smith O'Brien in 1843, before he became a Nationalist or even a Repealer, moved in the London Parliament that an inquiry should be made into the causes of Irish discontent, the English minister, Sir James Graham, opposed his motion fiercely. He said that the disaffection should be repressed by every means. " Any hesitation now, any delay, any irresolution, " he added, " will multiply the danger a hundred-fold. I appeal then to both sides—not to one but to both.—I appeal to both sides and say, if you falter now, if you hesitate, now in repressing the rebellious spirit which is at work, the glory of this country is departed—the days of its power are numbered, and England, this all-conquering England, must be classed with those countries from which power has dwindled away, and present the melancholy aspect of a falling nation." His appeal was of course successful, and the motion was promptly rejected.

The Naval and Military Gazette, about the same time said. " There are now stationed in Ireland 35,000 men of all arms, but widely scattered over the island. In the event of a rebellion, and who can say we are not on the eve of one? we feel great solicitude for the numerous small detachments of our gallant soldiers. * * * It is time to be up and doing. * * * The day we fear is near when, quite peaceably, every Repealer will come armed to a meeting, to be held simultaneously as to day and hour, all over the island, and then try to cut off, quite peaceably, every detachment of her Majesty's loyal army." *The Westminster Review* asked: " Is it absolutely certain that we can beat this people?" and one of its contributors remarked: " If something is not done, a fleet of steamboats from the United States will, some fine morning, be the Euthanasia of the Irish struggle."

There was in fact some reason to apprehend that America would aid her sister nation in a struggle against British despotism, if one should break out. The President of the United States, John Tyler, was a "Friend of Ireland." His son Robert Tyler presided over a Repeal convention held in New York City in September, 1843, at which there appeared delegates from thirteen states and one territory, and which occupied three days in deliberating upon the best methods of assisting the cause of Irish liberty. Money was being liberally subscribed here in aid of the movement. Boston alone, in the first six months of 1844, sent $10,000 to Ireland, and other cities were not far behind. A dispute arose between the United States and Britain, a little later, over the Oregon boundary, and President Polk, himself an Irish-American who had succeeded President Tyler in

March, 1845, declared that the right of the United States to
the territory of Oregon, up to a certain parallel of latitude,
was " clear and unquestionable." Sir Robert Peel became
very nervous and sent what he called a " message of peace "
to Ireland, an additional grant to Maynooth College. He
succeeded in securing the assent of the London Parliament
to this measure, by saying that there was rising " in the far
western horizon a cloud (the Oregon boundary question),
small indeed but threatening future storms."

In the year following (1846), however, a failure of the potato crop in Ireland to some extent relieved the apprehensions of the British Ministers. Over 300,000 people perished of hunger, or of typhus fever caused by hunger, in the
latter months of that year. It is hardly necessary to say
that had the Irish lived under a native government, a humane government, in fact under any government except
that by whose rule they were cursed, this partial failure of
the crops would not have led to the death of a human being, for during every one of the " famine " years, more food
was exported from Ireland to England, than would have
fed twice the population of the former country. But the
landlords, the great majority of whom lived in England, had
to receive their rents, and the taxes imposed by the London
Parliament had to be paid, even if hundreds of thousands
of Irish should perish of hunger, while the last sight that
met their dying eyes was that of English soldiers and officials seizing upon and putting on board ships bound for
British ports the crops which they toiled so hard to raise.

The year '47 witnessed still more appalling scenes: but
the subject is too horrible to dwell on; suffice it to say here
that in three years '46, '47, and '48, the best authorities
declare that over *a million and a half* of human beings died
in Ireland of " famine " in the midst of plenty. The number was not quite as large as had been predicted in " politi-

cal circles " in England; there it was complacently estimated that there would be at least "two millions of Irish
corpses"as a result of British law, produced starvation before the close of the last mentioned year.

The London Parliament indeed voted some small sums of
money for the relief of this terrible distress, but it at the
same time compelled the people to give up the food which
they had raised at the point of the bayonet, in order that it
might be sold in England to supply the British treasury with
funds and the landlords with their rents.

Meanwhile British Ministers pretended to sympathize with
their victims in Ireland, and appealed on their behalf for alms
to the world. The Irish insisted that they wanted no alms,
only the right to take care of themselves. At a public meeting in Dublin, presided over by the Lord Mayor, a resolution was passed declaring " That for purposes of temporary
relief as well as permanent improvement, the one great want
and demand of Ireland was that foreign legislators and Ministers should no longer interfere in the management of her
affairs."

Assistance was sent to Ireland from all quarters, but in
many cases it was prevented from reaching the people.
The Sultan of Turkey sent $10,000, but half the sum was
returned to him, not for the reason that it was not needed,
but because the English Queen, who derived so large a proportion of her income from Ireland, could not spare to help
her alleged " subjects " more than half the Sultan's contri-
bution, and would not allow him to give more than herself.

Munificent contributions were sent from America. A
committee in Philadelphia raised in a short time $48,000
in cash, and in provisions, to the value of $20,000. New York
contributed nearly a quarter of a million of dollars, and Boston
and the New England States about the same amount.* At

---

* The aid sent from America during this terrible famine was a generous

Washington a meeting in aid of the suffering Irish people was held at which the Vice-President of the United States, George M. Dallas, took the chair, and our government sent two ships of war to New York and Boston to convey provisions to Ireland. But when those vessels reached the Irish ports, they found British ships sailing out loaded with food from the very districts in which the " famine " was greatest.

No wonder that Lester says * "this was not a famine, which means in the proper sense of the term a calamity sent by the Almighty upon the fruits of the earth. It was all *legal assassination—foulest of all murder.* Would not a Coroner's jury of Americans, sitting at an inquest over such dead, *be compelled by their oaths as honest men to render a verdict of wilful murder against the Queen of England?*" Nor need we be surprised at Mitchel's assertion that " All the nations of the earth might be defied to feed or relieve Ireland, beset by such a government as this (of Britain)." †

At a meeting of the Irish confederation, held to thank the people of the United States for their generosity, Mitchel said:

" Americans give us the produce of their own industry and energy. We have no claim upon them;—America never wronged us, never robbed us;—no American ever sought, save by fair competition, to ruin our trade that his might flourish;—America has not the spending of our rents and revenues;—Americans do not thrive by virtue of our beggary, and live by our death;—Americans do not impose upon us laws that breed famine and pestilence, nor locust

---

return "after many years" for the relief which the Irish had forwarded to the starving people of Massachusets in 1676. Then a ship from Dublin brought to Boston a full cargo of provisions valued at about £1,000 sterling, which was divided among one hundred and sixteen suffering families of that city.

* Glory and Shame of England.

† Last Conquest of Ireland (perhaps).

swarms of officials that exasperate famine and pestilence. In your thanks to the Americans let your whole hearts go with them. Let your acknowledgments be as ample and unconditional as their generosity (hear, and loud cheers). They have laid us under an obligation; and if Heaven be good to us it shall be discharged (loud cheers). But Englishmen can well afford to give Ireland alms out of the spoils of Ireland. They are rich and may well be generous, because we have been such fools as to let them have our bread to eat and our money to spend for generations;—because we have consented to use everything they can make, and to make little or nothing for ourselves;—because we have sacrificed our tradesmen's wages and our peasant's lives to the insatiable spirit of English—*commerce,* let me call it; beggars must keep a civil tongue in their heads: let it not be supposed that I mean to derogate from their merits, or to limit our thanks, when I tell them that, whether they know it or not, they are living upon Irish plunder; that, *although the loss of one crop be a visitation from Heaven, Irish famine is a visitation from England*—that the reason why we want relief, and they can give it, is just that our substance has been carried away, and that they have it."

In 1841 there were, according to the census returns, 8,175,125 people in Ireland, and the census commissioners estimated that the population in 1851 would amount to 9,018,799. But when the census was taken in the latter year, it had fallen to 6,550,000, a loss of nearly two millions and a half. 1,188,000 had emigrated from 1847 to 1851 inclusive, over three quarters of a million of whom came to this country, leaving not far from a million and a half to be accounted for. They were in famine and famine-fever graves. And the London *Times* cried out exultingly "The Celts are gone, gone with a vengeance; *the Lord be praised.*"

On March 4, 1857, James Buchanan, born of Irish parents at Stony Batter, Franklin county, Pa., took the oath of office as President of the United States, he having received 174 electoral votes, to 114 cast for John C. Fremont and 8 for Millard Fillmore.   During his administration Minnesota and Oregon were admitted as States into the Union, and the Atlantic Cable was laid.

The election of Abraham Lincoln to the Presidency in 1860, led to the deplorable conflict between the people of the North and South.   Leading statesmen in the latter section, had long maintained the doctrine of State Sovereignty, and held that any State could withdraw from the Union at its own pleasure.   They now seemed to fear that the institution of slavery was in danger, and succeeded in inducing several of the States to secede and form a separate government.   On April 12th Fort Sumter was fired upon by the forces under Beauregard, and three days after the President issued a proclamation calling for seventy-five thousand men to put down the rebellion, and summoning Congress to meet on July 4.   It is not intended here to dwell on the part which the Irish bore in the Civil War, as the limits of this outline will not permit of it, and the publishers of FORD'S NATIONAL LIBRARY contemplate the issue shortly of a volume especially devoted to the subject.

But men of the Irish Race may well be proud of the heroism displayed by those of their blood who came from East and West to "rally round the Flag" and maintain inviolate the integrity of the Union.   The memories of Shields and Kearney, of Corcoran and Meagher, of Logan and Mulligan, of McMahon, Matt. Murphy, Guiney, Moore and many others, as well as of the brave men who fought under them, should never be forgotten by those who honor bravery, and esteem fidelity to duty.   Whether under McClellan on the Peninsula, with Grant from the Wilderness to Appomattox, or on many a hard-fought field of the West and South, the Irish-American soldiers of the Republic well maintained the reputation which in other days the men of their race had won, from " Dunkirk to Belgrade, " among the best swords-men of Europe.

And if the Starry Flag needed defenders to-morrow, the Irish-American Chief of the army of the United States, Phil. H. Sheridan, active, skillful and daring as he is modest, would find himself at the head of regiments of citizen-soldiers of his own blood, as prompt to respond to the call of duty, and as brave and faithful in its performance as any he has commanded. The Sixty-ninth of New York, the banner Irish-American regiment of the Republic, under its veteran Colonel James Cavanagh, is second to none in the Republic as a military organization. The Ninth Massachusetts well maintains the reputation won by it during the Civil War, and the Hibernian Rifles of Illinois, the Third regiment California National Guards, and scores of companies throughout the Union, continue to show that the old spirit of the race is still as vigorous as ever, and its devotion as much to be relied on.

At the Presidential election of 1880 Jas. A. Garfield was chosen President of the United States; Chester A. Arthur, son of Rev. W. Arthur, of Ballymena, Antrim Co., Ireland, being elected Vice President. They took the oath of office on March 4, 1881. On July 2 of that year President Garfield received a fatal wound at the hands of an assassin and died on Sept. 19, following, being succeeded as President by General Arthur. The latter was born at Fairfield, Vermont, in 1830, and died at New York, Nov. 18, 1886.

CHAPTER XXI.

THE numerical strength of the Irish race in America has been variously estimated, but the conclusions arrived at with regard to this question by Patrick Ford, appear upon investigation to be the most accurate and reliable. He has bestowed great attention on the subject, and examined closely all available sources of information. Mr. Ford says,* (writing in 1874): " The plan to be followed out in order to reach a correct conclusion in the matter is: (1.) Find the total population of the thirteen colonies at the close of the War of Independence. (2.) Divide that population into its constituent elements—English, Irish, French, German, etc. (3.) Find out the natural product of that colonial population to-day supposing, of course, no European immigration had set in or affected it. (4.) Find the produce of the population of the States and Territories once held by France and Spain; as well as (5) the number of French-Canadians, and Irish-Canadians who are now settled in this country, but who were never registered on the " emigration " lists, and who, of course, cannot be counted in the product of colonial population. (6.) Next find the figures of the total European immigration to the United States since 1790. (7.) Divide that immigration into nationalities. (8.) What nationality has contributed longest and largest in the

---

* *Irish World*, July 25, 1874.

way of immigration? (9.) In what ratio does population increase? (10.) What is the product of Irish immigration from 1790, in the United States to-day? (11.) What is the product of all the nationalities. This is the plan which we adopted. After much labor and patient research we arrived at the following result:

"*Table showing the relative proportions of the constituent elements of the population of the U. S. in* 1870.

1. Total white population of the thirteen Colonies
   at the close of the Revolutionary War   3,172,000
2. Relative proportions of the constituent elements
   in the Colonial population:
   Celtic (Irish, Scotch, Welsh, French, etc.) 1,903,200
   (Irish separately)   1,141,920
   English, (so-called Anglo-Saxon)   .   841,800
   Dutch and Scandinavians .   .   .   427,000
3.—Product, in 1870, of the population of 1790. 9,496,000
4.—Product, in 1870, of the separate elements of
   the population of 1790:
   Celtic   5,697,000
   (Irish separately)   3,418,200
   English   2,504,000
   Germans, Dutch and Scandinavians   .   1,295,000
5.—Product, in 1870, of population gained by acquisition of new territory since 1790 .   1,500,000
6.—Product, in 1870, of Irish and French immigration from Canada   2,000,000
7.—Total strength of Colored element in 1870   4,504,000
8.—Total immigration to U. S. from 1790 to 1870 8,199,000
   Irish Immigration from 1790 to 1870 .   3,248,000
   English immigration, from 1790 to 1870   796,000
   Immigration of all other elements   4,155,000

9.—Product of total immigation to U. S., from
1790 to 1870 23,000,000
Product of Irish immigration (from 1790) 9,750,000
Product of English " (from 1790) 2,000,000
Product of all other " (from 1790) 11,250,000
10.—Total population of United States in 1870 38,500,000
11.—Joint product, in 1870, of Irish Colonial element and subsequent Irish immigration (including that from Canada) . . 14,325,000
Joint Product, in 1870 of English Colonial element and subsequent English immigration . . 4,522,000
Joint Product, in 1870, of all other Colonial elements and all subsequent immigration (including colored population) 19,653,000

Total Joint Product. } 38,500,000

12.—Total Celtic element (Irish, Scotch, French, Spanish, Italian), in United States in 1870 24,000,000
Total Irish element in United States in 1870 14,325,000
Total English element in United States in 1870 4,522,000
Total of all other elements (not Celtic nor English) in the United States in 1870 9,978,000

" Of the authorities which we have searched to aid us in forming our calculations, the principal are: Blodget's *Statistical Manual;* Dr. Seybert's *Annals; Colonial Lectures*, by Merrivale; *Progress of Western Nations*, by Bury (an English baronet); Tucker's *Tables of Population;* Bromwell's

History of Immigration; Eighty Years' Progress (the joint production of eminent men); Grahame's *History of North America.*

" The ratio of increase of the American population as laid down by the most approved writers, and as accepted in *Appleton's Cyclopædia*, is (leaving out immigration) 1.38 per cent. annually. That is every hundred persons in the population have increased 1.38 yearly in excess of deaths. Adopting this standard, we find that the colonial population of 1790 would, by natural increase, have reached every decade from that up the following figures:

" *Table 2.—Showing what the population of 1790 would have been at each succeeding tenth year—without immigration.*

Year.					By natural increase.
1790	.	.	.	.	.	3,172,460
1800	.	.	.	.	.	3,638,500
1810	.	.	.	.	.	4,173,000
1820	.	.	.	.	.	4,786,010
1830	.	.	.	.	.	5,489,080
1840	.	.	.	.	.	6,395,420
1850	.	.	.	.	.	7,220,220
1860	.	.	.	.	.	8,280,870
1870	.	.	.	.	.	9,497,330

"According to this estimate—which is presumably correct —had there been no immigration permitted since 1790 the population of the United States, at the close of 1870, would have been a little short of nine and one-half millions. Such a number probably does more than represent the natural product of that Colonial population to-day: while all the rest of the white inhabitants of the Union have been acquired by immigration and by cession of Territory, since the year in which that first census was taken. Conceding that the nat-

ural increase of the population of 1790 amounts in 1870 to
something over nine millions, we have now to determine
how that number is distributed among the elements, according to origin.   If the elements increased at a uniform
rate, it would be easy to make this distribution.   If the
Anglo-Saxon race increased as fast as the Celtic, then we
would have only to give each a share, in the population of
1870, proportionate to the share it had in 1790.   But such
is not at all the case; and for this reason, that the elements
do *not* increase at a uniform rate.   The Irish race is the most
prolific of any in the world.   All statisticians admit the
fact; and ethnologists pronounce the rapid increase of the
Irish people a phenomenon.   *   *   *   But lest any exception should be made to this conclusion, we shall apportion
the figures as if all the elements had increased at a uniform
rate:

"*Table 3.—Showing the natural product, in 1870, of each separate element of the population of 1790.*

	Element in 1790	Element in 1870
Celtic (Irish, Scotch, French, and Welsh) .	1,908,200	5,697,000
Irish separately	1,141,920	3,418,000
English or so-called Anglo-Saxon	841,800	2,504,000
Dutch and Scandinavians . .	427,000	1,295,000
Total.	3,172,000	9,496,000

" Thus we see that the white population of 1790, if left in
undisturbed possession of its Thirteen Colonies, would to-
day amount to something less than one-fourth of the actual
population of the United States !   The other three-fourths
—excepting the colored race—are composed of immigrants
and their descendants.   This general conclusion is not dependent on our assertion.   It is definitely and specifically
laid down in *Appleton's Cyclopædia.*   The total English or

so-called Anglo-Saxon element in this country to-day is about five millions—or less than an eighth of the entire population. This figure will surprise some. But it will surprise those most who have given the subject least attention. To those who say the English element must be greater, we simply put the question: Why must it? How are you going to make it greater? Oh! but it is commonly supposed that this is an English country. We are aware of the supposition. But there are several popular errors afloat, and this is one of them. * * * Let those who say the English element in the United States must be greater than is here given, produce their proofs. Let them exhibit their statistics. If they can do this, very well—if they cannot do this —if they have nothing to show—then let them not insist on others believing that which they themselves are unable to substantiate. Ignorance is often excusable; but ignorance, when it becomes dictatorial, only merits contempt. Supposition must always yield to facts.''

Mr. Ford brings forward an overwhelming array of facts and statistics in support of his conclusion, which must be acknowledged as correct by all who take the trouble to investigate the question. Since 1870, not far from a million more of Irish immigrants have arrived in the United States, and although emigration from Ireland to this country, has fallen off considerably from what it was many years ago, and is now exceeded by that from Germany, it is fair to assume, looking at our vast population, that the proportion of the various elements cannot be appreciably altered. It may be asserted then, with confidence, that as the total population of the United States has risen from 38,500,000 in 1870, to almost sixty millions to-day, the Irish element here having at least increased in equal proportion, now numbers not less than twenty-three millions.

In this brief sketch of the Irish race in America, it was

unavoidable that many subjects of great interest and importance should have been passed over. The Irish pioneers in
the Western States, their adventures, progress, the settlements which they founded, and the great communities which
have sprung from them, the genius and skill of Fulton, Colles
and O'Reilly, and many others; the contributions to science
and learning of Adrain, Allison, Thomson and other eminent Irish American scholars; the wisdom and practical
knowledge of social questions displayed by men like Matthew Carey, his son Henry C. Carey, and his grandson
Henry Carey Baird; the generosity of Margaret Haughery,
Bryon Mullanphy and those of our own day—all these and
many other subjects of great interest cannot be touched on
in these pages.

In Canada there are over a million of the Irish race, for
the most part still true to their old traditions and principles, and though living under the flag of Britain, soon it is
hoped to be flung away, yet one in sentiment and feeling
with their kindred in this Republic. In the capital of Newfoundland, where live so many of the descendants of those
who fought on the Hills of Wexford in '98, in the old city
by the St. Lawrence, on whose heights Montgomery fell,
in the commercial metropolis of the Dominion, Montreal,
where the children of the Gael though born upon Canadian
soil, glory in the name of "Young Irishmen," in Toronto
where, however few, the men of our race were always fearless
and faithful, in these cities and in many a town and village
on the banks of the St. Lawrence, beside the great lakes of
the West, or in the backwoods, are to be found those who
have sprung from Ireland, are proud and prompt to avow it,
and willing, anxious as their brothers here, to aid her cause
and humble her enemy.

In the Southern continent, over a quarter of a million of
Irish Argentines, constantly increasing in numbers and re-

sources, forming national clubs, and helping forward every movement made for Ireland's advancement, give proof that the spirit and vigor of the race has not deteriorated under the "Southern Cross."

For ourselves here on this free soil, we yield to none in our devotion to the institutions, and in obedience to the laws of the Republic. We have no jealousies or prejudices against any element of the community. We hold, however, that to use the phrase which John F. Finnerty has adopted as his motto, "Europe not England is the Mother Country of America," and that pretensions or assumptions to the contrary are absurd and mischievous. If there be any among our fellow citizens, who question our right to aid our kindred across the sea in their struggles against that despotism to whose overthrow America owes her freedom, prosperity and progress, we say to them in the words of the adopted son of Washington, "Americans recall to your minds the memory of that heroic time when Irishmen were our friends, and when in all the world we had not yet a friend beside." This Republic has never suffered, nor will it ever suffer through its friendship for Ireland, and those who have come here from that Old Land may repeat now, as ever, what John Boyle O'Reilly has said in his own grand way in the *Exile of the Gael*:

" No treason we bring from Erin—nor bring we shame nor guilt !
The sword we hold may be broken, but we have not dropped the hilt !
The wreath we bear to Columbia is twisted of thorns, not bays :
And the songs we sing are saddened by thoughts of desolate days.
But the hearts we bring for Freedom are washed in the surge of tears:
And we claim our right by a People's fight outliving a thousand
      years !"
" What bring ye else to the Building ? "
                              " O, willing hands to toil :
Strong natures tuned to harvest-song, and bound to the kindly soil ;

Bold pioneers for the wilderness, defenders in the field—
The sons of a race of soldiers who never learned to yield.
Young hearts with duty brimming—as faith makes sweet the due :
Their truth to me their witness they cannot be false to you !"

And every patriotic American will echo the poet's closing words:

" It is well, ay well, old Erin !   The sons you give to me
    Are symbolled long in flag and song—your Sunburst on the Sea ?
    All mine by the chrism of Freedom, still yours by their love's belief :
    And truest to me shall the tenderest be in a suffering mother's grief.
    Their loss is the change of the wave to the cloud, of the dew to the
        river and main :
    Their hope shall persist through the sea and the mist, and thy streams
        shall be filled again.
    As the smolt of the salmon go down to the sea, and as surely come
        back to the river.
    Their love shall be yours while your sorrow endures, for God guardeth
        His right forever !"

INDEX

317

ABOUT
THE AUTHOR

The following is from *The Journal of The American Irish Historical Society*, Volume XV, 1916, pp. 51–62.

PROCEEDINGS AT ANNUAL MEETING.

THE PRESIDENT-GENERAL: Doctor, we will be pleased to hear you.

DR. COYLE: *Mr. President and Gentlemen:* It has happened since the last meeting of this Society that a great and very noble figure in American Irish life has passed from amongst us, and I have thought it advisable to put into the records of our Society something of the life of Edward O'Meagher Condon.

EDWARD O'MEAGHER CONDON.

BY JOHN G. COYLE, M. D.

Edward O'Meagher Condon was the eldest child of Thomas Condon and Ellen O'Meagher, natives of Mitchelstown, County Cork, where Condon was born about 1840. His parents sailed for America while the boy was under two years of age and in delicate health. The better to assure the steadiness and safety of his diet, his fond parents took with them on the ship a goat, whose milk the child had been consuming. The episode of the transportation of the goat afforded many a quip to Condon in his later life.

The Condon family settled at St. Johns, Newfoundland, where they remained for some years. Young Edward was sent to a "Dame School," such being the common name applied to a school conducted by nuns. Other children were born to Mr. and Mrs. Condon during their stay in St. Johns. The elder Condon was a contractor, and better opportunities for his business appearing to exist in Quebec, the family removed to that city, where Edward received further education.

After a stay of some years in Quebec, Thomas Condon removed with his family to Toronto, where Edward finished his education and entered the employ of a prominent architect, and he completed his training for that profession. Condon, the elder, built St. Mary's Cathedral in Toronto, and an asylum at Aurelia, Ontario. In Toronto, Edward O'Meagher Condon met his future wife, Miss Sarah Quinn, daughter of Hugh Quinn and Catherine Devlin. She was but sixteen years of age at that time. The courtship which then began lasted for several years before opportunity came to crown it at the altar.

The American Civil War broke out and the struggle enlisted much interest on the part of the Canadian Irish and Scotch. Young Condon watched the progress of the strife with increasing interest and a growing desire to take part in it with the thousands of others of Irish birth who were rallying to the cause of the Union.

When Col. Michael Corcoran, who led the sixty-ninth New York to the front at the outbreak of the war and was captured at Bull Run, July 21, 1861, returned to New York after thirteen months spent in Southern military prisons, the Irish colonel was promoted by President Lincoln to the rank of Brigadier-General, dating from his capture. Corcoran's long stay in prison was partly because he would not give parole not to fight again, if released. As soon as he had returned, he announced that he would raise a brigade for service in the Union cause.

Edward Condon hastened to New York to offer his services under the gallent Corcoran. His father and his family removed to Cincinnati, Ohio, about the same time. Condon enlisted as a private and served in the One Hundred Sixty-fourth New York Volunteers, a regiment also known as the Corcoran Guard and Corcoran Zouaves, entering the service of the United States on November 19, 1862. Col. John E. McMahon commanded this regiment. When Col. John E. McMahon died on March 3, 1863, his brother, Col. James P. McMahon, succeeded him. A third brother of the McMahons was Gen. Martin T. McMahon, who served valiantly in the war, and died several years ago, while holding the position of judge of the Court of General Sessions in New York City.

The One Hundred Sixty-fourth New York, with Condon in its ranks, served until the end of the war, taking part in twenty-nine battles, beginning at Deserted House, Virginia, January 30, 1863, and ending at Appomattox Court House, where Gen. Robert E. Lee surrendered to Grant. At the battle of Blackwater, Condon was wounded in the breast. During this engagement three color-bearers were shot down. Condon rushed forward, seized the colors and held them until the close of the day. At Cold Harbor, Col. James P. McMahon was killed, June 3, 1864, and every man on Condon's left was killed, so that he was left standing alone.

On the fateful night when General Corcoran, stricken with apoplexy while preparing for the Christmas holidays, lay dying in his headquarters, with his young wife sobbing at his bedside, the soldiers of the Legion asked permission to say farewell to their commander. In single file they passed around the dying General's bed, each in turn silently saluting. Among them was O'Meagher Condon, whose saluting had caught a falling tear from the young soldier's moist eyes.

For some months after the war Condon served as a quarter-master. Then, freed from the turmoil and trouble of war, his heart called him to Toronto, where he made up for his long absence by the ardor of his wooing. On May 24, 1866, Edward O'Meagher Condon and Sarah Quinn were married with nuptial Mass, celebrated by Father White, who had joined them. One child, Helen, was born before Condon took the great step which made him famous around the world.

With many other Irishmen, who had seen service in the Civil War, he had the belief that the hour had come for a successful revolution in Ireland. The ex-soldiers believed that their ex-

perience would be highly useful in organizing and directing the
volunteers who would be expected to form the Fenian army.
Condon joined the Irish Revolutionary Brotherhood and went
to Ireland in 1867 to take part in the "rising." He was in
charge of the district at Macroom, County Cork. But, unfortunately, the plans were not sufficiently perfected, either to supply
the eager revolutionists with arms or to assure quick and simul-
taneous co-operation at various points throughout Ireland.

There was especial difficulty about securing firearms. After a
long period of anxious waiting, the men who were to take the
field, in some places dispersed, in others actually did battle with
police and soldiery. Condon received word to leave Cork, the
message coming from the Fenian leaders. He then went to
England, where he was directed to Manchester. Here in 1867,
a Fenian convention was held. Men attended from Scotland,
from various parts of England as well as Manchester. Condon
vouched for the fidelity of those whom he personally knew.

The difficulty at Manchester was that of securing arms.
There were some resolute men, but not enough firearms could be
secured to precipitate a revolt of any size. Some of the Fenians
were very short of funds and had difficulty in getting enough on
which to subsist. The police learned of the presence of Fenians
in the city and began a careful search for the plotters. Among
the men who had come from America were Col. Thomas Kelly
and Capt. Timothy Deasy. They were arrested as they were
coming from the wake over the child of a friend.

Their arrest and the police statements as well as the news
printed concerning their arrest told the Fenians that their plans
were known and that many men were under suspicion. Captain
Murphy, one of the leaders of the Irish Revolutionary Brotherhood, was representative of Scotland in the convention and had
general charge of affairs in that country. Col. Rickard O'Sullivan Burke had charge of the southern counties of England and
Captain Condon was in charge of the northern counties. As
the arrest of Kelly and Deasy had taken place in the district of
which Condon had charge he felt that bold and prompt steps
should be taken to prevent the condemnation of the two
suspects. He procured a lawyer to represent them, but immediately took a more daring and resolute method to secure
their freedom.

Condon organized a rescue party for the freeing of Kelly and Deasy. He telegraphed a code message to Murphy and Rickard Burke. The message read "Your uncle is dying." Murphy was not at the address the message went to, but Burke received his and responded at once. With Captain Michael O'Brien he joined Condon on September 17, 1867, and both coincided with his view that an effort should be made to free Kelly and Deasy by force. Condon sent a friend to Sheffield to purchase four revolvers. These represented the sum total of firearms employed in the famous rescue.

On the morning of September 18, Condon with Rickard Burke, Michael O'Brien, and a party hastily gathered for quick action, learned that Kelly and Deasy were to be transferred to Bellevue Jail. Condon's party prepared to attack the prison van on its way from the magistrate's court to the jail. Owing to the fact that there had been a fight in front of the court house, where a Manchester Fenian was arrested, Kelly and Deasy were put in irons and Police Sergeant Brett, who was in charge of the police squad, instead of riding outside on the step of the van, as was his custom, locked himself in with the prisoners, while a strong force of police surrounded the van.

The road to Bellevue Jail passed under a railway arch. As the van started from the court house, a cab went ahead of it. This cab contained a messenger who apprised Condon's party by signal of the coming of the van. The Fenians were gathered under and near the arch, and as the van appeared, they rushed out and stopped it, a shot disabling one of the horses making the stoppage certain. The police resistance was quickly overcome. But Sergeant Brett, inside of the van, refused to open the door. He was warned that the lock would be forced or shot away, but he bravely refused to open the door. A revolver shot was sent through the lock and the bullet killed Brett. A woman prisoner within the van took Brett's keys and open the door. Kelly and Deasy were immediately freed and promptly fled and were never captured. Assistance quickly came to the police around the van, from Bellevue Jail, which was not far away from the scene. The rescuers fled in small groups. Condon and others were overtaken and captured. Kelly and Deasy reached Liverpool and thence safely got to America. The Manchester police made nearly eighty arrests, but the great majority of those arrested had nothing to do with the rescue and were released. One of the innocents was a sailor, who bore an Irish name and was visiting his sweetheart at Manchester.

Twenty-seven persons were put on trial for complicity in the crime of shooting Brett and conspiring to free Kelly and Deasy. Five were sentenced to death, these being Condon, Allen, Larkin, Michael O'Brien, who used the name of Gould, and Maguire. The other prisoners were sentenced to prison for varying terms.

When O'Meagher Condon was about to be sentenced, the judge asked him, as was customary, what he had to say. In reply Condon said that he regretted that human life had been taken in what they deemed a necessary act. He hoped that the other prisoners would have a fair trial and that the blood of those condemned would satisfy the craving that seemed to exist for vengeance. He added, "I have nothing to retract—nothing to take back. I can only say 'God save Ireland.' "

The three men beside him repeated the cry, "God save Ireland." During the trial the court officer had cried out several times, "God save the Queen." To Condon it seemed, as he truly said, "I felt it would not be unfitting that my last public utterance in life should be fidelity and expression of faith in God, fidelity to Ireland and defiance of the enemy."

The cry of O'Meagher Condon in the dock at Manchester has rung around the world. It was the aspiration of the patriot, the prayer of the man of faith, the hope of the trustful Christian. From the judge upon the bench about to execute human law, the voice of Erin appealed through Condon to the Supreme Judge of mankind. If Condon and his fellows might not be the instruments through which Ireland's freedom could be won, let not a stricken nation's cause go yet unheard, but might the God of Nations make it His Divine Will to lift from the darkness and woe of her bondage the isle of sorrows and once more permit her to resume the glories and enjoy the treasures of freedom.

The Manchester incidents and the fate of the men who were executed stirred T. D. Sullivan to write the ballad, "God Save Ireland," which, sung to the tune of "Tramp, Tramp, Tramp, the Boys Are Marching," a Union war song, has become the national anthem of Ireland, taking rank with "The Wearing of the Green" as a stimulant to Irish patriotism.

Maguire, who was condemned to death, was pardoned because the evidence against him was shown to be perjured. Condon, because of American appeals made in his behalf, was fortunate enough to have his sentence commuted to imprisonment for life. Allen, Larkin and O'Brien were put to death on the scaffold on November 23, 1867. Annually, their fate is commemorated in "Manchester Martyrs" meetings in various parts of the world. The song, "God Save Ireland" pictures the three men as crying out on the scaffold, "God Save Ireland." But Captain Condon said that several of those present at the execution told him no such scene occurred. What did happen was that the three prisoners recited their prayers quietly, in low but audible tones, until the springing of the trap prevented further utterance.

Condon went to prison and served eleven years at hard labor, during which his child, Helen, died at the age of seven years. In 1879, owing to a resolution passed by the United States Congress and appeals on his behalf made by many public men, the British Government released him. He was forbidden to return to Great Britain for a number of years.

When Captain Condon returned to the United States he was given receptions and welcomed by the Irish societies in general. President Rutherford B. Hayes appointed him to a position in the government service. Condon remained in this place during the administrations of Hayes, Garfield and Arthur. He actively supported the great Land League movement then in progress and contributed his talents as a writer and speaker to the cause.

During the first Cleveland administration Condon was a victim of the spoils system and went out of office. Patrick Ford of the *Irish World* asked him to join the staff of that journal. While on the *Irish World* Condon wrote the book that is associated with his name, "The Irish Race in America." This is a remarkably interesting, accurate and carefully compiled statement of Irish deeds and Irish progress in the United States. His remuneration for the work was small, although the sales were large. Paper-covered editions were most popular and issued, of course, at a low price. The work is to be found in the gradually increasing library of the American Irish Historical Society.

After Condon left the *Irish World* staff he founded a weekly in Philadelphia, devoted to Irish and American Irish matters, but, finding that his associates were not congenial, he left the editorship and management of the paper and returned to New York.

When President Harrison succeeded Grover Cleveland, the Republican leaders felt that a considerable part of the victory was due to the support of the *Irish World*. Mr. Patrick Ford was asked if he desired anything. With characteristic modesty, Mr. Ford wished nothing for himself, but spoke for Edward O'Meagher Condon. It was understood that Condon was to be made Consul at Rome. It proved, however, that the appointment of another to this post had been promised, so Captain Condon accepted a place in the Supervising Architect's office in the Treasury Department, where he remained until his death, except for a short period of time, when he served as inspector of construction in the New York Fire Department to accommodate Austin Ford, a nephew of Patrick Ford, who was a fire commissioner.

While maintaining a residence in New York, where he dwelt with his wife and a daughter, Miss Eva Condon, born after his return from prison, Captain Condon was stationed in various parts of the country, where construction of important Federal buildings was in progress. His history was known to all interested in Irish matters and his views upon Irish politics were often sought and widely quoted.

He took up the study of Irish as a member of the Gaelic Society of New York City and acquired a reading knowledge as well as a fair spoken use of the language. Always interested in philology, his knowledge at times appeared almost uncanny, so unexpectedly did he employ it to illuminate some historical fact or to point an argument. He enjoyed the personal friendship of many of the Irish leaders, including Parnell, Davitt, Dillon, Redmond, Devlin and many others.

In 1909 Captain Condon visited Ireland and England. He was accorded most enthusiastic receptions. From many platforms he declared his complete approval of the efforts of the Irish people towards the securing of Home Rule. It was a cause he had advocated in this country and had contributed both time and money to advance.

In England he visited the prison which is the successor of Salford Jail, in which were buried the bodies of Allen, Larkin and O'Brien. When the new prison was erected, the bones of the buried prisoners were dug up and transported to the new jail and there reinterred. Winston Churchill, then Home Secretary, gave Condon permission to enter the prison and thus, forty-two years after the death of his comrades, Edward O'Meagher Condon knelt above their dust and prayed that they might be in the Kingdom of Heaven.

At Manchester, which is largely dominated by the Irish, was enacted the extraordinary scene of the former convict being attended with honor by the mayor, the aldermen, police and people. He was made the guest of the officials as he went over the places where he lived such exciting days in 1867. He replied to the warmth of the public greetings by the same modesty and brevity of speech and the same soundness of his observations which always distinguished the man.

His last public appearance in New York was at a Thomas Moore Memorial meeting, held on May 28, 1915, at Aeolian Hall, where he was one of the speakers. A member of Shields-Corcoran Post, No. 69, G. A. R., once two separate posts, each named for an Irish General in the Civil War, Captain Condon attended the Grand Army of the Republic annual encampment at Washington in the late summer of 1915. The oppressive heat and fatigue deprived him of vitality. Gradually he failed in strength. Not until actually ill in his home, did he discover that a picture hanging in his room, to which he had not given any attention, was a picture of Portland Harbor, England, showing plainly the prison which he had been confined for eleven years.

One effect of his prison confinement was an intolerance of a closed room. In his last sickness, he demanded that the window be kept open, no matter how cold the room might be, or how strong the draught might blow.

Even when suffering from great difficulty of breathing and other symptoms of distressing character, his mind was alert on problems and news concerning Ireland and her hopes of self-government. He discussed the world situation with keen insight and wide knowledge of nations and races. He was preparing an elaborate dissertation to show that England's population to-day was more than half Celtic by race and descent. He had accumulated many notes and much material about this subject, in which his interest was keen and constant.

Not until a day or two before his death did he dispense with his daily shave, the donning of a high standing collar and a well-made cutaway coat. His will was iron, his courage, whether in sickness or in health, unsurpassed. Fortunately, he went to the end fortified by the rites of his faith, and after many days of suffering, sank into a peaceful and painless coma which closed his life on December 16, 1915.

Numerous expressions of regret and sympathy from many parts of the world came to his widow and his daughter, among them a message from the Irish leader, Mr. John E. Redmond. After Mass at the Church of St. Jean Baptiste, Lexington Avenue and Seventy-sixth Street, New York City, his body was interred in Calvary Cemetery on December 18.

In person Edward O'Meagher Condon was a well-formed man, about five feet, eight inches tall, erect and obviously soldierly in bearing. His mustache, eyebrows and hair in early and middle manhood were a very dark brown, almost black. His cheekbones were rather prominent, his mouth and chin firm, his eyes, somewhat smaller than the average, were of a dark hazel color. There was resoluteness without pugnacity visible in his appearance and bearing. His manner was courteous, his speech fluent, when he chose to let his thoughts take oral expression. He was careful in statement, always fair to friend or opponent, and a manly man.

Edward O'Meagher Condon's life is a notable part of Irish history in the nineteenth century. He suffered for two countries, Ireland and America. His patriotism was unquestioned, his merits many, his faults few, indeed.

He was one of the few remaining Irish patriots who directly link the present with the Ireland before the disestablishment of the Irish Church. His career was diversified, active and notable. He is a great figure in Irish history, a prominent one in American Irish life. His breadth of view, his fairness of judgment and his ability to keep step with the trend, political, industrial and otherwise of the Irish in Ireland not only distinguished him—for such attributes are not common since aged men are inclined to live in the past and disparage the present—but these qualities gave to Condon's utterances and writings a persuasiveness and a weight of appeal which enabled him to win many converts to the cause of Home Rule for Ireland.

His busy active life has ended. He has gone without seeing the fulfillment of his hopes, an Irish Parliament in Dublin. But he was made thousands know the record of the Irish in America. He has renewed in many souls a dormant patriotism for the land of their birth or the land of their fathers. He was a voice speaking from the past, breathing the traditions and the spirit of the Irish race. He was an historian of accuracy and of power. He was a romantic figure, unconscious of romance, devoid of egoism, but making a magic appeal to the undying spirit of the Gael.

He lived a full life, a robust life, a life that makes the heart pulsate in sympathy with his sufferings and his aims, the blood stir in quicker stream at the memory of the American soldier, the Irish patriot, the upright Christian gentleman, Edward O'Meagher Condon.

THE PRESIDENT-GENERAL: We are much indebted to Dr. Coyle for his touching account.

DR. SULLIVAN: May I add, on 11th Street I secured a copy of Condon's "Irish in America," and, in front, inside, is a letter from Jefferson Davis, the President of the Confederacy, answering Condon when he asked him about the proportion of the Irish in the Rebel army. He writes him a very courteous letter, tells him he is unable to say, but he might secure something from the former Secretary of State. That is attached inside a copy of O'Meagher Condon's "Irish in America."

I want to say, too, if I might, that here is a copy of the "Irish People" of November 30, 1867, and in that is O'Meagher Condon's and the other men's addresses in the dock, and I took that out some months ago to bring here to show to Dr. Coyle and also Captain O'Brien. In the corner is a little item of a half-dozen words telling about Captain O'Brien's escape from Clonmel jail. This is a paper of 1867 that I have secured, and sometime may give to the Society. It has the general address here, in this paper. The men had not been hung at that time, or, rather, they had not been murdered (applause).

THE PRESIDENT-GENERAL: I want to say that, while Dr. Coyle was reading that splendid paper of his, there was passing through my mind a very glorious picture of that time, the time of the Manchester rescue and escape, when I was in England and a Fenian Center in London, I knew all those men (except the local Manchester men)—Condon and Burke and Murphy, and I inwardly thrilled at the thought of it. We did not know when we were meeting each other in the processes of this conspiracy of ours to free our land, to do something for it, of the proportions these deeds would take in the future. We were simply men working for a principle, and it is one of the beautiful things of history,—of the study of history—to know of the flowering of simple deeds. The utterance of that cry of Condon, "God save Ireland," which has blossomed and gone around the world, came to us in London, at the time, like the benediction of dying men, and I remember well that when we, in defiance of a very bitter public opinion in London, held a parade for the grand Manchester Martyrs, that the words, "God save Ireland," rang along the line, and to find it now the cry of the world is very inspiring.

I only add, in the way of a small correction, that Captain Burke's name was "Rickard," not "Richard" Burke; a very small correction to make; but I knew Rickard Burke at the time, and nobody ever called him "Richard" or "Dick." He was "Rickard Burke."

Now, Gentlemen, we will meet this evening for the dinner, and inasmuch as there is much to be done and much ground to be covered, we hope that everyone will be there on time because of what was explained to you about the demonstration of our opportunity of exchanging conversation by word of mouth with our fellow members in San Francisco, who will be sitting down to dinner about the time that we will have finished. That will take up a lot of time. It will be very interesting; and we must, therefore, sit down at seven o'clock. I ask you all to be on time.

Gentlemen, we adjourn.